"As Leah Schade makes clear, we need to
to green the planet. She provides some
do that in a sound and transformative w
— Bill McKibben, Author of *The Comfort*
  Scale of Creation

"Preachers can no longer avoid addressing the issues of climate change
and environmental injustice. Finally, we have a substantial book to
support us in this calling. Deeply grounded in environmental ethics
and eco-feminist theology, Leah Schade provides both a theoretical
framework and practical strategies to help preachers speak to the crisis
facing God's creation. Schade has provided an essential resource for the
urgent situation we face. Every preacher should read this book. Now."
— Charles Campbell, Duke Divinity School and Coauthor of *Preaching*
  Fools: The Gospel as a Rhetoric of Folly

"In *Creation-Crisis Preaching*, Leah Schade provides both a compelling
case for, as well as a fully developed guide to, preaching on creation.
Writing as a Lutheran pastor, feminist theologian, and ardent
environmentalist, Schade plumbs the depths of history, theology, and
homiletics to help preachers provide their hearers with a new frame of
reference by which to enter into a deeper relationship with God's good
Creation and, ultimately, each other."
— David Lose, President, Lutheran Theological Seminary and Author
  of *Preaching at the Crossroads*

"*Creation-Crisis Preaching* is bold and prophetic. Grounded in the
gospel and a theology of the cross that names God's hidden yet
startling presence in the midst of suffering, Dr. Leah Schade draws
on the profound insights of ecofeminist theology to help preaching
address and engage environmental injustice. She shows us how our
own sermons can be a moment where God's Creation is even now
'flowering, leafing, and fruiting' in the fecund, liminal space between
eco-crucifixion and eco-resurrection."
— David Schnasa Jacobsen, Boston University

"How is the Word of God in Scripture to be proclaimed as hope in the midst of eco-catastrophe? What does it mean to preach Jesus Christ living, crucified, and risen in light of the linked oppression of Earth and women? How is the preacher to proclaim what God is doing to bring about eco-resurrection? Schade's daring venture at the intersection of ecofeminist theology and homiletics plunges the reader into these courageous and vital questions. Her response is theologically compelling, faithful, forthright, and hope-inspiring. Articulating a Lutheran ecofeminist Christology and its implications for preaching, the author charts a course to preaching that is faithful to the Gospel and responsive to the cries of the Earth and people who suffer with its degradation. This remarkable book is a gift to the church and the world, and is a work of abiding love—love for the church, the Word of God, the Earth, and its creatures (human included). While grounded in Lutheran traditions, Schade's guidance in this book will be relished by people of other Christian traditions and beyond. It is a must-read for all who hunger to hear and proclaim God's word of life in our day."
— Cynthia Moe-Lobeda, Pacific Lutheran Theological Seminary

"Can one preach a good word in season and out of season, when seasons may not be around for too long? Can one communicate the good news in a world of broken dreams and shattered hopes, when the world as we know it is facing human-made catastrophes on an unprecedented scale? Can the legacy of Lutheran thinking be of value in addressing ecological issues and themes? Not one to shy away from penetrating and pertinent questions amidst the messiness of everyday life, Pastor Schade is warmly commended for her passionate and pastoral advocacy of a creation-centered approach to the ongoing calling to faithful preaching."
— J. Jayakiran Sebastian, The Lutheran Theological Seminary at
   Philadelphia

"Leah Schade's *Creation-Crisis Preaching* is a profoundly moving vision of a new Christian homiletics focused on Earth's bounty as God's gift to all of us, human and more-than-human alike. Firmly rooted in the splendor of Pennsylvania's upper Susquehanna Valley, and its degradation from hydraulic fracturing, Schade's pastoral vision is biblically sonorous and liturgically prophetic. Beautifully written and persuasively argued, this exercise in green preaching will offer readers a road map for the future of a church that is recovering its love of creation."
— Mark Wallace, Swarthmore College, Author of *Green Christianity*

"With this slingshot of a book Leah Schade has alerted the people, named the danger, and taken aim to help topple the creation-killing Goliaths of our day. She calls the preacher to claim the Biblical privilege and power for environmental story and truth-telling, and then lays out possibilities for those who would be, and should be champions for the stewardship and healing of the earth. In light of this eco-crisis, my attention to Scripture and my preaching have changed since reading this very timely and important book. You will find the depth of her scholarship compelling, her theological and urgent imperatives to address this eco-crisis convincing, and her illustrative sermons captivating."
— Claire Burkat, Bishop, Southeastern Pennsylvania Synod, ELCA

"In the quest to wake up family and friends to the reality of our growing climate crisis, oddly the most effective voices have come from the most unlikely places. With grace, wisdom, and humor, rural Pennsylvania pastor, Dr. Leah D. Schade uses her voice and storytelling skills to address the biggest challenge facing us today. I can't think of a better resource to tackle hope deniers."
— Peterson Toscano, Host of the Climate Stew Podcast

"Environmental issues have become a critically important subject. However, prophetic and practical sermons in this vital area are scarce. Leah Schade, an eco-homilist, attempts to solve this problem as she provides ways for preachers to effectively communicate environmental concerns. *Creation-Crisis Preaching* juxtaposes theology and science effectively, bridging the gap between religion and ecology. The use of theological and scientific language in this book connects earth's problems to heaven's promise. If you are looking for resources and hope during this ecological crisis look no further."
— Wayne E. Croft, St. Paul's Baptist Church, West Chester, Pennsylvania

"Author Leah Schade is a leading theological voice on eco-preaching and has crafted an intriguing ecofeminist model for preaching. She provides an excellent guide to the issues confronting Creation today and examines how preaching can and should engage these concerns. The use of imagery, language, and concrete suggestions brings the Earth and the preacher into dialogue, in challenging and helpful ways. Providing sermon examples makes this book an even more important partner for the conversation."
— Karyn L. Wiseman, The Lutheran Theological Seminary at
    Philadelphia

"An excellent resource for pastors who wonder about their role in honoring and caretaking God's creation. Drawing on the Lutheran emphases on theology of the cross and the centrality of the resurrection, Dr. Schade provides both a compelling case for why 'creation-crisis preaching' is necessary, and also a solid guidebook on how to do it. Full of rich imagery, confident truth-telling, and resurrection hope, this book inspires new directions for preaching."
— Michael Scholtes, Prince of Peace Evangelical Church, Bangor, Pennsylvania

"Those who preach in the current era of environmental disasters, toxicity in food and water, and atmospheric carbon overload need *Creation-Crisis Preaching* by Leah Schade. Lacing ecofeminist insight into classic Reformation perspective, Schade guides preachers to name crucifixion in creation, coach resistance to exploitation, and assert resurrection precisely where it seems unlikely. The volume is full of specific strategies and examples. Anyone who wants to preach effectively and with relevance needs this book."
— Gilson A.C. Waldkoenig, Gettysburg Seminary

"Leah Schade is an advocate for the integrity of God's creation and invites preachers into her craft. She combines feminist exegesis, theological reflection and her own passion to help preachers help congregants hear anew God's voice in creation and their role in loving, defending and preserving it. Her creative sermons model preaching techniques that bring creation to voice and leave the hearers pondering the awesome ways of God. A needed and important contribution to homiletics and creation care."
— Amy Reumann, Director, Lutheran Advocacy Ministry in Pennsylvania

"Leah Schade is to be congratulated. In one volume she has given us current analyses of environmental issues, a robust eco-theology that is informed by her Lutheranism, gender studies, and ecology, as well as examples for addressing the environmental crisis in the public arena and the congregation. An invaluable resource for anyone interested in being the 'persistent widow' against the status quo in the greening of God's good creation."
— Karl Krueger, The Lutheran Theological Seminary at Philadelphia

"This is one of the most creative books on preaching you will find. Leah Schade draws many strands of theology and homiletics into the orbit of feminism and care for the Earth. She pioneers an interdisciplinary ethic that cries out to be proclaimed. She explores the radical changes necessary for us to address the global crises we face. Her generative reflections on the cross and resurrection invite solidarity with the most vulnerable of Earth's creatures and offer hope that inspires us to action and transformation. The study is punctuated by stories and sermons that illustrate well the proposals she makes. I learned a great deal from this book and I recommended it enthusiastically for teachers and students in preaching, theology, feminism, and environmentalism."
— David Rhoads, Lutheran School of Theology at Chicago

"By responding to the looming environmental crisis, Leah Schade demonstrates the potential for the renewal of Christian preaching. She shows how an ecologically inspired homiletics enables the voice of the Earth to be heard. She shows how an ecotheology is necessarily a feminist theology. And she shows how this ecofeminist theology opens the pathway to a 'shape-shifting Jesus' who still contains the power to surprise. This is an important book that announces Schade as a desperately needed pastoral and prophetic voice of environmental consciousness."
— Jeffrey W. Robbins, Lebanon Valley College, Author of *Radical Democracy and Political Theology*

"*Creation-Crisis Preaching* provides a dense introduction to the theological and philosophical background on which Rev. Schade builds an argument for a new ecofeminist theology. The book is strongest when she takes that theoretical background and shares with her readers her actual, pulpit-delivered sermons—a wide variety of them, many using the Revised Common Lectionary—that she has delivered in three widely different contexts over recent years, from wealthy suburban Philadelphia, to urban, African-American Philadelphia, to rural, poor, farming-hunting-and-fracking areas of Pennsylvania. By interrupting those sermons with internal commentary, linking the text to the theoretical grounding, she paints examples of how challenging theology can scaffold, build, and direct homily."
— Cricket Eccleston Hunter, Director, Pennsylvania Interfaith Power & Light

"It is in the interface between two different ecologies (e.g., where a forest interacts with a savannah) that one finds the most abundant and complex life forms. In this creative nexus of ecofeminist theology and homiletics, Schade similarly creates a rich landscape of insight by bringing together things often kept separate. The work provides helpful overviews of pertinent theory in the fields of ecology, homiletics, and gender studies. The author, mindful of producing a practical resource for the church, always suggests real-life applications within the ecological crisis that defines the contemporary church's *kairos* moment. It is an excellent hermeneutical introduction to a serious and neglected 'text' for today's preachers."
— Erik Heen, The Lutheran Theological Seminary at Philadelphia

"A healthy ecosystem depends upon the interdependent flourishing of its parts. In *Creation-Crisis Preaching* Leah Schade makes a winsome case for the mutually reinforcing contributions of environmentalism and feminism, ecological consciousness and a Lutheran Christian theology of the cross, cycles of nature and the surprising newness of resurrection, homiletical theory and practice. From her experience as an interdisciplinary scholar, a preacher grounded in a local religious community, and an environmental activist, Schade challenges, invites, and inspires others to work that is simultaneously demanding, urgent, and joyful."
— John Hoffmeyer, The Lutheran Theological Seminary at Philadelphia

"A must-read for all preachers, seminarians and theologians committed to environmental concerns. Richly illustrated with sermons, stories and art, the book offers a pastoral theology of creation from an ecofeminist-Lutheran perspective that is academically well-grounded and practically insightful. As a creative contribution to an eco-Christology readers may find the concepts of eco-crucifixion and eco-resurrection profoundly intriguing and meaningful."
— Paul Rajashekar, The Lutheran Theological Seminary at Philadelphia

"Rev. Dr. Leah Schade wrestles with the question of preaching truly good news in the face of the bad news of serious anthropogenic ecological disruption. Animated by ecofeminist insight and Lutheran accents on living word and theology of the cross, the book also highlights Schade's distinctive preaching voice. This work will provoke needed conversation about how the life-giving Gospel can be spoken when the Holocene epoch itself is threatened."
— Benjamin W. Stewart, Lutheran School of Theology at Chicago

"This is a book about proclaiming the cross and resurrection, about Martin Luther's theology of the cross, finding God in the depths of suffering and oppression. Leah Shade has extended that traditional Lutheran emphasis, in our time finding those depths of suffering in the exploitation and debasement of the created world and the systematic oppression of women, a region called ecofeminism. Her exploration of this region is both provocative and stimulating. The book takes its life from her preaching, from imaginative, challenging yet accessible sermons. The cross borne by the created world and women must be proclaimed, faced by all people of faith, if there is to be not reform but resurrection."
— Bob Robinson, The Lutheran Theological Seminary at Philadelphia

"Rev. Dr. Leah Schade's book *Creation-Crisis Preaching* is the perfect companion for Pope Francis' recently released Encyclical 'Laudato Sii'. Scripture is faithfully reinterpreted thru a 'Green Lens', guiding fallen humanity away from fulfilling the prophecy in Genesis 3:17—'Cursed is Earth because of you'—and back into right relationship with all Creation. Two hundred pages of well-documented, thought-provoking, faith-affirming yet faith-challenging didactic catapults the reader into a hopeful, almost 'Franciscan' perspective."
— William Thwing, past President, Pennsylvania Interfaith
    Power and Light

"Dr. Schade does a brilliant job of helping preachers not only to preach toward amelioration of the creation crisis but also of helping them to understand how creation itself literally contributes its voice to proclamation. Schade offers fascinating insights, practical advice, and boldly creative sermons that will be priceless for pastors committed to making a significant difference toward ending the creation crisis. By God's power, this book will help us to avoid catastrophe."
— David Von Schlichten, Seton Hill University

"Norman Wirzba says the environmental crisis demands pastors preach nothing but the doctrine of Creation. Leah Schade provides the theoretical and practical tools needed to do so. Accessibly and with wonderful clarity she inspires as well as instructs on the homiletic challenge before us. One might argue over technical ecological points, but the road she lays out for ministry of Word is one we must travel and she provides a meaningful, coherent and cogent road map."
— Thomas W. Martin, Susquehanna University

"Dr. Schade has done an extraordinary work to help preachers in their attempt to proclaim better care for the environment. In a very interesting and provocative way she draws on ecofeminist theology that recognizes comparisons of how the society has interacted with women and the ecological environment over the centuries. Her understanding of ecology as being that which involves humans and our natural surrounding encourages the preacher to proclaim the 'oneness' that humans and the rest of creation enjoy. Her work embellishes the great scholarship done by other theologians and activists to bring about attention to the dire need for the care and maintaining of a healthier ecological environment. As a skilled homiletician she offers many themes and images to assist preachers in their proclamation. She raises the need for preachers to nurture a greater appreciation and care for the whole of God's creation. Her perspective and approach are very much needed for this present age."
— Charles Leonard, The Lutheran Theological Seminary at
    Philadelphia

"Dr. Schade's book is a timely contribution to theology and praxis, to ways of thinking about and responding to the environmental crisis. Meaning of creation and our stupor before the degradation of nature are among her concerns. A timely resource for preachers, naturalists, and anyone concerned with earthy life and ethics, she proclaims a 'word of hope, empowerment, and courage.' It should become required reading for theology students, environmentalists, and the general public."
— Nelson Rivera, The Lutheran Theological Seminary at Philadelphia

Creation-Crisis Preaching

Ecology, Theology, and the Pulpit

Leah D. Schade

CHALICE
PRESS

ST. LOUIS, MISSOURI

www.ChalicePress.com

Print: 9780827205413   EPUB: 9780827205420   EPDF: 9780827205437

Library of Congress Cataloging-in-Publication Data
Schade, Leah D.
  Creation-crisis preaching : ecology, theology, and the pulpit / Leah D. Schade.
  —1st [edition].
     pages cm
  Includes bibliographical references and index.
  ISBN 978-0-8272-0541-3 (pbk.)
  1. Preaching. 2. Creation—Sermons. 3. Ecotheology—Sermons. I. Title.

BV4211.3.S345 2015
261.8'8—dc23
                          2015013658

Contents

Acknowledgments   xiii

Foreword by John S. McClure   xv

Introduction: Why Creation Needs Good Preaching, and Good   1
    Preaching Needs Creation

    Eco-Crucifixion and Eco-Resurrection?
    "Nature" or "Creation"?
    Creation Care: The Message, the Messenger, and the
        Mode of Delivery
    The Case for an Ecofeminist Homiletic
    A Theology of Preaching for an Eco-Homiletic
    Chapter Overview

1. Environmental, Theological, and Biblical Foundations   17

    PART ONE: A Brief Overview of "the River" of the
        Environmental Movement
    PART TWO: Ecological Theology – A Brief Overview
    PART THREE: Scriptural Eco-hermeneutics

2. Flowering, Leafing, Fruiting—Strategies for Approaching   38
    Environmental Preaching

    PART ONE: The Convergence of Environmentalism and
        Ecological Theology Viewed through Social Movement
        Theory
    PART TWO: Three Approaches for Environmental Preaching
    SERMON: "Welcoming Children into God's Creation"

3. Who Is My Neighbor? Mapping a Preaching's Eco-Location   62

    PART ONE: Beyond the Human: Criterion for Determining
        Who Is "My Neighbor"
    PART TWO: Guiding Questions and Exercises in Mapping Our
        Neighbors
    SERMON: "An Earth Day Sermon"
    SERMON: "A Resurrection Sermon for an Earth-Kin
        Congregation" (A Sermon for an Outdoor Setting)

4. Ecofeminist Theology and Implications for Preaching   92

    PART ONE: What Is Ecofeminism?
    PART TWO: An Overview of Ecofeminist Theology
    Initial Implications of Ecofeminist Theology for Preaching
    An Ecofeminist Hermeneutic for Preaching

5. Developing an Ecofeminist Christology for   117
   Creation-Crisis Preaching

   Sophia-Mer-Christ
   Ecofeminist Christology – A Tense Discomfiture
   Sallie McFague and Theological Models
   Mary Solberg's Lutheran Feminist Theology of the Cross—
       An Ecofeminist Appropriation
   Celia Deane-Drummond's Ecological Theology
   Summary

6. Preaching a Shape-Shifting "Trickster" Resurrection   139
   in the Face of the Creation Crisis

   PART ONE: Rediscovering the "Witty Agency" of Creation
   SERMON: "The Gardener—An Easter Sermon"
   PART TWO: Preaching the Trickster in the Face of Ecological
       Injustice
   SERMON: "The Easter Surprise of Riverdale" (A Sermon for
       Holy Humor Sunday)

7. Earth, Water, and Wind: A Trilogy of Creation-Crisis   163
   Sermons

   An Ecofeminist Homiletic
   Values and Commitments for an Ecofeminist Homiletic
   A Trilogy of Creation-Crisis Sermons
   SERMON: "Earth Speaks: What's Next?"
   SERMON: "I Am Water, I Am Waiting"
   SERMON: "I Am Ruah: A Sermon on Climate Disruption
       Preached from the Perspective of the Holy Spirit"
   Conclusion

Bibliography   188
Index   195

Appendices and study guide can be downloaded for free at:
www.creationcrisispreaching.com

Acknowledgments

I express my sincere gratitude to the following:

The congregations of Reformation Lutheran Church in Media, Pa.; Spirit and Truth Worship Center in Yeadon, Pa.; and United in Christ Lutheran Church in Lewisburg, Pa. My colleagues and mentors in ministry: The Rev. Bishop Claire Burkat, The Rev. Bishop Robert Driesen, The Rev. Dr. Larry Smoose, The Rev. Pat Davenport, The Rev. Robert Kilby, and my colleagues in the Upper Susquehanna and Southeastern Pennsylvania Synods. Special thanks to my "spiritual midwife," Joy Mills.

My excellent dissertation committee: my advisor John Hoffmeyer, Nelson Rivera, and Karyn Wiseman. My mentors and teachers at the Lutheran Theological Seminary at Philadelphia, especially Katie Day, David Grafton, Erik Heen, Phil Krey, Karl Kreuger and the library staff, Jon Pahl, Paul Rajashekar, Robert Robinson, Kiran Sebastian, Mrinailni Sebastian and Storm Swain, as well as the staff of the seminary.

My mentors and colleagues in the Academy of Homiletics, especially those who helped guide this project along the way: John McClure, James Kay, Sally Brown, Heather Murray Elkins, Charles Campbell, Melinda Quivik, and Suzanne Duchesne.

Special thanks to David Rhoads and the members of Lutherans Restoring Creation.

Friends and colleagues in the Interfaith Sacred Earth Coalition of the Susquehanna Valley, Shale Justice, Responsible Drilling Alliance, Protecting Our Waters, Susquehanna Valley Progressives, Rivertown Coalition, and the Tire Burner Team. A special thanks to the Milton Public Library and to Carol and Paul Parowski, both of whom provided beautiful space and hospitality during a critical phase of writing this book. And with gratitude and prayers for Deborah Eck and her Riverdale neighbors.

To the ingenious artist Anthony DiLorenzo – I hope my use of your inspiring work honors the spirit in which you created it. Special thanks to Rev. Ken Hilston for the use of his photographs and to

Father Francis Gargani and the Redemptorist community of Mount St. Alphonsus for their hospitality and gracious spirit.

The staff at Chalice Press who have been wonderfully supportive throughout this entire process: Brad Lyons, Steve McKnight, Gail Stobaugh, K.J. Reynolds, Bill Watkins and John Carey.

Benjamin Hollenbach, who read the initial draft of this book and offered invaluable critiques and edits.

My parents Carl and Peggy Jacobs, who cultivated my love of God's Creation as well as my faith. My father- and mother in-law, Jim and Carolyn Schade, who have given so much support to me and my family. My husband Jim – I could not do what I do without you being the husband, father and best friend you are.

To my children, Rachel and Benjamin. This book is for you, for your children, and your children's children. May it inspire you and the generations who follow to continue the "Great Work" of our time. And may it serve as a witness that while we inherited a broken world for which we are answerable in passing on to you, there were some of us who responded to the call and did all we could to bring about healing, reconciliation and hope.

Foreword

by John S. McClure, Vanderbilt Divinity School

During the week that I began to write this Foreword, Sen. Jim Inhofe (R-Okla.), decided to prove on the floor of Congress that global warming is a false idea dreamed up by an ideologically driven elite. He went out onto the street and brought a snowball into the Senate and spoke about how the unseasonably cold weather outside made a mockery of theories of climate change. Into this highly politicized situation of both willful ignorance and "deer in the headlights" apathy regarding environmental abuse Leah Schade has penned her new, extremely helpful book, *Creation-Crisis Preaching: Ecology, Theology, and the Pulpit*.

In this situation, preachers find that they need help. In the first place, most of us are not experts on climate change, fracking, or many other environmental issues. We know all about biblical criticism, pastoral theology, and denominational polity, but we do not feel competent to engage head-on the many permutations of environmental devastation all around us.

In the second place, we are not certain where to put our oar in the water. Should we preach about the larger issue of care for the environment and our role in that process? Should we become involved in a local environmental campaign and preach out of personal, on-the-ground experience? Should we preach environmental "issue" sermons, or should we layer in a regular set of messages about the environment as the church year or lectionary presents us with the opportunity? Should we develop an environmental "aspect" to our usual theology, or do we need to rethink our entire theological construct so that it is informed by an environmental hermeneutic? Should we draw an ethical "line in the sand" and push for a particular ideological stance, or is it best to move slowly, negotiating an environmental perspective that is responsive to our shared life as followers of Christ?

In the third place, we are not sure of our goals. Are we building a community of environmentalists who will work in unity for change? Are we providing "hints and helps" for daily life that will help each of us do our part? Are we providing new theological perspectives that might "leaven the loaf" in the public conversation about the environment? Are we operating as public theologians, claiming space for the churches within a larger global movement?

Faced with such complexities, and already absorbed in our own set of congregational and homiletical concerns, many of us simply barrel along with our heads down. We find occasional openings to mention our own commitments and those of our denomination regarding environmental issues. We support Christian education opportunities and forums on environmental topics. And we try to model good environmental habits in our personal and congregational lifestyles.

In the pages of this book, Leah Schade helps us to sort out and address many of the often-debilitating issues listed above. As she does so, she speaks from experiences as a preacher and committed practitioner. As an ordained Lutheran pastor, passionate and skillful preacher, and anti-fracking activist, she speaks "as one with authority" about what it takes to be active and involved in changing the rhetoric used to frame environmental discourse. At the same time, she is a skilled interdisciplinary scholar, deftly integrating Christian social ethics, ecofeminism, Lutheran Christology, and homiletics. In *Creation-Crisis Preaching*, she develops new ways of thinking about preaching and the church's practices of communication in the public arena that are powerful, workable, and potentially game-changing. She encourages preachers to get involved in the difficult business of reframing both public discourse and the church's discourse around environmental issues.

If you are like me, reading this book will both trouble you and leave you hopeful. Instead of incessantly nagging at the reader, convicting us of the many things that we are not doing, the tone of this book is not only positive but *redemptive*. This is because Schade permits theology, and more specifically Christology, to lead the way. Whereas many scholars place their theological focus, quite logically, on the doctrine of Creation, she weaves together hard ecological narratives of political and public abuses of power and privilege with the narrative of Jesus' *life and crucifixion*. At the same time, the book opens up rhetorical and activist possibilities and weaves them together with new understandings of Jesus' *resurrection*. This focus on Christology, and the work of Christ between Good Friday and Easter, is one of the most refreshing and helpful dimensions of the book. As

I read the book, I found myself being educated not only about our environment and its potential devastation, but also about the depth of God's *redemptive* love for the world through Jesus Christ.

Creation-Crisis Preaching is also immensely practical, providing a useful homiletical model for those who desire to preach from a theologically informed ecological perspective. This model holds up under real-world testing, bearing the marks of Schade's own experience as a preacher-activist. Schade is not in favor of the "one-off" school of preaching in which preachers suddenly load up on an unsuspecting congregation. She favors weaving together pastoral theology with activism (or least public commitment). Ultimately, however, her interests are theological and rhetorical. She wants preachers be on the watch for ways to *reclaim the entire discourse around the environment*. In a way similar to the great pastoral theologians of the New Testament, who used ideas and images at hand to shape theological discourse (mustard seeds, finishing a race, judgment and acquittal, etc.), Schade wants preachers to take the stuff of our environmental experience today, consider it carefully theologically, and use it to reframe the entire environmental conversation. She believes that preachers can become the front line in the battle for environmental language and rhetoric.

These are difficult and back-breaking times for the Earth that sustains us. We are surrounded by debates regarding oil pipelines, fracking, climate change, emissions control, "clean coal," and so on. In this potentially apocalyptic situation, Schade sounds an urgent call for better theological reflection and ethical forms of worship and preaching that include both the difficult naming of the sinful reality of ecological violence, and the claiming of a redemptive pathway forward. In my opinion, this book represents a milestone in the field of homiletics – heralding a new generation of ecologically informed preaching. I have learned much from Leah Schade, and I am sure that you will as well.

Introduction

Why Creation Needs Good Preaching, and Good Preaching Needs Creation

The old adage for preachers, paraphrased from a quotation by Karl Barth, is that we should preach with the Bible in one hand and the newspaper in the other.[1] As I have opened my local newspaper, *The Daily Item* ("Serving the Central Susquehanna [Pennsylvania] Valley since 1937"), each day since 2011, I have been struck by the increasing number of articles that directly address or simply mention some environmental issue. Central Pennsylvania is a politically conservative, small-town, agrarian, blue-collar, Republican, conservative Christian area of the state. It is certainly no bastion of flaming-green, tree-hugging liberalism. Yet more and more articles, editorials, and op-eds address environmental topics: from climate change to hydraulic fracturing; from climate refugees to intersexed and cancerous fish in the river; from shuttered coal plants to disputed natural gas pipelines—all samplings of issues that regularly make headlines. National newspapers, news magazines, and online news venues carry similar articles and reports on the environment. The news is rarely positive.

Contamination of drinking water, air pollution, loss of species and habitat, and catastrophic weather events due to climate change have implications for every human being on this planet. Yet how often do clergy address environmental issues in their sermons? If you are a religious leader who regularly preaches in a congregation, how many times have you mentioned environmental issues in your preaching in the past year? If you regularly attend worship services as part of a congregation, how many times in the last six months have you heard a sermon that spoke about ecological issues?

According to research conducted by Lifeway, a Christian nonprofit organization, "The majority of Protestant pastors (52%) address environmental issues once a year or less... Eleven percent say they never speak to their church members about the environment."[2] Only 25 percent say they speak on the subject several times a year, and

1

a mere 12 percent say they address the issue at least once a month. In addition, a 2014 survey conducted by the Public Religion Research Institute (PRRI) and the Academy of Religion (AAR) indicated that "most Americans who attend religious services at least once or twice a month hear little from their clergy leader about the issue of climate change. Just over one-third of Americans say their clergy leader speaks about climate change often (11%) or sometimes (25%). More than 6-in-10 Americans say their clergy leader rarely (29%) or never (33%) references climate change."[3]

Given this reticence in addressing environmental issues from the pulpit, it is not surprising that a recent study by sociologist John M. Clements, et al., finds that between 1993 and 2010 there is "no clear evidence of a greening of Christianity among rank-and-file Christians in the general public."[4] Even more troubling in their findings is the fact that Christians today actually have less regard for ecological issues than those who practice no religion. According to Clements, after seven years of the repeated assertion by a few religious leaders that Creation care is not only consistent with, but in fact is demanded by Christian values, "Overall, mainline (and evangelical) Protestants still reported lower levels of environmental concern than did non-Christians and nonreligious respondents."[5]

This stagnation in ecological concern and the corresponding dearth in environmental sermons do not bode well for Creation, nor do they speak well of contemporary preaching. As Lynn White's prescient essay "The Historical Roots of Our Ecological Crisis" made clear over forty years ago, the dire state of the world's ecological systems is due in large part to disastrous Jewish and Christian theological interpretations of biblical texts that promote humanity's domination over Earth.[6] According to White, humans are experiencing an ecological backlash due to the profoundly negative way our interpretations of Scripture have affected our environment.[7] In addition, war, industrialization, agriculture,[8] deforestation, the burning of fossil fuels, overpopulation, and pollution have all combined to "foul the nest," and threaten not only our species' survival but the survival of every other species on Earth as well.

This book, then, begins with two premises: (1) there is a dire need for all Creation, inclusive of humanity, to hear the Good News of the Christian faith in this age of planetary environmental devastation; (2) contemporary Christian preaching, if it is to be responsible to one of the primary justice issues of our time, and if it is to be relevant in the lives of our hearers, must address Creation care on a regular basis. Stated in a more positive way, there is enormous potential for the renewal of Christian preaching, the Church, and Creation through an effort to include Creation both as subject within, and "listener" of, our sermons.

Yet preaching good news in the face of environmental devastation, the climate crisis, extreme energy extraction, and the related issues of economic injustice can feel overwhelming to pastor and congregation alike. Catherine Keller describes the problem this way:

> [W]arnings of social, economic, ecological, or nuclear disaster have become so numbingly normal that they do not have the desired effect on most of us, who retreat all the more frantically into private pursuits... How can we sustain resistance to destruction without expecting to triumph? That is, how can we acknowledge the apocalyptic dimensions of the late-modern situation in which we find ourselves entrenched without either clinging to some millennial hope of steady progress or then, flipping, disappointed, back to pessimism?[9]

Especially for the preacher, the dual temptations either to legalistically preach about "saving the earth" or to irresponsibly encourage waiting passively for a messianic solution can lead to an "apocalyptic either/or logic—if we can't save the world, then to hell with it. Either salvation or damnation."[10]

This book will explore ways to preach through this double-bind in environmental sermons that are equally pastoral and prophetic. The goal of this book is to help religious leaders develop an environmentally literate approach to preaching that honestly and creatively names the reality of our ecologically violated world, while emphasizing God's activity in bringing hope and restoration. More specifically, this book articulates a *Lutheran ecofeminist Christology* that probes the meaning of Jesus' life, crucifixion, and resurrection in light of the dual oppression and destruction of women and Earth, and then provides a *homiletical model* for how to preach from this standpoint.

For a Christian, any "issue preaching" must bring us to the person of Jesus Christ and what his ministry, preaching, teaching, healing, miracles, death, and resurrection mean for the very real bodies of human beings, animals, plants, and even Earth itself. Because I am a Lutheran, I am particularly keen to discover how ecofeminist theology squares with the *theology of the cross*. I firmly believe in the Lutheran conviction that God is found in the very place where we are least likely to look—the apparently God-forsaken place of the cross. I will argue that, in this day and age, God is found particularly within what might be identified as an *eco-crucifixion* that is going on all around us, felt most keenly by women and their families. Because I am a Lutheran homiletician, I am compelled to find a way to preach the *eco-resurrection*, even when most signs indicate that Good Friday may be the fate of our planet.

Eco-Crucifixion and Eco-Resurrection?

Why use the term *eco-crucifixion*? Some may take offense in my using a strongly Christian symbol—indeed, the preeminent Christian symbol—to describe what is happening to Earth. I recognize that my use of this term may be interpreted as an attempt to Christianize the environmental crisis. My work among interfaith grassroots environmental groups has sensitized me to this issue. Christians, too, may resent such a co-opting of this symbol that is deeply spiritual and carries so much personal and communal meaning. Hence, I do not use this term flippantly or without caution. Rather, this word choice arises out of my understanding of what constituted Jesus' crucifixion: the torture and death of an innocent being for the purpose of strengthening and furthering the power of what Walter Wink calls the "domination system."[11] I see a direct parallel to what is happening to Earth and women, for which preaching will play a key role in illustrating.

I draw support for this idea of a crucified Earth from the work of Mark Wallace, who makes the case that the "cruciform Spirit" embodied in and through Earth suffers just as Jesus did on the cross, this time under the continual siege of "ecological sin." (This will be more fully explicated in Chapter 7.) Wallace warns of a "permanent trauma to the divine life itself" through the crucifixion-like ecocide that humans continually inflict upon Earth and its inhabitants.[12] His powerful equating of God's suffering through Jesus on the cross with God's suffering through the embodied Spirit in Earth is meant to spur "a conversion of the heart to a vision of a green earth, where all persons live in harmony with their natural environments . . . [and] work toward a seamless social-environmental ethic of justice and love toward all of God's creatures."[13]

What is missing in Wallace's analogy, however, is the resurrection. In fact, as we will note in the chapters ahead, the resurrection is curiously absent from the work of many ecological and ecofeminist theologians, leading to what a Lutheran might identify as a kind of environmental "works righteousness," wherein we mistakenly believe there is something we as humans can do to earn salvation – ours or this planet's. Because of the enormity of the environmental problems facing Earth and its inhabitants, and the full burden of ecological sin that rests squarely on the shoulders of humanity, the task of healing and liberating both Earth and women can seem overwhelming, especially if we rely solely on our human capacity to turn things around and effect change. Thus a question to explore is the degree to which Lutheranism can dialogue with ecofeminism and expand not just the concept of the crucifixion, but our understanding of the power of God in the resurrection. When we have witnessed instances of environmental devastation, the term *eco-crucifixion* may be appropriate to describe the experience of the kind of death we are seeing and experiencing planet-wide. At the same time, we will also spend a good deal of time discussing what it means to proclaim an *eco-resurrection* that arises through God's grace.

"Nature" or "Creation"?

While we are on the subject of terminology, let's take a moment to clarify how I will be referring to the natural world. *Nature* is the term used within a scientific framework that utilizes an explanatory model based on empirical data. In contrast, *Creation* is a theological term used within a religious framework to denote that which is *created* by God. This is not to say that there is a mutually exclusive dichotomy between the two terms, or that one is to be privileged over the other. Rather, the theological term of Creation builds upon the empirically observable phenomenon of nature and "functions within Christianity as an axiological claim [as] the moral and aesthetic point of the symbolically mediated relationship between creation and nature."[14] As W. David Hall explains, "[T]he fundamental significance of the idea of creation is that the universe is invested with value, that is, creation is good, and that this value makes a claim on us."[15] Hall affirms that both the scientific term *nature* and the theological term *creation* are valid and have their place in human understanding of the world, but they should not be confused and folded into one another.

What the concept of Creation gives us is "a buttress against the tendencies toward devaluation within anthropocentrism" that can, in turn, contribute to both an ecological and comprehensive ethic.[16] As Hall explains: "The Christian view of the world is one of a realm invested with value and a proper object of respect because it is the creation of a good and perfect deity. This recognition of the world as a realm of value says important things about the place of humanity and human use of the world."[17] What the biblical narrative tells us is that "humans have the capacity to take a consciously responsible attitude toward the nonhuman world. Indeed, it is this capability to be consciously oriented in the world that makes ecological ethics a possibility."[18]

Thus, I generally use the term *Creation* instead of *nature*. Obviously when quoting or referring to the works of other ecotheologians who use these terms interchangeably, I will use their terminology. But for my purposes, I will heed Hall's admonishment to use the theological term for the world—*Creation*. In addition, I make the decision to capitalize the word so as to denote the level of respect I am affording the other-than-human world as a *subject* rather than object. I will do the same with the term "Earth" when addressing it as an entity (as opposed to lowercase *earth*, which is a synonym of *soil*). Capitalizing the term indicates that this is an entity with a name and worthy of such. This will be especially important when considering how both Earth and Creation are each a subject and "character" in the biblical narrative, and thus in preaching.

Creation Care: The Messenger, the Message, and the Mode of Delivery

The work of Clements and his associates on the lack of "greening" among Christians in America supports my assertion that preaching has a role to play in raising the level of environmental consciousness among Christians. They note that as the greening trend among Christian leaders and organizations deepens and broadens, they expect to see a measurable shift in the level of environmental concern among Christians.[19] The researchers suggest:

> [S]cholars may perform a series of experiments designed to systematically examine those factors expected to facilitate or inhibit the diffusion of green Christianity from religious leaders and organizations to rank-and-file members. Essential

here may be three characteristics: *the messenger, the message, and the mode of delivery* [emphasis author's]. For instance, who is more influential in changing the attitudes, beliefs, and behaviors of rank-and-file Christians: the leader of their local congregation or a well-known national Christian spokesperson? How do different characteristics of the message content matter (e.g., the use of Holy Scripture, the invocation of different values, etc.)? Finally, how does the effectiveness of a message to embrace green Christianity vary depending on its mode of delivery: in a church newsletter, *in a homily* [emphasis author's], via Bible study, etc.?[20]

My book responds to the last question by contending that sermons (or homilies) can indeed enhance the effectiveness of the message to embrace green Christianity. Research from the 2014 PRRI/AAR survey on religion, values, and climate change confirms this assertion, in that "Americans who say their clergy leader speaks at least occasionally about climate change also score higher on the Climate Change Concern Index. More than 6-in-10 Americans who report hearing about climate change from their clergy leader at least occasionally are very (38%) or somewhat (24%) concerned about climate change, compared to approximately 4-in-10 (39%) Americans who attend congregations where the issue is rarely or never raised."[21]

Given the fact that the majority of religious leaders do not address environmental issues in their sermons more than a few times a year (if at all), it may be that what is needed are models and frameworks to help preachers craft sermons that are informed by an environmental hermeneutic, consistent with ecological theology, attentive to the context of their hearers, and creatively inspired to include the "voice" of Creation within preaching. This book aims to offer just that. More specifically, I insist that environmental preaching intentionally incorporate the joint and interrelated oppression of women and Creation if it is to be faithful to Jesus' command to tend to "the least of these" on our planet. Thus this book offers the unique lens of ecofeminist Christology through which to interpret both Scripture and the environmental context of our time.

The Case for an Ecofeminist Homiletic

How does ecofeminist theology connect with the discipline of homiletics? Just as the field of justice and ethics preaching has recently seen the development of homiletics from the standpoints of traditionally underrepresented and unheard constituencies (the disabled, Native Americans, lesbian/gay/bisexual/transgender, victims of sexual violence, and so on), so I believe the time has come for the ecofeminist voice, speaking with and alongside Earth and women, to take its place within the theory and praxis of preaching. My hope is that by bringing together the disciplines of homiletics, ecology, and gender studies in the spirit of interdisciplinary scholarly practice, a conversation will begin that sparks ongoing collaboration. Certainly this mutual engagement will lead us to points of tension and controversy (which will be discussed in these pages). Nevertheless, I make the case that by bringing the approach of ecofeminist theology to the field of homiletics, both preachers and ecofeminists will mutually benefit—and be mutually challenged.[22]

For example, the holistic, healing, and prophetic work of ecofeminism will reach a larger, wider, and theologically grounded audience through the preaching of clergy committed to its principles. At the same time, ecofeminist theology will be challenged to more deeply reflect on theological tenets that thus far have been underdeveloped so that it may more profoundly resonate with people of faith. The discipline of homiletics, by the same token, will find its praxis enriched and better equipped to speak to the contemporary questions of the ecological crisis by paying attention to this particular intersection of women and the environment. Thus it is preaching that stands at the center point of the crossroads of church and society, as well as science and religion, always finding ways to create dialogue between theology and the world in which theology can bring discernment, understanding, and hope. As Richard Lischer states:

> Preaching functions as a corrective of theology. When theology moves toward synthesis with its dialogue partners of other disciplines, preaching recalls for it its character as *theology*, reflection on God. When theology becomes preoccupied with the symmetry of its own system or the cogency of its method, preaching reminds it of the catastrophic core of judgment and grace that called theology into being.[23]

Ultimately, my aim is to begin a mutual engagement between ecofeminism and homiletics that results in "sustained intellectual exchange that includes informed and detailed debate," which may enable us to become a more "productive scholarly community."[24]

Some may wonder if there is a need for an ecofeminist Christology within preaching and homiletics. A brief glance at the bibliography at the end of this book will demonstrate that, in fact, there has been very little attention paid to ecotheological concerns within either the academy or mainstream preaching publications. At the very least, I believe the claim can be made that the connection to ecotheology is in its nascent stage,[25] and that attention to ecofeminist theology within homiletic circles does not yet exist. Many of the homiletic resources addressing environmental concerns contain sermons and essays affirming that Earth and its other-than-human creatures have rights, deserve respect, and should be treated as equal partners in God's Peaceable Community.[26] Yet none of them specifically address the intersection of feminist and ecological issues from a homiletical perspective. I believe this to be a fundamental oversight within these monographs.

For example, take the otherwise fine volume *The Season of Creation: A Preaching Commentary*,[27] a collection of essays that connect biblical scholarship with ecological theology for the purpose of designing worship and sermons around the recently initiated "Season of Creation," a three-year lectionary cycle made up of twelve Sundays that seeks to connect congregations with Creation. In this book, some of the hermeneutical essays employ the metaphors of earth-as-mother, earth as giving birth to humanity, and earth as experiencing labor pains, while other essays mention the need for ecojustice in preaching. However, completely overlooked is the opportunity to connect ecojustice issues to the specific plight of women, and to trace the oppression of Earth to that of the patriarchal oppression of women.

In fact, in his essay on "Humanity Sunday," Norman Habel repeatedly assigns blame for our world's eco-crisis to the generalized concept of anthropocentrism without taking into account the ecofeminist argument that it is not necessarily human-centeredness that is the problem. Ecofeminists such as Wendy Lynne Lee point out that the notion of humans being able to decenter themselves is rather illogical, since centeredness is an "ineradicable feature of human consciousness."[28] Lee argues that "human-centeredness is not the enemy of environmental responsibility, but its most vital ally."[29] It is, rather, androcentrism, and particularly male chauvinism, that is at the root of the hubristic belief that males were created to rule and dominate not just nature, but those whom they deem to be lowest in the hierarchy, namely females. Thus it is the phenomenon of male dominance that "produces particular *patterns* of environmental destruction, nonhuman animal exploitation and cruelty, and social injustice," which ecotheologians such as Habel and others are either ignorant of, overlook, or simply ignore.[30] I argue that the silence within ecotheology and in the pulpit on this aspect of male domination and patriarchal aggression toward God's Creation and women must be corrected. This book aligns with Lee's assertion that the task of "an ecologically inspired feminism [is] to identify these patterns, spell out their place in the logic, and dispel the illusion of their naturalness and/or divine sanction."[31]

A Theology of Preaching for an Eco-Homiletic

Before we begin to explore the possibilities for developing an ecofeminist Christology for preaching, I must articulate how I understand the task of preaching and its relevance to contemporary questions and issues. Influenced by Lutheran theology, I work with the understanding that "[i]t is supremely through the words of the preacher that the Word of God in the Scriptures is made alive in the present."[32] Further, "[T]he Word of God spoken is itself the Word of God in preaching or God's own speech to us. Thus preaching has a dual aspect: divine activity and human activity, God's Word and human speech."[33] This dual function of preaching will be reflected in my development of an ecofeminist theology for preaching. I will emphasize both the human activity of the preacher who takes the suffering of women and Earth into consideration when proclaiming God's Word, as well as God's action of calling people to awareness, repentance, and hope in the midst of ecological despair. As well, the proclamation of what *God* is doing to bring about an eco-resurrection will be a key feature of this type of preaching.

What is the role of preaching in the community? L. Susan Bond notes, "Preaching is a sacramental activity that makes Christ present to the community… Preaching is nothing more and nothing less than the invocation of the dangerous memory, the subversive presence, and the transformed future of the God we know in Jesus/Christ."[34] Similarly, Lischer states, "Preaching is the church giving voice to its experience of God's salvation."[35] This process goes hand-in-hand with theological reflection on the significance of God's Word for the world. Lischer points out, however, that such proclamation must be engaged with other dialogue partners: "Beyond the preacher's pastoral experiences lies theology's perennial dialogue with psychotherapy, anthropology, philosophy, ideology, politics, the arts, science, medicine, cybernetics, and ethics. This dialogue not only informs preaching; it makes it possible—and intelligible."[36] He explains that the sermon brings together a confluence of the disciplines of "exegesis, biblical theology, systematics, dogmatics, symbolics, apologetics, history, comparative religion, practical theology, liturgy, the wisdom of the nontheological disciplines, [and] the experience and personality of the minister... It is a fragment, a moment in the whole, yet contains the whole."[37] This will be evident in developing approaches to Creation-crisis preaching in which the sermon may be thought of as a kind of synecdoche—one small instance of the proclamation of God's Word to the world in which the whole of its universal and particular significance is present.

I make the argument that it is possible to defend a commitment to preaching that is responsible to the gospel while also being responsive to ecofeminist theology. Further, I contend that the preacher's attention to ecofeminist theology is not merely an imposition of external ideological concerns on the Church's proclamation. Rather, it arises out of, and is a natural extension of, the gospel's concern for "the least of these" and the Good News about the coming of God's Peaceable Community. I am particularly interested in creating a dialogue within the area of justice and ethics preaching between ecofeminist theology and homileticians.

Most importantly, this project will emphasize a Lutheran understanding of preaching—not just the cross, but also the resurrection, for "only because of the resurrection does Christian preaching assume the significance and importance so desperately claimed for it... [A] Christian theology of the cross, no matter how poignant and realistic it is in its description of the Crucified One, cannot stop short of resurrection."[38] It is the promise of the resurrection that gives the commission and power to preach, observes Lischer.[39] I will build on that premise and make the argument that a proclamation of the resurrection for the sake of Creation and women is a subject that has not been sufficiently explored within homiletics. Therefore, this project offers another voice and range of issues to consider within the discipline of homiletics that will extend work already done, while expanding preaching in ways that are relevant to contemporary concerns for the joint rights of women and Earth.

Chapter Overview

Chapter 1 provides a brief overview of the "river" of the environmental movement in the United States and shows how ecological theology naturally springs forth from the environmental movement, particularly as it has emerged out of my own Lutheran tradition. This chapter will also explore the fertile soil of the interpretation of Scripture through an ecological lens and offer a way of preaching that enables the voice of Earth to be heard.

Chapter 2 asks, What are possible strategies for approaching an ecological homiletic? It begins by consulting social movement theory and examines the role of religion—specifically, the function of preaching—within the environmental movement. At the same time, we begin to see how the social movement theory concepts of framing, meaning construction, and the rhetoric of change can provide a means by which to understand and analyze our Creation-crisis preaching. The second part of the chapter offers three approaches for preaching drawn from the stages of a deciduous tree: *consciousness-raising* (flowering), *call for action* (leafing), and *sustainable change* (fruiting). The purpose is to offer an analytical framework for understanding the preacher's intention for particular sermons, the discursive and rhetorical devices used to accomplish the sermon's goal, and criteria by which to measure the sermon's effectiveness. This section provides preachers with ways to think about their own creative, rhetorical, and performative strategies for ecotheological preaching. A sermon illustrating these very notions concludes the chapter.

Chapter 3 offers guidelines for preachers to situate themselves at the intersection of their local eco-habitat and institutional nexuses of business, government, society, and culture. This eco-location for preaching is in response to the question, "Who is my neighbor?" By surveying our landscapes and extending the concept of "neighbor" to our Earth-kin and to those entities that connect to each other in biotic, social, and spiritual ways, we can begin mapping our neighbors. This chapter will be buttressed by the work of four key homileticians—Rebecca Chopp, Lucy Atkinson Rose, Anna Carter Florence, and John McClure—to support this mapping of the other-than-human neighbors in our midst. Each provides important theoretical concepts to undergird Creation-crisis preaching. The chapter also includes two sermons to give concrete examples of contextual green preaching.

Chapter 4 brings the concepts of ecofeminist theology into conversation with preaching. The chapter begins with an overview of ecofeminist theology, its emphases, and its principles—which include the critique of patriarchy, hierarchy, instrumentalism, dualism, and "othering." It also provides a critical examination of the associations that people make between women and nature. The chapter concludes with initial implications of ecofeminism's impact on the practice of preaching. Here we see John McClure's concept of "exiting" as particularly helpful in connecting ecofeminism with homiletics.

This ecofeminist homiletic is developed around the focal point of Christology in chapter 5 that includes an artistic rendering of Jesus by Anthony DiLorenzo, which I have titled "Sophia-Mer-Christ." The image provides the frame for a Christology that addresses the intersection of women and Earth within a shape-shifting Jesus. This chapter will also examine a feminist theology of the cross developed by Mary Solberg to provide the foundation for an ecofeminist Christology. Celia Deane-Drummond's theology of evolution will round out the implications of Jesus' incarnation, crucifixion, and resurrection for an ecofeminist Christology that is infused with wisdom and wonder.

Chapter 6 draws on the motif of the shape-shifting "trickster" to add yet another perspective to ecological theology and the ecofeminist Christology developed in the previous chapter. The goal is to provide an expansive way to think about preaching Jesus's incarnation, crucifixion, and resurrection, while also moving our conceptions of nature beyond that of passive recipient or docile victim of abuse. Utilizing Charles Campbell's and Johan Cilliers' homiletical notion of "preaching fools," this chapter challenges us to find creative ways to proclaim the hidden power of God that surprises us with justice and hope. Two sermons are included in this chapter. One illustrates the image of Jesus as the shape-shifting "gardener" on Easter morning. The other is a more prophetic sermon proclaiming the risen Christ in a community destroyed by fracking and its related industries.

The final chapter begins by outlining the guiding principles that shape an ecotheological homiletic for preaching informed by ecofeminist principles, and offers a trilogy of sermons informed by these criteria and principles. Each sermon is "preached" from the perspective of one of the other-than-human characters in the biblical narrative. The sermons are each preceded by an explication of the eco-hermeneutic used for the biblical texts and are followed by an explanation of how the principles of ecofeminist theology were applied. This chapter will help to demonstrate what is possible for homiletic theory and praxis incorporating the values of ecotheology and ecofeminism. The concluding argument of the book is that by using an ecofeminist theology of the cross and resurrection, we will be addressing the needs of the world in terms of justice and ethics, making our preaching more relevant, and offering the proclamation of the gospel in a uniquely contextual and life-giving way.

Notes

[1] "Take your Bible and take your newspaper, and read both. But interpret newspapers from your Bible." Karl Barth, quoted in *Time* magazine ("Barth in Retirement," May 31, 1963). See http://content.time.com/time/subscriber/article/0,33009,896838,00.html, accessed May 11, 2015.

[2] Mark Kelly, "Lifeway Research Studies Global Warming Beliefs among Protestant Pastors" (April 16, 2009), accessed July 13, 2014, http://www.lifeway.com/Article/LifeWay-Research-studies-global-warming-beliefs-among-Protestant-pastors. According to the website, "The phone survey sampled randomly selected Protestant churches. Each interview was conducted with the senior pastor, minister or priest of the church called and responses were weighted to reflect the geographic distribution of Protestant churches. The completed sample of 1,002 phone interviews provides a 95 percent confidence that the sampling error does not exceed ±3.2 percent. Margins of error are higher in sub-groups."

[3] Robert P. Jones, Daniel Cox, Juhem Navarro-Rivera, *Believers, Sympathizers, and Skeptics: Why Americans Are Conflicted About Climate Change, Environmental Policy, and Science: Findings from the PRRI/AAR Religion, Values, and Climate Change Survey* (Washington, D.C.: Public Religion Research Institute and American Academy of Religion, 2014), 4.

[4] John M. Clements, Aaron M. McCright, Chenyang Xiao, "An Examination of the 'Greening of Christianity' Thesis among Americans, 1993-2010, " *Journal for the Scientific Study of Religion* 53:2 (2014): 373.

[5] Ibid., 388.

[6] Lynn Townsend White, Jr., "The Historical Roots of Our Ecologic Crisis," *Science* 155, no. 3767 (March 10, 1967).

[7] There are, of course, other contributions to our current ecological crisis that will be discussed in the next chapter, in which I critically engage White's thesis. What is significant about his proposal, however, is that it is the first time religion is indicted as a major contributor to the ethical failings that have led to the current state of our planet.

[8] White made no distinctions between different types of agriculture in his critique. It must be noted that co-op and family farms committed to organic, chemical-free and humane agriculture and animal husbandry are very different from "factory farms," monoculture, and industrialized agriculture.

[9] Catherine Keller, *Apocalypse Now and Then: A Feminist Guide to the End of the World* (Boston: Beacon Press, 1996), 14.

[10] Ibid.

[11] See Walter Wink's *The Powers* trilogy, especially *Engaging the Powers: Discernment and Resistance in a World of Domination* (Minneapolis: Fortress Press, 1992).

[12] Mark I. Wallace, *Finding God in the Singing River: Christianity, Spirit, Nature* (Philadelphia: Fortress, 2005), 129.

[13] Ibid., 136.

[14] W. David Hall, "Does Creation Equal Nature? Confronting the Christian Confusion About Ecology and Cosmology, " *Journal of the American Academy of Religion* Vol. 73, no. 3 (September 2005): 784.

[15] Ibid.

[16] Ibid.

[17] Ibid., 806.

[18] Ibid., 808.

[19] Clements, "An Examination of the 'Greening of Christianity,'" 389.

[20]Ibid.

[21]Jones, Robert P., *Believers, Sympathizers, and Skeptics*, 4.

[22]Eckert and McConnell-Ginet, in their field of sociolinguistics, have advocated for an "interdisciplinary community of scholarly practice" in their particular area of language and gender studies. Their insights apply to my own project of bringing ecofeminist theology and homiletical theory into conversation for the purpose of mutual enrichment. See: Penelope Eckert and Sally McConnel-Ginet, "Communities of Practice: Where Language, Gender and Power All Live," in *Language and Gender: A Reader*, ed. Jennifer Coates (Malden, Mass.: Blackwell, 1998).

[23]Richard Lischer, *A Theology of Preaching: The Dynamics of the Gospel*, rev. ed. (Eugene, Oreg.: Wipf and Stock, 2001), 9.

[24]Eckert and McConnel-Ginet, "Communities of Practice," 493.

[25]It is notable that there has been a marked increase in the number of essays and articles that address ecological issues in preaching journals and papers presented in the Academy of Homiletics beginning in 2007. While there are certainly a number of factors influencing this uptick, it is worth noting that the widely viewed documentary *An Inconvenient Truth*, about former Vice President Al Gore's campaign to bring global climate change to the world's attention, was released the previous year, in 2006. There are also several websites indicating that individual congregations, religious bodies, and worldwide faith groups have begun to embrace the tenets of ecotheology and religious environmentalism. For example, there is the Yale Forum on Religion and Ecology; "Many Heavens, One Earth," an event organized by the United Nations and the Alliance of Religions and Conservation (ARC), designed to promote environmental evangelism among people of faith—the largest international gathering of its kind; Regeneration Project's Interfaith Power and Light campaign; and the Jewish Climate Change Campaign. There are also some web-based resources that offer examples of ecologically themed sermons. Three examples of these websites include: www.letallcreationpraise.org, www.interfaithpowerandlight.org, and www.lutheransrestoringcreation.org.

[26]This term, "God's Peaceable Community," is a variation on the phrase, "God's Peaceable Kingdom," the title of artist Edward Hick's famous 1826 painting of Isaiah 11:6–8. *Rhoads*

[27]Norman C. Habel, David Rhodes, and H. Paul Santmire, eds., *The Season of Creation: A Preaching Commentary* (Minneapolis: Fortress Press, 2011).

[28]Wendy Lynne Lee, "Restoring Human-Centeredness to Environmental Conscience: The Ecocentrist's Dilemma, the Role of Heterosexualized Anthropomorphizing, and the Significance of Language to Ecological Feminism," *Ethics and the Environment* 14, no. 1 (2009): 29.

[29]Ibid., 41.

[30]Wendy Lynne Lee, *Contemporary Feminist Theory and Activism: Six Global Issues* (Ontario, Can.: Broadview Books, 2010), 196.

[31]Ibid., 196.

[32]Dennis Ngien, "Theology of Preaching in Martin Luther," *Themelios* 28.2, Spring 2003 (accessed March 6, 2013, http://www.biblicalstudies.org.uk/pdf/themelios/luther_ngien.pdf).

[33]Ibid.

[34]L. Susan Bond, *Trouble with Jesus* (St. Louis: Chalice Press, 1999), 150.

[35]Lischer, *A Theology of Preaching*, 79.

[36]Ibid., 9.

[37]Ibid., 15.

[38]Ibid, 16, 19.

[39]Ibid., 21.

1

Environmental, Theological, and Biblical Foundations

"Living water" will be a recurring theme throughout this book, both in terms of scriptural references and regarding the very real need for clean water for all living things. Water also provides the underlying metaphor for this chapter on environmental, theological and biblical foundations for Creation-crisis preaching. Recognizing that "living water" is only as healthy as the ecosystem through which it flows, we begin by examining the foundations that undergird and inform our "green" preaching: the environmental movement, ecological theology and a "green" hermeneutic for interpreting Scripture. Part One of this chapter will present a brief overview of the environmental movement, including a basic review of its history, followed by a closer view of where the movement is today—often called the "fourth wave" of environmentalism. Specifically, I will discuss Michael Zimmerman's analysis of the divergence between "reform environmentalists" and "radical ecologists," as well as his suggestion of ecofeminism as a viable response to critiques of deep ecology.

In Part Two, ecological theology naturally "bubbles up" around the environmental movement, allowing for discussion of how the two intersect and mix, especially regarding their critiques of those aspects of society that have led to the eco-crisis we currently face. The concentration will be on examining Lynn White's now-famous essay, "The Historical Roots of Our Ecological Crisis," which implicated the Judeo-Christian tradition as a main contributor to our ecological ills. This will be followed by a focus on ecotheology within American

Lutheranism over the past fifty years, particularly regarding the work of H. Paul Santmire.

Part Three will follow an important stream within the field of religion and ecology—that of eco-hermeneutics for Scripture. This will be prefaced with a hermeneutical framework based on the work of Hans-Georg Gadamer. Following will be the work of Norman Habel and Dieter Hessel, which provides the eco-hermeneutic for developing a way of preaching that enables the voice of Earth to be heard.

PART ONE: A Brief Overview of "the River" of the Environmental Movement

The Susquehanna River of central Pennsylvania is not just important to the state's and our country's history. It is also part of my personal history. I have fished its waters for catfish and bass, explored several of the creeks that feed into it, and paid attention to the way it has been used (and misused) for human consumption, agriculture, recreation, travel, energy, and commerce over the last four decades. Ask someone to identify on a map where the Susquehanna ends, and she will easily point to the Chesapeake Bay. But ask where it begins, and the answer is not so clear. With both a West and North Branch, it is difficult to say where the river actually starts. If you look at a satellite view you will see that the lines of the two branches come together into one larger confluence, which then flows through the southern part of the state and empties into the Bay in Maryland. The farther upstream you follow these branches, you see that they split into a multitude of creeks and streams, all branching out across the landscape like the roots of a tree.

Like a river whose many tributaries defy the marking of a definitive beginning, the exact start of the environmental movement in the United States evades precise pinpointing.[1] From a bird's eye view of history, one may identify numerous contributors to modern-day environmentalism. The conservation movement of the late 1800s, led by figures such as John Muir, Henry David Thoreau, Gifford Pinchot, and Theodore Roosevelt, raised to public consciousness the need to protect natural areas, either for recreation, "wise use," or preservation of their pristine state.[2] Scientific knowledge and technological development during that time also exercised a great influence on environmental consciousness, for good and for ill. For example, there was simultaneously the ability of human beings to create synthetic chemicals that threaten biological life at all levels (grimly described in Rachel Carson's seminal book *Silent Spring* [1962]), and greater study and understanding of how chemicals affect human and ecological health. Similarly, technological developments in fossil fuel extraction led to all manner of pollution and political strife worldwide. All the while, these forms of energy gave human beings the ability to travel the globe and even fly to the moon and see this precious, fragile blue and green orb in the context of the vastness of space, providing human beings a new means and perspective to appreciate its wonders.

In the 1970s several events occurred and issues arose that indicated that a true movement around ecological and environmental issues was afoot.[3] The proliferation of nuclear weapons, as well as nuclear power plants and their attending risks of disasters and radioactive fallout, were the impetus behind the start of international organizations such as Greenpeace and Friends of the Earth. Concerns about population explosion and the ability of the planet to sustain life under such a heavy consumptive burden became part of the public conversation. Species extinction, endangerment, and loss of habitat, together with concerns about pollution, acid rain, and global warming, led to international conferences, policy decisions, and popular events such as Earth Day, which all concentrated on protecting and preserving both human and other-than-human life. Today, there are several trends in ecology and environmental science that have raised a heightened sense of urgency, including studies of overpopulation, resource and energy use, and the climate crisis.

Christopher Rootes describes the evolution of the environmental movement as a progression from conservation (e.g., hunters concerned with protecting habitat for game) to preservation (e.g., those concerned about protecting environments for the spiritual and aesthetic relationship between humans and nature) to "reform environmentalism,"which recognizes that "humankind is part of nature and that the health of human populations is intimately bound up with the health of ecosystems."[4] As ecology became an academic discipline, environmentalism became more a part of mainstream discourse, yet it did not usually undertake extensive analysis of the social or religious origins of environmental problems. According to Rootes, the modern environmental movement in the past fifty years was built upon six conditions: (1) increasing understanding of environmental impacts; (2) increase of the extent of higher education leading to greater public awareness; (3) increasingly effective technology; (4) the mass media; (5) the critique of consumerist capitalism; and (6) an emphasis on the systemic sources of environmental problems.[5] Key actors during this evolution were the New Left (which quickly disintegrated after the 1970s), student movements, and the Green parties that arose in Europe in the 1970s. Protests against toxic industrial waste as well as nuclear waste eventually led to the development of the environmental justice movement. Groups such as Greenpeace and Friends of the Earth were emblematic of these movements.

The environmental movement first came to widespread public consciousness on Earth Day in 1970. That first event, "in which 20 million Americans participated in a wide variety of actions designed to highlight environmental issues, can be seen both as the culmination of the environmental critique that developed during the 1960s and as a critical point in the transition toward the institutionalization of environmentalism in the US."[6] Since that time, we have entered what Rootes calls the "fourth wave" of the environmental movement. Deep ecology, part of this fourth wave, "starts from the proposition that all living things are part of a single natural system in which no part is of more intrinsic value than any other."[7] Unlike its anthropocentric predecessors in the environmental movement, deep ecology is "resolutely ecocentric even to the point of hostility to humankind as the perpetrator of greatest damage to other elements of the ecosystem."[8]

Another strand within the fourth wave has been environmental justice, which raised awareness of environmental racism. Activists within this part of the movement connect the "brown" issues of pollution, toxic waste, and public health to the poorest communities (which are usually populated with people of color), which have no recourse to resist this kind of public health oppression imposed on them.[9] Sociologist Robert D. Bullard, for example, has documented the way in which government and business elites in the United States have targeted black communities for polluting industries, municipal landfills, and toxic-waste dumps, even while these enterprises are touted as job-creators for these impoverished communities. This results in lax enforcement of pollution standards and environmental regulations, even while health risks to workers and residents increase.[10]

Ecofeminism, yet another strand in the fourth wave of environmentalism,

> has emphasized the special affinity between women and women's roles in society and interests in environmental protection... [E]cofeminism has developed principally as a critical discourse within environmental philosophy and has given rise to few and relatively small organizations in western industrialized countries. In such less-industrialized countries as India and Kenya women have played important roles in environmental activism.[11]

Finally, Rootes identifies ecotheology as the newest and perhaps fastest growing strand of environmentalism in the United States, where "it is invoked as a critique of the previously dominant Christian view that human domination over the natural world was divinely ordained and justified unlimited human exploitation of the natural environment."[12] Before exploring ecotheology in detail, some space must be devoted to understanding a critical distinction between reform environmentalists and radical ecologists, because this will provide an important template upon which to place ecotheology.

Fourth Wave Environmentalism: Reform Environmentalists and Radical Ecologists

In his book *Contesting Earth's Future: Radical Ecology and Post-modernity*, Michael Zimmerman describes a critical divergence within environmentalism — that of "radical ecologists" from "reform environmentalists." According to Zimmerman, "reform environmentalists" are much more conservative and anthropocentric in their views. For example, they may seek to reduce pollution and promote "wise use" of natural resources, but stop short of calling for fundamental change in society's instrumentalist view of nature, wherein nature is seen as a means to an end to satisfy human needs, wants, and profits.[13] In contrast, radical ecologists insist that "unless far-reaching changes *do* occur in this and related views — as well as in authoritarian political and socioeconomic arrangements associated with them — modernity's attempt to gain wealth and security through technological control over nature could trigger off ecological catastrophes capable of destroying humankind and the rest of terrestrial life."[14]

Zimmerman identifies three major branches of radical ecology: deep ecology, social ecology, and ecofeminism. Regarding the first, deep ecologists blame the ecological crisis on "anthropocentric humanism that is central to the leading ideologies of modernity, including liberal capitalism and Marxism."[15] They seek to dispel the false notion that humankind is separate from, distinct from, and ontologically superior to the rest of nature. In their view, "[A]ttempts to gain control of nature have also led to attempts to control human behavior in ways that limit freedom and prevent 'self-realization.' In general, deep ecologists call for a shift away from anthropocentric humanism toward an ecocentrism guided by the norm of self-realization for all beings."[16]

Social ecologists are more specific in their critique, narrowing their focus down from overarching anthropocentrism to the social structures rooted in authoritarianism, as seen in both capitalism and state socialism. Social ecologists critique the "[w]anton destruction of nature [which reflects] the distorted social relations at work in hierarchical systems, in which elites subjugate other people while pillaging the natural world for prestige, profit, and control."[17] Social ecologists insist that human beings are, in a sense, nature becoming conscious of itself, and that the way to preserve human life is for people to see themselves fully embedded in the natural systems that sustain them. According to Zimmerman, "[S]ocial ecologists call for small-scale, egalitarian, anarchistic societies, which recognize that human well-being is inextricably bound up with the well-being of the natural world on which human life depends."[18]

The third type of radical ecology Zimmerman describes is ecofeminism. Ecofeminists explain the ecological crisis as "the outcome of patriarchy that follows the 'logic of domination.'... Wild nature, then, like 'headstrong' women, must be tamed, ordered, and otherwise rendered pliant to masculine will. According to ecofeminists, only dismantling patriarchy will free human relations and nature alike from the dark consequences of the logic of domination."[19]

Zimmerman's book critically analyzes and assesses all three strands and asserts that "radical ecologists have no choice but to enter into a *contest* to determine which of many competing views will shape the future of human society and the living Earth."[20] He uses the term "contest" in the most positive sense of the word, explaining that it encourages the best in all contenders. In Zimmerman's view, a vital contributor to that contest is that of ecofeminism, which he sees as containing helpful correctives to both deep and social ecology. For Zimmerman, the concern about deep ecology stems from the ecofeminist "charge that progressive views of history are accounts of the rise to power of the masculine ego. Some ecofeminists read deep ecology's ideal of wider identification [with nature] as grounded in a masculinist concept of self which seeks to obliterate difference by reducing everything 'other' to 'same.'"[21] He looks to ecofeminism to develop a post-patriarchal "progressive" view of history.

Part Two: Ecological Theology—A Brief Overview

If the environmental movement is similar to a river whose exact beginning is difficult to locate, then ecological theology may be compared to a spring that bubbles up from the ground at a certain spot, but whose true origins are so deep and diffuse, its actual genesis defies precise determination. As H. Paul Santmire states, "Ecological theology is a relatively new movement in the world of christian[22] thought and practice and therefore is neither widely understood nor easily defined, even by those who are variously involved in the movement."[23] One could make the argument that any summary of ecological theology should include a survey of the history of the theology of nature as found in the writings of early Christian theologians and trace its development through the millennia to the present day. Fortunately, Santmire has already done this work in his volumes *The Travail of Nature: The Ambiguous Ecological Promise of Christian Theology* and *Nature Reborn: The Ecological and Cosmic Promise of Christian Theology*. Other scholars would recommend taking a wider view of how different religions have related to the natural world and the modern study of environmentalism and ecology. That, too, has been well covered by authors and editors such as Celia Deane-Drummond, Roger Gottlieb, Laurel Kearns, and Catherine Keller.

For our purposes, we'll focus on an article written by Lynn Townsend White in 1967, which is widely regarded as being the first to introduce the idea that Judeo-Christian tradition may be a main contributor to the current ecological crisis. In the nearly fifty years since the publication of that essay, his critique has reached across the globe, meeting and joining other voices in the religious realm that speak *of* Earth and *for* Earth in the context of biblical hermeneutics, theological inquiry, liturgical studies, feminism and gender equality, and ethics and justice issues.[24] And because some of the presuppositions he introduced have had lasting influence on consequent ecological theologians, some of which are problematic to ecofeminist theologians, it is pertinent to undertake a critical assessment of his work.

"The Historical Roots of Our Ecologic Crisis"

White's essay, "The Historical Roots of Our Ecologic Crisis," sought to find the underlying presuppositions that have led to our ecological crisis. First, he identified Western science and technology imposed in thoughtless, arrogant, and empirical ways as sharing much of the guilt for the crisis. The roots can also be traced back to medieval peasants who developed "ruthless plowing," which changed the relationship between humanity and earth from one of interdependence to that of exploitation. But, according to White, there is an even deeper cause: religion, which, in his view, has deeply and devastatingly conditioned our oppressive relationship to nature. Specifically, Judeo-Christian religion has conditioned humanity toward this oppressiveness and bears "a huge burden of guilt" for paving the way for scientific and technological power to get out of control. White's essay laid the blame for the ecological crisis firmly at the feet of the biblical traditions that create "Christian attitudes toward man's relation to nature...[in which] we are superior to nature, contemptuous of it, willing to use it for our slightest whim."[25]

In White's analysis, beginning with the Creation narrative itself, the anthropocentric attitude of the Judeo-Christian religion affected the way humanity treated the environment:

> By gradual stages a loving and all-powerful God had created light and darkness, the heavenly bodies, the earth and all its plants, animals, birds and fishes. Finally, God had created Adam and, as an afterthought, Eve to keep man from being lonely. Man named all the animals, thus establishing his dominance over them. God planned all of this explicitly for man's benefit and rule: no item in the physical creation had any purpose save to serve man's purposes. And, although man's body is made of clay, he is not simply part of nature: he is made in God's image.[26]

While White raises some important points to consider, subsequent scholars have found his critique to be overgeneralized and lacking in a more nuanced and detailed understanding of the text. For example,

Sallie McFague counters, "It is simplistic to blame the Hebrew and Christian traditions for the ecological crises, as some have done, on the grounds that Genesis instructs human beings to have 'dominion'; nevertheless, the imagery of sovereignty supports attitudes of control and use toward the nonhuman world."[27] McFague's assessment proves correct, especially after a closer reading of Genesis, which yields a more complex theological rendering of the interrelationship between God, humans, and nonhumans on this planet. As we will see, White's critique is too general and not informed by proper, detailed study of the text (although this may be due to the fact that at the time when White was writing, the subdiscipline of ecological hermeneutics within biblical studies had not yet emerged).

In his sweeping view, White does not distinguish between the Priestly and Yahwist accounts in Genesis, which need to be examined and contrasted. When teasing apart the two accounts, carefully considering the concerns, choice of words, and differing emphases of these authors, one discovers a more nuanced reading of Genesis. Granted, biblical scholars such as von Rad and Brueggemann have shown that the Priestly version of the Creation story (1:1—2:4) does, indeed, establish a paradigm of hierarchy and domination for humankind over and above the earth and its creatures.[28] However, what White failed to realize is that the Yahwist account of Creation provides a model for humans caring for and working alongside Earth as partners in God's Creation. In Genesis 2:15 we read, "The LORD God took the man and put him in the garden of Eden to till it and keep it." As Carol Newsome points out, this is God creating a relationship between Earth and earthling—not of human over Earth, but human within and beside Earth. "The image that Genesis has of the original human relationship to the environment is one that involves interaction but of a very modest sort. The forest of Eden is imagined as what we would call a permaculture, where human attention is part of the ecosystem, but of a nature rather like 'light pruning and raking.'"[29]

Nevertheless, while White may have missed the mark in pinpointing the origin of the ecological crisis on the theology of Genesis, his observations of the way Christianity became hostile toward the natural world are much more on target. He noted that as Christianity spread into the Mediterranean and northward into Europe, its adherents engaged in de-spiritualizing the pagan practices of honoring all aspects of Creation. Thus it became "possible [for

Christianity] to exploit nature in a mood of indifference to the feelings of natural objects."[30] Add to this the Latin West's approach to science and technology, which eventually removed the necessity of God in Creation, and nature is rendered completely vulnerable to conquest because of "man's transcendence of, and rightful mastery over, nature."[31] White warned that the ecological crisis will continue to worsen until "we reject the Christian axiom that nature has no reason for existence save to serve man."[32]

Indeed, Christianity itself is not to be rejected—just those tenets that serve to drive our planet further into the breach. Instead, a "recycling" of images, stories, and myths are necessary for the rehabilitation of our religion and, in turn, God's Creation. In White's words:

> Both our present science and our present technology are so tinctured with orthodox Christian arrogance toward nature that no solution for our ecologic crisis can be expected from them alone. Since the roots of our trouble are so largely religious, the remedy must also be essentially religious, whether we call it that or not. We must rethink and refeel our nature and destiny.[33]

White's proposed solution was to learn from Saint Francis of Assisi "the virtue of humility, not merely for the individual but for man as a species."[34] His hope was that, inspired by Saint Francis, humanity will be able to see all creatures as brothers and sisters joining in praise of God, thus respecting, honoring, protecting, and learning from them. For White, the answer is not to jettison Christianity, but in fact to embrace the "transcendent Creator, who, in the ultimate gesture of cosmic humility, assumed flesh, lay helpless in a manger, and hung dying on a scaffold."[35]

Ecological Theology, Panentheism, and Subscendence

One of the most basic questions we need to answer in developing a theology for Creation-crisis preaching is how we understand the relationship between Creator and Creation. Traditionalists may feel some nervousness that this project will result in animism (the belief that natural objects and phenomenon contain the whole of the Divine), which would lead to a pagan idolatry of Creation. This is certainly not my intention, because there is indeed a differentiation between who God is and what God creates. I would argue, however, that the pendulum has swung so far to the extreme of detached theism that a rupture in the relationship between humanity, God, and Creation has resulted. It is high time for a move in a direction that would re-envision the natural world as sacred and thus deserving of human nurture and love. Thus I turn to *panentheism* as a way to emphasize God's immanence in Creation while retaining God's transcendence and distinction from Creation. This position holds that Creation is part of God but does not constitute the whole of God.

Mark Wallace's work on *Christian animism* is helpful here. He notes the apparent disjointedness between the historic Christian proclivity to view the material world as inferior to the soul and spirit. This results in a world- and flesh-denying belief that is at odds with classic animists who see all of the created world as infused with goodness and God's presence. What Wallace points out is that there is a distinction between paganism/heathenism/pantheism and the kind of Christian animism he envisions. Where Christian animism differs is its emphasis on panentheism, whereby God's Spirit is infused within the created world but cannot be limited to or contained within that creation. Rather than continue to emphasize God's transcendence, Wallace introduces a new term, *subscendence*:

> God flowing out into the Earth, God becoming one of us in Jesus, God gifting to all creation the Spirit to infuse all things with divine energy and love. Now nothing is held back as God overflows Godself into the bounty of the natural world. Now all things are bearers of the sacred; everything that *is* is holy; each and every creature is a portrait of God.[36]

Thus Wallace creates a dialectic of "ensoulment" (Earth blessed as the living realization of divine grace) and "enfleshment" (God pouring out Godself into the carnal reality of lived existence).[37]

As will be seen in the sermons throughout this book, the concepts of panentheism and subscendence will undergird the theological premises of Creation-crisis preaching. This is not to say that there are no other theological frameworks for understanding the relationship between God and Creation when thinking about green preaching. Others, for example, may hold to a strictly transcendent theology and think about the "voice" of Earth and nonhuman entities in a purely metaphoric or poetic way. My approach in this book does not preclude other frameworks and allows that there are other entry points for approaching homiletics from an ecotheological perspective.

My development of the present project, however finds its footing in the notion of God's immanence in Creation in a panentheistic way, being "in, with and under," as Luther described.

Ecological Theology: A Lutheran Perspective

One of the first theologians to respond to the call to overlay the concerns of our modern ecological crisis upon the Christian faith, and vice versa, was H. Paul Santmire, a Lutheran scholar whose 1970 book *Brother Earth: Nature, God, and Ecology in a Time of Crisis* was among the first to articulate an ecological theology. A pioneer in what was a nascent field at the time, Santmire helped to organize a conference at Wellesley College entitled "An Ecological Reformation of Christianity?" in 1974.[38] He went on to write several books that provide a helpful background for understanding a theology of nature traced through the writings of Christian thinkers throughout history. Though often laboring alone or with a handful of other like-minded scholars in this new field of thought, [39] Santmire's work is emblematic of the steadfast Lutheran engagement with ecotheology over the last fifty years. As Santmire observes:

> From the outset, particularly in the United States, lutherans have been deeply involved [in ecotheology]. One might even argue that american lutherans have played a central role in the cultivation of this new field, both at the reflective, theological level and in the wider dimensions of church life, especially by the production of two theologically substantive social teaching statements (1972, 1993) and by the emergence of a host of practical ministries in lutheran circles that have embodied and, in some sense, tested the viability of the theological reflection and the social teaching statements.[40]

Unlike our metaphorical river of environmentalism and bubbling spring of ecological theology, the emergence of American Lutheran ecotheology, according to Santmire, can be pinpointed to a precise year: 1962, when a relatively obscure American Lutheran theologian named Joseph Sittler addressed the World Council of Churches Assembly in New Delhi and called for a "Christology of nature." At the time, the predominant view of nature among Christians, including Lutherans, was a continuation of that which had arisen during the period of Protestant Orthodoxy[41] and continued through the theo-anthropocentric theology of Karl Barth. Christians saw nature "mainly as the stage for human history and as the world of resources given to humans by God for the sake of human well-being and human justice."[42] In contrast, Santmire and other Lutheran ecotheologians such as Larry Rasmussen (eco-ethics), Ted Peters (eschatology), Terence Freitheim (biblical studies), and Gordon Lathrop (liturgical studies) began the shift toward a theo-cosmocentrism. In this new paradigm,

> the chief objects of theological reflection are God and the whole created world... Human creatures, according to this way of thinking, are fully and irrevocably imbedded in nature, notwithstanding the fact, variously expressed, that humans, even as they are essentially interconnected with all other creatures, nevertheless have a divinely bestowed vocation that in some sense differentiates them from all other creatures, just as all other creatures also have divinely bestowed characteristics that in some sense differentiate them from one another, in the one created world of "nature" (Joseph Sittler) or the one created earth-community (Larry Rasmussen).[43]

In this paradigm there is a move away from seeing humans in a hierarchical, domineering relationship with Earth and its creatures toward seeing them as being in kinship with all God's Creation. Values such as caring, loving, communion, and cooperation with nature replace those of objectification, commodification, abuse, and destruction. This has implications for humans' relationship not just with nature but also with each other. For if the ethic of care is inclusive of both humans and other-than-humans, concerns for justice become expansive in all directions across the web of life.

One of the highlights of Lutheran ecotheology in terms of its relevance for the Church as well as the larger society is the 1993 social statement co-authored by Santmire for the Evangelical Lutheran Church in America entitled "Caring for Creation: Vision, Hope, and Justice."[44] With clear biblical foundations and sharp analysis of the ecological crisis of our time, the document engaged in comprehensive and sophisticated ethical discourse—one that provided a helpful theological framework for interpreting what the human relationship with nature is intended by God to be. This included a global and social justice perspective that lifted up the need to care for the poor and oppressed in light of the interrelated degradation of nature.

Another movement of note within American Lutheranism has been that of grassroots environmentalism. New Testament scholar David Rhoads has been an inspirational and indefatigable force behind the establishment of the Lutherans Restoring Creation movement and the website "The Web of Creation." Rhoads has also worked in conjunction with other ecotheologians worldwide to create the website "Let All Creation Praise," based on an experimental liturgical lectionary that focuses on ecological theology and ecojustice issues. The site also includes resources for worship planning, preaching, prayers, rituals, and orders of worship with Creation-care themes.

Santmire also notes with admiration that much of this grassroots Lutheran environmentalism was able to take hold because of a long and robust history of outdoor ministry within the Lutheran Church. Church camps and places such as Holden Village in Washington State helped create a hospitable setting for grassroots Lutheran environmentalism to go mainstream, observes Santmire.[45] Today Lutheran colleges, universities, and seminaries are taking seriously the role of being both leaders and models of "greening" their curricula and campuses.[46]

As Santmire points out, however, the history of Lutheran ecotheology has been dominated almost exclusively by white, academically-oriented men. He notes that "this situation must change."[47] As of 2012, he believed that as the second chapter of American Lutheran ecotheology was beginning to be written, things *were* changing. He envisions a more global focus for Lutheran ecotheology in the years ahead, and hopes for more women to arise within this discipline.[48]

Part Three: Scriptural Eco-Hermeneutics

Before explaining the recent development of ecological hermeneutics within the study of biblical interpretation, I wish to briefly describe the hermeneutical framework that I have found helpful in developing an ecological hermeneutic for preaching. In his tome *Truth and Method,* the philosopher Hans-Georg Gadamer has provided a key concept that will aid in the discussion of preaching and ecotheology—that of the *fusion of horizons.* Having this model for "understanding understanding" in place will better enable the navigation and interweaving of the various "horizons" within this project of ecological preaching.

Hermeneutics According to Gadamer

Hermeneutics is the study of understanding and interpretation. Within the word, one may recognize the name Hermes from Greek mythology. "Hermes served as a messenger of the gods, charged with the task of transmitting divine communication into a form human intelligence can grasp. Retaining this basic meaning, hermeneutics in the modern period was viewed initially as a discipline concerned with the art and science of the interpretation of ancient texts in ways that were meaningful to people in the present."[49] Thus hermeneutics can mean either the way in which a particular text is interpreted and the art and science by which a text is made meaningful, or it can refer to the study of the interpretive process itself.

The singular contribution Gadamer made to the discipline of hermeneutics was his claim that the interpreter is not just a subject over against a text (be it a piece of art, a work in literature, and so on), but is actually and simultaneously an object addressed by the text as subject. As Bjorn Ramberg puts it in his summary of Gadamer's thought: "It is not really we who address the texts of tradition, but the canonic texts that address us. Having traveled through decades and centuries, the classic works of art, literature, science, and philosophy question us and our way of life. Our prejudices…are brought into the open in the encounter with the past."[50]

In Gadamer's hermeneutical circle, when you stand at a particular perspective and encounter a particular "other" (such as a text, person, work of art, etc.), you see what he calls a "horizon" of that distant other and all the meaning it has accumulated up to the point of your encounter with it. At the same time, the other is encountering your horizon as well, along with all your "prejudices" (pre-judgments) that you bring to the point of encounter. It is at that point of encounter where the "fusion of horizons" occurs. According to Gadamer, this is the movement of the two horizons toward a shared point of understanding and meaning. As he explains, "In a tradition this process of fusion is continually going on, for there, old and new are always combining into something of living value, without either being explicitly foregrounded from the other."[51] This is not to say that there is a complete overtaking of one horizon by the other. Rather, there is a tension between the two horizons that is a natural result of the "otherness" encountered by each of the two horizons. The task of hermeneutics, then, takes place in the interplay of interpretation and understanding in the dialectical exchange between the two horizons.

Preaching Informed by the "Horizon" of Creation

A key concept for Gadamer is "historically effected consciousness" wherein all understanding is affected, not just by an event or text in the past, but also by the accumulation of interpretation and tradition radiating forth from that event/text through history. Thus our consciousness is inevitably shaped by all that has come before us. The fusion of horizons as brought about by this historically effected consciousness has important ramifications for preaching that is informed by ecotheology. Any preacher can be seen as standing at the nexus between various horizons encountering each other. The Bible, the cumulative tradition of exegesis over the centuries, the contemporary context of a particular congregation, the Holy Spirit we assume to be guiding our interpretation, the listeners on a particular Sunday, and the preacher herself/himself are all intersecting at the point of a fusion of horizons that is the sermon.[52] But for the preacher concerned with ecotheological issues, one other horizon will come to bear—the horizon of God's Creation. In fact, it is a literal horizon, that which is experienced *on Earth*. This has been a scantily explored realm in both hermeneutics and homiletics, but it warrants serious attention for preachers committed to ethical preaching appropriate for the environmental crisis that affects Earth and Earth's inhabitants today. Such a horizon brings with it an accumulation of historically effected consciousness that predates the existence of human beings, and yet is greatly affected by its encounter with the human subject today. When such a preacher brings this horizon of God's Creation into an encounter with the reading of Scripture, the result is biblical eco-hermeneutics.

Biblical Eco-hermeneutics

Biblical ecological hermeneutics is an emerging field that began in 2000 with the work of Norman C. Habel and Peter Trudinger publishing The Earth Bible series. Both men went on to become co-chairs of the Section on Ecological Hermeneutics of the Society of Biblical Literature, which seeks to encourage biblical exegesis informed by the "Earth Bible Principles." Their chief aims are:

> to declare, before reading the text, that we are members of
> a human community that has exploited, oppressed, and

endangered the existence of Earth community; to become progressively more conscious that we are also members of the endangered Earth community in dialogue with ancient texts; to recognize Earth as a subject in the text with which we seek to relate empathetically rather than as a topic to be analyzed rationally; to take up the cause of justice for Earth and to ascertain whether Earth and Earth community are oppressed, silenced, or liberated in the text; and to develop techniques of reading the text to discern and retrieve alternative traditions where the voice of Earth and Earth community has been suppressed.[53]

Six ecojustice principles were developed in dialogue with ecologists as well as theologians and biblical scholars. We will want to keep these in mind as we consider scriptural exegesis for Creation-crisis preaching. The principles are as follows:

1. *The principle of intrinsic worth:* The universe, Earth, and all its components have intrinsic worth/value.
2. *The principle of interconnectedness:* Earth is a community of interconnected living things that are mutually dependent on each other for life and survival.
3. *The principle of voice:* Earth is a subject capable of raising its voice in celebration and against injustice.
4. *The principle of purpose:* The universe, Earth, and all its components are part of a dynamic cosmic design within which each piece has a place in the overall goal of that design.
5. *The principle of mutual custodianship:* Earth is a balanced and diverse domain where responsible custodians can function as partners with, rather than rulers over, Earth to sustain its balance and a diverse Earth community.
6. *The principle of resistance:* Earth and its components not only suffer from human injustices but actively resist them in the struggle for justice.[54]

While I will be delving into these principles more as the book unfolds, for now I want to stress Habel and Trudinger's insistence that "there is no 'orthodox' ecological hermeneutical method. Rather within the current environmental crisis, in dialogue with the growing field of ecology, and in line with recent hermeneutical approaches such as feminist and postcolonial readings, ecological hermeneutics is a work in progress."[55] What this ecological hermeneutic demands, however, is a "radical reorientation to the biblical text."[56] This is not simply joining ecology to a theology of biblical criticism in order to render it as a particular object of study. Rather, Earth is seen as a *subject* in the text, capable of encountering the text from its own horizon, with an attending hermeneutic of suspicion (here one will recognize a feminist influence on this approach). Ultimately, one of the key tasks of ecological hermeneutics is "to retrieve the perspective or voice of Earth and Earth community of whom we humans are but one species."[57] Key to my project will be to bring an *ecofeminist* perspective to these ecojustice principles.

The task of biblical ecological hermeneutics, however, brings up an obvious question: *How* do Earth and its inhabitants make their perspectives known in a discourse that uses traditional human language? Gadamer's hermeneutical framework can be helpful here as well. In his chapter "Language as the Medium of Hermeneutic Experience," he explains that in order for two individuals of different languages to speak to each other, they must initially engage in translation. "Thus every translation is at the same time an interpretation," he adds.[58] In trying to "converse" with other-than-human nature, we have to "translate" because it does not speak to us in human language. This will involve imaginative and creative engagement with animals, plants, and entire ecosystems to "hear" what they might say. This is already being done by naturalists, biologists, and environmental scientists who "listen" to species and ecosystems by way of observation, collection and analysis, and interpretation of data. In fields other than science, examples of "listening" to Earth can be found in any of The Earth Bible series volumes, in which theologians and biblical scholars work from an eco-centric hermeneutic to interpret the text from Earth's point of view.

Admittedly, this task of dialoguing with the other-than-human realm is fraught with the potential for misunderstanding, misguided motives, and manipulation. Questions about discernment will need to be asked as we wonder who gets to speak for Earth— environmentalists? land developers? impoverished women? advertising firms? theologians? Agreeing on a criteria for discerning the "true" voice of Earth and Earth's inhabitants will be a tremendous challenge. Nevertheless, it behooves us to at least try to understand what the other-than-human other is trying to communicate to us. It will be one of the chief tasks of Creation-crisis preaching to help listeners find common ground for communicating with each other about how we may proclaim God's Word of justice, hope, reconciliation, and healing for the Earth community, inclusive of humanity. We turn to this task in the next chapter.

Notes

[1] I am cognizant that this overview is ameri-centric and thus lacking in global scope. In many ways it was the threats to local environments posed by American imperialism throughout the globe (deforestation, commandeering of natural resources, building of dams, and other instances of what ecofeminist Vandana Shiva would call "mal-development") that prompted a need for concerted environmental attention in other countries.

[2] Gifford Pinchot coined the term "wise use" in 1910 as a way to describe the idea of sustainably harvesting natural resources. It also included the notion of multiple uses for public land, ranging from recreation to timber harvesting to wildlife habitat preservation. In modern times, however, the term was co-opted by some anti-environmental groups opposed to the environmental movement on the grounds that land use is to be unfettered by legislation and the political agenda of environmentalists. (See James McCarthy, "First World Political Ecology: Lessons from the Wise Use Movement," *Environment and Planning,* 2002, vol. 34, pp. 1281–1302.) The Wise Use movement is also driven in part by the theological argument that God gave the earth to human beings for their benefit. (See: Chris Crews, "Contesting the Anthropocene: Fundamentalism, Science and the Environment," WPSA Paper Presentation, March 29, 2013. Accessed February 18, 2015, http://www.academia.edu/3090128/Contesting_the_Anthropocene_Fundamentalism_Science_and_the_Environment; and Stephenie Hendricks, *Divine Destruction: Dominion Theology and American Environmental Policy,* [Hoboken, N.J.: Melville House, 2005].)

[3] There is a distinction between *ecology* and *environmental studies,* and it is one of scope. Ecology refers to the study of living things within a biome and their relationships with each other and nonliving entities. Environmental studies include ecological considerations, but apply them to the realm of human interaction, including the social and political aspects of such relationships.

[4] Christopher Rootes, "Environmental Movements," in *The Blackwell Companion to Social Movements,* ed. David A. Snow, Sarah A. Soule, and Hanspeter Kriesi (Malden, Mass.: Blackwell Publishing, 2007), 612.

[5] Ibid., 613–14.

[6] Ibid., 614.

[7] Ibid., 615.

[8] Ibid.

[9] It is worth noting one exception to communities of color being subjected to environmental toxins—that of slickwater hydraulic fracturing (fracking), which is happening in rural, low-income areas typically populated by whites. This issue of fracking will be addressed throughout this book.

[10] Robert D. Bullard, ed., *Dumping in Dixie: Race, Class, and Environmental Quality,* 3rd ed. (Boulder, Colo.: Westview Press, 2002). See also: Ronald Brownstein, "The Toxic Tragedy," in Ralph Nader, Ronald Brownstein, and John Richard (eds.), *Who's Poisoning America: Corporate Polluters and Their Victims in the Chemical Age* (San Francisco: Sierra Club Books, 1982); Robert D. Bullard, "Solid Waste Sites and the Black Houston Community," *Sociological Inquiry* 53 (Spring 1983), 273–88; Robert D. Bullard, "Environmentalism and the Politics of Equity: Emergent Trends in the Black Community," *Mid-American Review of Sociology* 12 (Winter 1987), 21–37; Commission for Racial Justice, *Toxic Wastes and Race in the United States: A National Report on the Racial and Socioeconomic Characteristics of Communities with Hazardous Wastes Sites* (New York: United Church of Christ, 1987); Julian McCaull, "Discriminatory Air Pollution: If the Poor Don't Breathe," *Environment* 19 (March 1976), 26–32; David Morell, "Siting and the Politics of Equity," in Robert W. Lake, ed., *Resolving Locational Conflict* (New Brunswick, N.J.: Rutgers University Center for Urban Policy Research, 1987), 117–36.

[11] Rootes, "Environmental Movements," 616.

[12]Ibid.

[13]This is in contrast to viewing Earth as having intrinsic value regardless of its worth to human beings.

[14]Michael E. Zimmerman, *Contesting Earth's Future: Radical Ecology and Postmodernity* (Berkeley: University of California Press, 1994), 3.

[15]Ibid., 2.

[16]Ibid.

[17]Ibid.

[18]Ibid.

[19]Ibid.

[20]Ibid., 13.

[21]Ibid., 232.

[22]Santmire does not capitalize the proper names of denominations or religions in his paper.

[23]Paul Santmire, "American Lutherans Engage Ecological Theology: The First Chapter, 1962–2012, and Its Legacy," in *Convocation of Teaching Theologians* (Columbus, Oh.: Trinity Lutheran Seminary, 2012), 1.

[24]Examples of scholars exhibiting ecological consciousness in these areas are Carol Adams, Thomas Berry, John B. Cobb, Jr., Daniel Cowden, Calvin B. Dewitt, Aruna Gnanadason, Mary C. Grey, Norman Habel (particularly his *Earth Bible* series), Dieter T. Hessel, Catharine Keller, Gordon Lathrop, Sallie McFague, James A. Nash, Larry Rasmussen, Rosemary Radford Reuther, H. Paul Santmire, and Mark Wallace.

[25]Lynn Townsend White, Jr., "The Historical Roots of Our Ecologic Crisis," *Science* 155, no. 3767 (March 10, 1967)., 1206.

[26]Ibid., 1205.

[27]Sallie McFague, "An Earthly Theological Agenda," in *Ecofeminism and the Sacred*, ed. Carol Adams (New York: The Continuum Publishing Company, 1993), 91.

[28]Gerhard von Rad, *Genesis: A Commentary*, trans. John H. Marks (Philadelphia: The Westminster Press, 1961); and Walter Brueggemann, *Genesis: A Bible Commentary for Teaching and Preaching* (Atlanta: John Knox Press, 1982).

[29]Carol A. Newsome, "Common Ground: An Ecological Reading of Genesis 2—3," in *The Earth Story in Genesis*, Earth Bible, vol. 2, ed. Norman Habel and Shirley Wurst (Sheffield, England: Sheffield Academic Press, 2000), 64–65. It is worth noting that Genesis 2:15 is not an inoculant to anthropocentric interpretation. This passage has often been used to support "wise use" and "responsible stewardship" stances that, while an improvement over neglect or scorn for the natural world, still support the "reform environmentalism" Zimmerman critiques as anthropocentric and ultimately damaging.

[30]White, "The Historical Roots of Our Ecologic Crisis," 1205.

[31]Ibid., 1206.

[32]Ibid., 1207.

[33]Ibid.

[34]Ibid., 1206.

[35]Ibid., 1207.

[36]Mark I. Wallace, *Green Christianity: Five Ways to a Sustainable Future* (Minneapolis: Fortress Press, 2010), 7.

[37]Ibid., 9.

[38]Cf. especially James A Nash, "Toward and Ecological Reformation of Christianity," *Interpretation* 50:1 (1996), 5–15.

[39]Santmire recalls: "We knew that something momentous was unfolding in the world around us and we felt called upon to address the then emerging crisis theologically, but most of us also felt very much alone and without viable theological resources with which to work," Santmire, "American Lutherans Engage Ecological Theology," 4.

[40]Ibid., 1.

[41]More on the theology of nature in Protestant Orthodoxy was in a paper I presented entitled "The Theology of Nature in Reformation Theology and Protestant Orthodoxy," at the Patristic, Medieval and Renaissance Conference of the Augustinian Institute at Villanova University, Villanova, Pa., October 2011.

[42]Santmire, "American Lutherans Engage Ecological Theology," 6.

[43]Ibid., 8.

[44]Available online at http://www.elca.org/Faith/Faith-and-Society/Social-Statements/Caring-for-Creation.

[45]Ibid., 19.

[46]Concern for ecological issues is beginning to permeate the highest levels of learning and research, as evidenced in the course offerings of religious studies programs and seminaries that either directly address or include readings on ecological issues (See: Sarah Hammond Creighton, *Greening the Ivory Tower: Improving the Environmental Track Record of Universities, Colleges and Other Institutions* (Cambridge, Mass.: MIT Press, 1998). In addition, the emergence of initiatives such as The Web of Creation (webofcreation.org), the Eco-Justice Working Group of the National Council of Churches, and The Green Seminary Initiative (greenseminaries.org), indicates that Christian academics and activists are discerning where research and scholarly works can most effectively aid the work of preserving the planet that birthed us and sustains us.

[47]Santmire, "American Lutherans Engage Ecological Theology," 26.

[48]In fact, several female Lutheran scholars, activists, pastors, churchwide staff, and grassroots organizers have been doing important work in the fields of ecological/environmental theology, biblical eco-hermeneutics, environmental ethics, and environmental advocacy. That list includes (but is not limited to): Lisa Dahill, Mary Minette, Cynthia Moe-Lobeda, Phoebe Morad, Amy Reumann, Barbara Rossing, Terra Rowe, Rebecca Sauer, Aana Vigen, Audrey West, and Nancy Wright.

[49]Richard R. Osmer, "Teaching as Practical Theology, " in *Theological Approaches to Christian Education*, ed. Jack L. Seymour and Donald E. Miller (Nashville: Abingdon Press, 1990), 223.

[50]Bjorn Ramberg, "Hermeneutics," http//plato.standford.edu/entries/hermeneutics (accessed December 26 2010).

[51]Hans-Georg Gadamer, *Truth and Method*, 2nd rev. ed. (New York: Crossroad, 1991), 306.

[52]Not only is the sermon a fusion of horizons between the past and the present, there is also the eschatological aspect of a fusing of horizons between the world we are experiencing now in all of its brokenness and sinfulness, and the "new creation" that is being proclaimed in an already-and-not-yet moment of Christ's salvific redemption made real for the hearers in the sermon. "But where exactly is the dividing line between the present world and the world that comes to be?" Gadamer asks (ibid., xxx). In other words, for the preacher looking to help mediate the arising of a new world that takes into account the diverse horizons of the people in her congregation, as well as the horizon of the coming kingdom of God, the hermeneutical task takes on an added dimension of openness toward the future as well as the past.

[53]Norman C. Habel and Peter L. Trudinger, *Exploring Ecological Hermeneutics*, Society of Biblical Literature Symposium Series (Atlanta: Society of Biblical Literature, 2008), 1–2.

[54]Norman C. Habel, "Guiding Ecojustice Principles," in *Readings from the Perspective of Earth*, ed. Norman C. Habel, The Earth Bible (Cleveland: Pilgrim Press, 2000), 2.

[55]Habel and Trudinger, *Exploring Ecological Hermeneutics*, viii.

[56]Ibid., 3.

[57]Ibid., 8.

[58]Gadamer, *Truth and Method*, 384.

2

Flowering, Leafing, Fruiting—
Strategies for Approaching
Environmental Preaching

In *Living Beyond the End of the World,* Margaret Swedish calls attention to the fact that despite decades of clarion calls by the environmental movement for change that would reign in the burgeoning worldwide eco-crisis, widespread embrace of the principles, attitudes, lifestyles, policies, and spiritualities that would enable such change have failed to take hold. Citing Mary Evelyn Tucker and John Grim, co-directors of the Forum on Religion and Ecology at Yale, she writes:

> There's a puzzling disconnection between our growing awareness of environmental problems and our ability to change our present direction. We have failed to translate facts about the environmental crisis into effective action in the United States. We are discovering that the human heart is not changed by facts alone but by engaging visions and empowering values. Humans need to see the large picture and feel they can act to make a difference.[1]

Swedish calls for a change in culture, ways of thinking, and the values that form the paradigm in which the current system of domination resides and holds people in thrall. A move away from this system must simultaneously replace it with something more viable, sustaining, and life-giving. She sees the need for a *movement* to be the impetus behind such a shift and suggests the story of the loaves and fishes—in which Jesus takes these meager provisions, blesses them, and shares them with the crowd, resulting in a miraculous feeding—as a parable for our time:

> The loaves and fishes—taking from the scarcity of the moment to provide what is needed by all—can suggest a great deal for us in a world where food, water, and energy are becoming crucial issues for much of humanity, where we must find a way to share these things without depleting what will be necessary so that future generations have food, water, and energy... What is lacking is the moral and ethical will to create such a world.[2]

I contend that preaching may be a resource for activating the moral and ethical will within congregations and in the larger society to address ecological injustice, and may provide an impetus for the kind of environmental social movement Swedish envisions. I find support for this assertion in the work of noted feminist homiletician Christine Smith, who affirms: "If preaching is to be a transforming act, then the power and integrity of our proclamations will surely be measured by their ability to mobilize communities to resist the reality that confronts us."[3] She states that preaching is not just about hearing and receiving the gospel, "but that it is an act that must enable and sustain persons to *be* good news in the larger world. To affirm preaching as resistance is to encourage the faithful community to be about God's redemptive activity in the world in concrete, particular ways."[4]

I begin this chapter "by the riverside" and will demonstrate how religion and the environmental movement inform, shape, and influence each other. This will be done by utilizing social movement theory to examine the role of religion in the environmental movement, specifically the issue of shale gas drilling, a particularly spurious contributor to the Creation-crisis. In the second part of this chapter, I will offer strategies for preachers to develop their own Creation-crisis preaching. This section will be helpful in a pedagogical sense by providing a heuristic method by which to approach ecojustice issues. Drawing from the seasonal cycle of a deciduous tree, the method gives preachers a three-fold process for framing sermons that address various aspects of the Creation-crisis. This chapter then ends where it began—alongside the river—and sets the stage for the process of eco-location and "neighbor-mapping" in chapter 3.

PART ONE: The Convergence of Environmentalism and Ecological Theology Viewed through Social Movement Theory

In the first chapter I started by asking where the Susquehanna River begins. That answer eludes us. But there is a place where the North and West Branches come together at the point where the counties of Northumberland, Union, and Snyder touch: Shikellamy Overlook State Park.[5] Standing atop Shikellamy Point, one can see the North and West Branches converge below. It is an awesome sight to observe the waters from the two branches—each with slightly different colorations, character, and flow speeds—come together in a seamless melding of flowing water.

Just below Shikellamy Point, at the site of Shikellamy Marina on the southern tip of Packer Island, on February 17, 2012, a group of members from the Interfaith Sacred Earth Coalition (a group that I helped to found in January of 2012) held a press conference to protest the passage of Act 13 in the Pennsylvania legislature, the so-called "fracking bill," which critics decried for its numerous inequities and failures to protect environmental and public health while ensuring the profitability of the oil and gas industry. According to Jan Jarrett of PennFuture, there are "seven deadly sins" in the legislation: the removal of the rights of municipalities to use their zoning powers to dictate if and where drilling may occur; failure to adequately protect groundwater; limitation of the power of the Department of Environmental Protection (DEP) from adequately regulating the drilling industry; failure to provide for adequate set-backs of wells from residential areas, schools, or hospitals; failure to protect small, ecologically sensitive intermittent streams or small wetlands; limitation of DEP's ability to put conditions on gas drilling operations that may harm a public resource such as a park or state forestland; and failure to establish a public record for tracking where gas drillers are disposing of the waste flowback water from the wells.[6] There is also controversy surrounding the law's provision that health care providers treating people exposed to drilling-related chemicals must sign confidentiality waivers to protect companies' "proprietary rights." According to *StateImpact* reporter Scott Detrow, "[T]he legislation requires drillers to provide the state with a list of chemicals used during hydraulic fracturing, with the exception of chemicals the energy companies deem 'trade secrets.'" The concern is that this puts a "gag order" on doctors that will negatively affect public health and leave doctors unprotected should they choose to reveal the chemicals to their patients or in research publications.[7]

With all this in mind, members of the Interfaith Sacred Earth Coalition gave several speeches by the riverside (including one given by me, which can be read in the free Appendix download available at www.creationcrisispreaching.com) calling for the bill's repeal on religious and ethical grounds. The group then held an interfaith water blessing ritual to recognize the sanctity of the river's water. After pouring water from the river into a large bowl and saying a blessing over it, the water was ceremoniously returned to the river. The event was featured on the front page of two local newspapers in what may be seen as an example of public theology, wherein faith, religion, and the social movement of environmentalism converged.[8]

This is just one example of the ways in which religion and the environmental movement inform, shape, and influence each other, like different tributaries converging into one larger confluence. The role that preaching plays in this movement can be understood in terms of social movement theory. While I can only present these concepts in broad brushstrokes, my goal in this chapter is to provide a framework for examining and analyzing the public theology of preaching. We will use these concepts in the second part of this chapter to establish three strategies for preachers to use in crafting sermons that address environmental issues.

Social Movement Theory and the Role of Preaching

Doug McAdam, in his book *Political Process and the Development of Black Insurgency 1930–1970,* examines both the classical model of social movements and the model of resource mobilization before proposing his own model of the political process.[9] From McAdam's work, we can distill five elements needed for a movement to emerge, gain traction, and have an effect on society.[10] One element is a *grievance*—an acknowledgment that something is wrong and that change is needed. But this is not necessarily enough to motivate people to participate. A second element is needed—a *moral imperative* that frames the issue in a way that raises public consciousness and stokes a level of anger that energizes people to act. Such energy must be harnessed, which necessitates the third element of social movements, that of *resources*: leadership, networks, connections, and institutional support to mobilize, fund, and direct the social change. A *shift in political opportunity* is the fourth element, whereby some event catalyzes a chain of events that enables the movement to capitalize on the grievances and moral imperatives that have been simmering. To use Malcolm Gladwell's term, this is the "tipping point" that spawns a wave of public outcry for change. But in order to keep this momentum from dwindling or losing its initial surge of energy, the fifth element is needed—a sense of *viability*. A short-term winnable goal must be achieved in order for movement participants to see that change is possible. This enables momentum to be sustained over the long haul with the hope that participants really can effect change, and that such change is within their reach.

What is the role of religion within social change? According to Hank Johnston and Bert Klandermans, religion varies from being a change-inhibitor (cautioning preservation of tradition) to change-agent (articulating the cry of the oppressed and critiquing the powers that enable the oppression).[11] For ecotheologians and religiously-oriented activists within the environmental movement, the latter role is emphasized. In terms of the five elements of social change theory, religion can make important contributions on many levels. Holy scriptures often contain rich resources for articulating grievances, lamenting unjust losses, and stoking righteous anger on behalf of the oppressed. Religious leaders are often skilled in framing moral imperatives that connect potential movement participants to the core values of their faith. And they have access to vast networks of people, funds, institutional support, and buildings to house meetings for the work of the movement. Religion can also be the site of a catalyst point, as has been the case with hate crimes leveled at houses of worship prompting movements for hate crime legislation. And, finally, religion contains the potential to intensify and add a moral and ethical dimension to the goals of a social movement by connecting them—via ritual, symbol, preaching, and teaching—to a transcendent level. For our purposes, I work with the premise of religion as change-agent and ally for social movements while also highlighting the expressive dimension of *preaching* in helping to interpret opportunities, mobilize support, and sustain commitment over time.

Framing and Rhetorical Strategies for Environmental Preaching

The function of a frame, according to David Snow, is to "define some existing problem, annoyance, or condition as an 'injustice' that demands correction or elimination rather than as a 'misfortune' that warrants only charitable consideration."[12] Frames give focus, articulation, and transformative power that convert and move a grievance into compelling motivation for action to address a situation that is unjust and ripe for change. For example, in an effort to oppose a proposed tire incinerator in my area of the upper Susquehanna Valley, a grassroots movement I helped to lead created yard signs that read "God's Country should not smell like burning tires." This provided a subtle theological frame implying that the incinerator would be an affront to God and the land created by God's hand. In an area characteristically Christian and politically conservative, this frame resonated strongly with local residents and helped galvanize the public in opposition to the burner (which was eventually defeated).[13] A common complaint about the environmental movement is that it has been hampered by grievances that are too vague, too large, and seemingly too overwhelming to tackle. I will argue that when the environmental movement and people of faith work together, much more traction is gained due to the frame provided by religious values and ethics. Further, I contend that one of the rhetorical means to create this frame is *preaching*.

Johnston sees a strong link between discourse and frames, in that frameworks - or mental structures - of social movement participants can be discerned through analysis of discourse "from the bottom up, from the text to the frame."[14] One way to gain access to frames is through micro-discourse analysis, examining the use of spoken and written language by movement participants in order to gain a "window of access" to the interpretative structures of individuals. As we will see, sermons are one example of micro-discourse and can be helpful for gaining insight into the shared values of both environmentalists and people of faith.

Within Johnston's schema, sermons would be categorized as a "speech situation," a "bounded episode of interaction in which there are specific social rules for what should and should not be said."[15] Preaching, as a rhetorical act in which the speaker and listeners observe unspoken but implicit "rules of engagement," would qualify as a "public speech situation" or "'public discourse'...where certain constraints in form and content are operative."[16] The social role of the preacher is another key component in micro-discourse analysis. The institutional authority of the pastoral office, the level of respect afforded to a preacher by her or his parishioners, and the social standing of the clergyperson within the larger community are all variables that affect the preacher's ability to effectively articulate a frame that engages listeners and compels them to action. Factors such as a preacher's gender, race, age, and socioeconomic location also go into the social perception of authority, which has an impact on the effectiveness of the preaching.[17] Viewed through the lens of social movement theory, a key function of religious preaching for social change is through *meaning construction*. Johnston and Klandermans identify three processes of meaning construction: public discourse, persuasive communication, and consciousness-raising during episodes of collective action.[18] Because preaching involves all three of these processes, it has a key role in meaning construction. As Johnston and Klandermans explain, "[A]t each level the processes forming and transforming collective beliefs take place in different ways: at the first level through the diffuse networks of meaning construction, at the second level through deliberate attempts by social actors to persuade, and at the third level through discussions among participants in and spectators of the collective action."[19]

As an example of meaning construction, we can consider the example of Father Geoff Curtiss at All Saints Episcopal Church in Jersey City, New Jersey, who led a ten-year community effort (1993–2003) to force owners of chromium processing plants to clean up the cancer-causing hexavalent chromium they had left at the sites slated for affordable housing. Through his sermons, public speeches, court testimonies, and meetings with the grassroots organization suing the company, Curtiss utilized the parable of the "persistent widow" (Lk. 18:1–8) in meaning construction that helped sustain the group for the long fight for justice. In the parable, a poor widow hounds a judge until he grants her justice against her adversary. In the case of Honeywell International and Pittsburgh Plate and Glass, the judge finally ordered the companies to undertake a $400 million site remediation to meet residential standards.[20]

Another concept that will be helpful for developing an ecotheological homiletic is distinguishing between a *rhetoric of inaction* and a *rhetoric of change*. William Gamson and David Meyer have noted that both kinds of rhetoric are present in the political realm of social movements. Drawing on the work of Albert O. Hirschman, they identify three central themes in the rhetoric of reaction/inaction that is opposed to change: jeopardy (change threatens what currently exists), futility (change is a waste of time and effort and will be ineffective), and perverse effects (change will make things worse).[21] Countering the rhetoric of inaction, "[M]ovement activists employ an optimistic rhetoric of change. Their job is to convince potential challengers that action leading to change is possible and desirable."[22] For each of the three themes urging inaction—jeopardy, futility, perverse effects—there are corresponding counter-themes that compel people to take action: urgency, agency, and possibility. The three themes are described this way:

- Urgency: "If we do not act now, the situation will not remain the same but will become more and more difficult to change. Action may be risky but inaction is riskier still. One must weigh the risks of action against the risks of inaction."
- Agency: "Windows that are currently open will not stay open for long. While there is no guarantee of success, the present offers opportunity enough to keep hope alive. Action now will open the window wider and keep it open longer, allowing more room for future victories."
- Possibility: "The promise of new possibilities counters the threats of perverse effects, [including] a vision of better policies, greater justice, and more humane social life."[23]

Through an emphasis on these themes of urgency, agency, and possibility, along with strategies of articulating a sense of viability, Creation-crisis preaching (and, really, preaching about nearly any justice issues) can find greater effectiveness. With these elements of social movement theory in mind, I propose three approaches to environmental preaching: consciousness-raising, calling for action, and discourse for long-term cultural and individual transformation. Examples of preaching included in this book show that these three approaches can assist in encouraging, exhorting, inviting, and creating the kind of ecological justice and action needed in congregations and their local communities. This theoretical background will also be helpful in developing homiletical pedagogy for guiding students of preaching into thinking about how they may preach on Creation-care and ecojustice issues.

Preaching Alongside and with the Susquehanna River

The public speeches made at Shikellamy Marina by the members of the Interfaith Sacred Earth Coalition (ISEC) exemplify the kind of environmental "preaching" that takes seriously the values of Creation-care uplifted by ecological theology, the value of sacred writings (the Holy Bible, for Christians) supporting a divine mandate to defend and protect Creation and those who are most endangered by its destruction, and the willingness to courageously speak in a prophetic voice against powers that have amassed great strength in terms of wealth and political authority. The group's choice of Shikellamy Marina for its location of public theological witness was informed by more than just scenic beauty. The convergence of the North and West branches of the Susquehanna River provided both a symbolic backdrop for the press conference and was actively incorporated in a ritualistic way through prayer and blessing. Thus the grievance against Act 13, the moral imperative to protect the river, land, water, and public health from the dangers of slickwater hydraulic fracturing, and the micro-discourses of the speeches could all be counted as examples of religion contributing to the environmental movement.

The day prior to this press conference (February 16, 2012), I spoke at another public event regarding the Susquehanna River. This event was a public hearing of the Susquehanna River Basin Commission in Harrisburg, Pennsylvania, to request that the commissioners deny permits to withdraw water from the Susquehanna River to be sold for the use of horizontal slickwater hydraulic fracturing.[24] After reading a letter to the commissioners signed by over sixty individuals (most of whom were clergy and self-identified people of faith, along with other nonreligious allies), I presented to the commissioners a bowl of water from the Susquehanna River prayed over and blessed by members of ISEC at our meeting five days prior to the hearing. Once again, the River was not just a symbolic set-piece; it became a tangible presence in the room as the commissioners puzzled over how to receive this gift.

"What do you want us to do with this?" one of them asked.

"I leave that up to you," I replied. "I trust that how you treat this bowl of water is how you will regard our river."

I can only surmise that, after the meeting, the bowl was unceremoniously emptied of its sacred contents and thrown in the trash—because, one month later, the SRBC voted to approve all but one permit for the withdrawal of water for hydraulic fracturing. Little did I know then that this political decision would have profound and devastating consequences for a little trailer park called Riverdale nestled along the banks of the Susquehanna River in Jersey Shore of Lycoming County, Pennsylvania. The residents of Riverdale were about to be caught up in a perfect storm of corporate greed, failed state politics, economic classism, and environmental devastation as the CEO of Aqua America took his cue from the SRBC and proceeded to purchase a tract of land to build a water withdrawal plant on the very site where the Riverdale community had lived for over thirty years. (In chapter 6, we will revisit this saga and see how the concepts of Creation-crisis preaching were used inside and beyond the church walls to address this injustice.)

Part Two: Three Approaches for Environmental Preaching

I have read, heard, or preached more than a hundred sermons that have dealt with environmental issues. I have also engaged in conversations with preachers about their processes of sermon creation and delivery when they address environmental or ecojustice themes. The results of my observations and conversations have revealed what I identify as three types of approaches to environmental preaching. I name these approaches *consciousness-raising, call for action,* and *sustainable change.* These approaches, while not mutually exclusive and often overlapping in a single sermon, are suggested as ways to frame environmental issues in relation to biblical, theological, and pastoral concerns. The point is to provide a way to understand environmental preaching in relation to social movement theory so as to illuminate how preaching helps with framing environmental issues, mobilizing support, encouraging the commitment of financial and human resources, and articulating a sense of viability, all of which are key elements of successful social movements.

Scholarly inquiry into homiletical theory that undergirds environmental preaching is scarce. As I mentioned in the Introduction, one can find a smattering of collections of ecologically-themed sermons and a few books dedicated to the subject of preaching about God's Creation. There are also some Internet websites that offer rich resources for ecologically focused ministry in worship, biblical study, education, and advocacy, as well as helpful suggestions for preaching and samples of ecological sermons.[25] But, as of yet, there does not exist a solidly researched heuristic framework for approaching environmental preaching, though interest in ways to approach environmental preaching are beginning to surface.

For example, The Reverend Peter Sawtell, executive director of Eco-Justice Ministries, in a post on the group's website, suggests that it is helpful to think of environmental preaching in terms of three "layers." One layer is "issue preaching," which directly addresses public policy and specific, concrete concerns, such as global warming, toxic waste, or wilderness preservation. He states, "While issue preaching has the capability of getting people involved in the world, it also has a high probability of making someone mad!"[26] Thus he recommends another layer, that of more "generalized themes." For example, "Sermons on the integrity of creation, the relationship between humans and nature, and celebrations of nature and life fit into this layer. In dealing with these subjects, the preacher as biblical scholar and theologian is the expert. Preaching on this level undergirds and supports issue preaching and has a lower probability of seriously offending members of the congregation," Sawtell explains.[27]

The third level is the "deep layer" that does not address environmental issues either directly or indirectly, but rather focuses on "profound pastoral issues that trouble, and can even paralyze, those who are in touch with the earth's distress." Such sermons would include more theological terms, such as sin, guilt, repentance, forgiveness, and grace, while speaking "to grief and loss in ways that bring us to active resistance, not to quiet acceptance."[28] He sees this layer as important for sustaining long-term commitment to environmental struggle in the church.

For example, returning to Father Curtiss' preaching in the midst of the decade-long legal battle with Honeywell, he found three themes that not only helped connect with listeners on the "deep layer" of underlying pastoral, ethical, and ecotheological layers, but also allowed for different points of entry and resonance in his congregation. Those themes were environmental racism, land use, and the beauty of creation. Speaking to the issue of environmental racism resonated with residents who knew that a connection existed within their polluted community between race, poverty, and high death rates from cancer. At the same time, he lifted up the role of land in the covenantal people's relationship with God, as well as the beauty and grandeur of the land surrounding their community within the Hudson River basin. These three deep layers are what Curtiss found to be most appropriate for his particular congregation of mainly young, upwardly mobile professionals who worshiped, and were committed to serving, in a community made up of primarily working class and poverty-stricken, racially diverse families whose health and well-being had been negatively affected by the pollution of the chromium processing plants.

Sawtell points out that there are appropriate times and places for focusing on these three different layers. While issue preaching is the most obvious way to address environmental justice, preaching from the other two layers is critical for grounding people in promise and hope, and thus giving them the spiritual resources for working on behalf of Creation. He stresses the importance of the deeper layers for helping the congregation develop "an emotional and theological base where direct issue preaching makes sense." He states that such deep-level preaching helps to establish a "frame in which preaching on specific issues is well grounded, and where tackling such issues is welcomed and expected."[29]

While I affirm Sawtell's three-layered configuration, I want to offer an alternative conceptual framework that incorporates social movement theory while also conveying the elements of this theory within its very form. I will outline three approaches to environmental preaching that correspond with the phases of a deciduous tree's yearly cycle: "flowering/pollinating" (consciousness-raising), "leaves" (calling for specific action), and "fruit" (transforming lifestyles and culture for long-term, sustainable change). These three approaches are not mutually exclusive, nor are they intended solely as a linear progression. One sermon may contain elements of one, two, or all three approaches. The point is to offer an analytical framework for understanding what a preacher's intention is for a particular sermon, the discursive and rhetorical devices used to accomplish the sermon's goal, and a criterion by which to measure the sermon's effectiveness.

Consciousness-raising: "Flowering/Pollinating"

As I sit at my desk, gazing at the springtime landscape outside my window, my eyes are awash with color from the newly opened flowers on the hawthorn tree in my yard. I watch bees and other insects hover and dart in and among the blossoms, cross-pollinating as they go. I see this pollinating as a metaphor for the approach to preaching I've identified as consciousness-raising. Sermons containing this approach use images, parables, narratives, and metaphors that attract attention and create "buzz" among the listeners. They also provide the impetus for cross-pollination as the listeners share the "pollen" from the sermon with others, distributing its effects by way of conversations and actions, and exchanging ideas, attitudes, and insights.

Consciousness-raising sermons can correspond with the social movement elements of *articulating a grievance* and *framing a moral imperative* that can direct awareness to an environmental issue. The frame of an ecological sermon could, for example, lift our eyes to the beauty, complexity, and fragility of Creation, which is deserving of our protection because of its sacramental quality and its intrinsic value in the eyes of the Creator. Or, the sermon can function as a venue for *meaning construction* by pointing to an ecojustice issue that the preacher feels warrants the attention of the congregation, and then connecting the issue to what it means to be a Christian charged with protecting "the least of these," such as a neighborhood suffering from pollution or a threatened species within a local habitat.

As with the first two elements of social change, the energy generated from these flowering/pollinating (consciousness-raising) sermons must be harnessed. I once heard Rabbi Marcia Praeger speak about this need for depth beyond consciousness-raising in a gathering of clergy to discuss climate change at Summit Presbyterian Church in Philadelphia in January 2011. Praeger is a Jewish Renewal rabbi, teacher, storyteller, artist, and therapist living and working in the Mount Airy community of Philadelphia. A graduate of the Reconstructionist Rabbinical College, she currently serves as rabbi of the Philadelphia P'nai Or Jewish Renewal Community. At this gathering she spoke to the necessity of *anger* as an important factor for moving people from the grievance stage to that of action. "How do we tap into the righteous indignation on behalf of the poor? Simply naming the evil can be very energizing." But, she cautions, "[R]aising consciousness without offering organizing vehicles that produce success results in negative backlash."[30]

In other words, for the pastor preaching on environmental issues, just raising a problem to awareness is not enough. Tapping into righteous anger without providing for any recourse to action will not only frustrate the listeners, but could result in the opposite effect of what the sermon intended—namely, apathy borne out of feelings of being overwhelmed by the size and complexity of the problems. What is needed, then, are concrete suggestions of ways to act, as well as offering opportunities to take steps on behalf of the victims of the named problem. This allows the rhetoric to shift from simply opening minds and hearts to actually moving hands and feet to take action in tangible ways.

Calling for Specific Action: "Leafing"

In a week or two, many of the flowering trees whose blooms I'm enjoying will lose their blossoms as they fade and fall. In their place will emerge leaves that do the work of photosynthesis, converting sunlight and water into food for the trees. The New Testament book of Revelation contains an image of trees with "leaves for the healing of the nations" (Rev. 22:2). Leaves are the energy-converters for the tree, offering shade and beauty of a different kind from the short-lived flowers. In the same way, environmental sermons must move beyond the short-lived approach of consciousness-raising into preaching that has longer-lasting effects and helps convert energy into action. This phase incorporates the social movement elements of engaging *resources* for change, and inviting listeners to engage with *opportunities* to live into the change we seek.

This is where the concept of framing in social movement theory is so critical. Snow reminds us that frames not only have an interpretive function but also serve to compel people to action. They are "agentic and contentious in the sense of calling for action that problematizes and challenges existing authoritative views and framings of reality."[31] Further, he states that there is a "dynamic rather than static character of collective action frames, [which] remind us that the flow of events—biographical, local, national, and international—have a way of intruding into our realities and forcing us either to incorporate them into our current understandings or modify those understandings accordingly."[32]

Sermons that incorporate this "leafing" stage call for change and invite listeners to take specific actions. For example, a sermon by the Reverend Dr. David von Schlichten delivered at St. James Evangelical Lutheran Church in Youngstown, Pennsylvania, on March 20, 2011, used a biblical frame of the famous John 3:16 passage to expand the congregation's understanding of salvation for *the whole created world*. He then used the concept of God's redemption of all Creation to serve as a model for humans to care for all Creation. He used this biblical and Christological frame within the micro-discourse of the sermon to create a justification for calling for collective action—in this case, inviting listeners to write down concrete actions they would take for following a Lenten discipline of caring for Creation, thus increasing their level of commitment and participation. Other examples might include asking listeners to sign a petition stating their support for a piece of environmental legislation, or signing up for a road cleanup, or taking part in a field trip to a local creek. In any case, these sermons might use more direct language to state the need for action in the face of environmental degradation and to call on listeners to respond in concrete ways.

Deep Transformation and Sustainable Change: "Fruiting"

After the hawthorn tree outside my window loses its delicate, white, spring blossoms, alongside the leaves appear clumps of small, round, hard berries that are like candy for the local squirrel population. In late summer, the red berries are consumed by the squirrels and blue jays, or they drop onto the grass. The flesh of the berry provides the wildlife with vitamins and nutrients. The seeds contained within the pulp, if they find proper soil and undisturbed conditions, may sprout into other seedlings that may one day become other hawthorn trees—perhaps even miles from this one. And the decaying fruit on the ground will eventually return to the soil, its nutrients being absorbed back into the tree itself.

So it is with environmental preaching that cultivates deep transformation and sustainable change. I suggest that much of today's preaching suffers from "Vitamin C (Creation) deficiency." Sermons with environmental themes preached once or twice a year may be attractive "flowers" and may even evoke substantive response from listeners ("leaves"). However, without preaching that enters the "fruit" phase—in which we are nourished by the nutrient- and vitamin-rich theological and biblical themes of Creation care, metabolize them, and spread them to "plant other trees"—we will only have lone ornamental specimens in a carefully cultivated arboretum of preaching. Imagine, instead, a forest of preaching that draws deeply from the soil of biblical eco-exegesis and ecotheological reflection in which, over time, lifestyles and cultures are changed, greened, and sustained by a long-term vision of God's care for Creation through our hearts, minds, and hands.

Such preaching incorporates the yet another element of social change—creating a sense of *viability* to see that change is not only possible but is, in fact, already initiated and nurtured by God. This type of preaching helps momentum to be sustained over the long haul and corresponds with Sawtell's third deep layer of environmental preaching that addresses biblical, theological, and pastoral issues that undergird the conditions of ecological crisis. While Sawtell's image is one of depth, in my metaphor of the "fruiting" phase I also see this kind of preaching as having breadth and long-term sustaining effects for environmental preaching. In this third approach to Creation-crisis preaching, the social movement elements of grievance, ethical/moral framing, resources/leadership, and viability are all present and dovetail with each other.

A profound example of the shift to this approach to preaching is found in a sermon preached by Steven Charleston, president and professor of theology at Episcopal Divinity School in Cambridge, Massachusetts, entitled "The Isaiah Factor: Prophetic Words that People Can Hear" (found in *Earth and Word: Classic Sermons on Saving the Planet*). The sermon was preached at the school during Earth Week, and its goal was to help those committed to preaching or speaking on environmental justice to reframe how the prophetic message is spoken to one's hearers. Charleston draws a comparison between Jesus' commentary on his parable about the Sower and the Seed, and the perpetual dilemma faced by "evangelists of environmental justice." In Matthew 13:14–15, Jesus, quoting Isaiah, notes that people listen to his parables but do not understand them or change their behaviors. Similarly, says Charleston, environmental evangelists encounter the phenomenon in which their message "is the one cause everyone agrees with but very few actually support."[33] He describes the scenario experienced by many who preach on environmental issues: "How many times after you have spoken to others about the urgency of environmental action have you received a warm response, only to watch it evaporate into benign neglect when it comes time to do something?"[34] As with Jesus and Isaiah, people hear the message but do not truly understand it. Nor do they perceive their own place in being part of the solution. "It may not be that their hearts are hardened on purpose," he explains, "but the effects are the same: Environmental ministries find few fertile grounds for growth in the life of the church."[35] Similarly, Charleston argues, the majority of those who listened to Jesus appeared to agree with him, but very few made the changes needed to live into the life to which he was calling them. He continues the comparison by saying that just as Jesus called for repentance, so environmental prophets insist on the need for repentance and change as well.

Where Charleston makes a significant shift in framing is in his move to equate environmental ministry with *healing*. He explains: "That last word from Isaiah ['I would heal them'] is the most important to Jesus and to you and me. The whole point and purpose of our environmental ministry is healing. We are not just in the business of advocacy or political action: we are very much engaged in a healing ministry."[36] Further, he equates this ministry of environmental healing[37] to that of an addiction recovery ministry. He states: "Our goal is to heal human beings from those things that keep them addicted to power and privilege… Repentance, for us, is recovery… Environmental action is intervention."[38]

Charleston then addresses the subject of choosing the best strategy for helping those caught in this addiction to "break through [the] denial to confront the reality for which they are personally responsible."[39] Overwhelming people with a barrage of scientific information and data and alarming statistics about the state of our world does not get at the "inner core of their addictions." What are needed, he argues, are convincing "emotional arguments." He suggests that environmental preachers use the same approach Jesus used — telling stories and parables: "Rather than moralizing at them, [Jesus] invited them into a new way of thinking. Instead of making a frontal assault on their defenses, he went around the corner and surprised them by getting them to think for themselves. Parables are invitations."[40]

Charleston thus encourages sermons that call for repentance, healing, and helping people face "our addictions to a level of privilege that cushions us from the need to change" by way of "a holy act of subversion: inviting people to accept personal responsibility by helping them see themselves in the environmental story. Most of all," he says, "it means letting them finish that story for themselves."[41] His prescription for a preaching treatment that helps facilitate this addiction repentance and healing could be summarized as follows: (1) create modern parables that communicate deep truths in Earth-centered language; (2) craft stories of everyday life with images easily accessible to everyday people; (3) illustrate an invitation to change with a call to repentance that sounds more like a promise than a stern warning; (4) allow space for hearers to decide what this call means to them.

A Word about Dormancy (Sabbath)

Another important phase in a deciduous tree's cycle is that of dormancy, when growth slows and the plant rests. While space limitations curtail an extended discussion of the need for Sabbath-rest for preachers, suffice it to say that especially for Creation-crisis preaching, we will need to intentionally take time off from our work on a regular basis (weekly, monthly, yearly). Key to this time of Sabbath-rest will be immersing ourselves in Creation, to be nurtured by the very planet and ecosystems we are striving to protect. Just as the stage of dormancy enables the tree to stay healthy, so will the preacher's health be sustained. Taking time to walk, sit, talk, explore and study also sets the stage for new buds of growth in the preacher's task. This will be more fully explored in the next chapter on "mapping."

An Eco-Sermon Example

Flowering, leafing, fruiting—with these three approaches to Creation-crisis preaching in mind, I offer an example of a sermon I preached that incorporated all three. The sermon raises to the listener's awareness the plight of a threatened natural area, calls for specific action to address that plight, and makes connections to larger biblical and theological themes to cultivate a deeper layer of transformation. You will notice the words *flowering, leafing* and *fruiting* inserted to mark those sections of the sermon.

SERMON: "Welcoming Children into God's Creation"
LEAH D. SCHADE
TEXTS: Jeremiah 11:18–20; Mark 9:30–37
> *(Readings from the Revised Common Lectionary for Year B, Seventeenth Sunday after Pentecost)*

"Jesus loves the little children." We sing that at the time of our children's sermon—because it's true! Just in the Gospel of Mark alone, children have a prominent place in five different stories. Why do you think this Gospel focuses so much on children? Well, let's think about children for a minute. What do we know about kids? *[Ask for responses from congregation...]*

Children are: helpless; without status; vulnerable; bestowed with a small view of the world, but big imaginations; inquisitive and curious. They know nothing but have everything to learn; love affection, love to be held; and need freedom to explore without fear.

So why does Jesus care so much about us welcoming children? Certainly, all these things we listed are true. But there's another reason. Jesus says that when we welcome children in his name, we are actually welcoming God into our midst.

Remember, Jesus is all about having God's kingdom established on Earth. And God's kingdom is all about caring for those most vulnerable. They say you can tell a lot about a society by the way they treat their oldest and youngest members. So if we are like the disciples—so concerned with who is the greatest that we ignore the needs of our children—then we are not following God's will.

[FLOWERING:]

And I would add that it's not just how we treat the most vulnerable in the human society that reveals our values. It's also how we treat the most vulnerable in *God's Creation*. How we treat fragile ecosystems, how we treat God's Earth in general, says a lot about how we treat our fellow humanity. For example, if we look at a beautiful forested mountain, and only value it for the coal or gas or oil beneath its surface, and are willing to sacrifice it for our short-term needs, then we are, in fact, not following God's will for ourselves or our children.

The well-being of children and the well-being of God's Creation are fundamentally linked. And throughout the next several weeks, that's what our sermons are going to be exploring. The preaching series is entitled "Of Lambs and Limbs" and will address the need for justice for children, trees, and other living things. Today I want to make a specific connection between the need to welcome children into God's Creation, and the need to protect one particularly beautiful and fragile part of God's Creation right here in Pennsylvania.

There's a book I love called *The Last Child in the Woods* by child advocacy expert Richard Louv. He writes about "nature deficit disorder," where he directly links the lack of nature in the lives of today's children to some of the most disturbing childhood trends, such as the rises in obesity, attention disorders, and depression. We keep kids inside, wired to their computers and televisions, which not only deprives children of important relationships with nature, but will result in generations of humans who have no interest in protecting or caring for God's Creation—because, "[C]hildren will not save what they do not love," he writes. And so he encourages giving children direct exposure to nature because it's essential for healthy childhood development and for the physical and emotional health of children and adults.

Where this connects with our land right here in Pennsylvania is in a place called Rock Run. Rock Run is an enchanting, beautifully wild area of Pennsylvania tucked away in the Loyalsock State Forest just north of Williamsport. And it is under threat to be destroyed by natural gas drilling. An oasis of 20,000 acres surrounds a 27-mile hiking path called the Old Logger's trail. All around the area drilling is proceeding at full force. But Governor Tom Corbett could direct the DCNR[42] to protect this still pristine area from natural gas development.

[LEAFING:]

Now, what does this have to do with you and me? What does this have to do with the church? Well, if we do not speak up for the land and speak out for the needs of our children to be able to inherit this land as citizens of Pennsylvania, unsullied by the drilling industry, then we will be shirking our responsibility both to protect God's Creation, and preserve the very land into which God wants to welcome them.

As one blogger wrote: "It is an area which, once encountered, leaves a lasting impression of serenity, unspoiled nature, and tranquil other-worldliness that is almost unknown in our modern world. To despoil this paradise with gas drilling or any other industry would be nothing short of ungodly. The surrounding area has suffered enough, leave the people some refuge." [http://keepitwildblog.blogspot.com/2012/09/dont-despoil-paradise.html]

As a Christian, I would add: How can we welcome the children into these places God has created if there is nothing left to welcome them into? Or if we have turned these sacred places into industrialized zones that are no place for children to play? Or if we have so poisoned and compromised the integrity of the area, that we have left our children with nothing but a memory and an Internet video reminding them of what it used to be?

I invite you after the service today to sign a letter to our governor, the head of the DCNR, and the company that wants to drill in this area, urging them to protect Rock Run and the Old Logger's Path. This is one way to put our faith into action. We have an opportunity to witness to our faith, and make our voices heard, reminding our leaders that the despoiling of the Rock Run area would be nothing less than the degradation of God's gracious gift of Creation. Psalm 24:1 witnesses to God as creator of the earth and all that dwells therein. Our leaders need to know that we, as Christians, believe all of Creation is worthy of protection, especially those areas that are particularly sensitive and whose ecosystems are fragile. Rock Run is one of those areas.

[FRUITING:]

The Holy Bible gives us several examples of mountains and waterways being special places in which God reveals God's self. This area of Loyalsock State Forest is a place where God's presence in Creation is experienced deeply by those who hike, swim, and fish there. A natural area such as this is not a domain to be conquered and exploited for short-term gain, but to be enjoyed, preserved, and explored as a wondrous, sacred trust.

Do we really want to cut down the tree with its fruit, as we heard in the Jeremiah text? Or do we want to uphold what Genesis 2:15 puts forth as our role within Creation: to serve and to keep God's garden, the Earth?

The letter will be downstairs with a sheet for you to add your name if you wish to remind our leaders that they have an opportunity to leave a legacy for this state and future generations that preserves the pure water, native fish populations, and unparalleled beauty of the forest. It is their responsibility as leaders in government and industry to protect this ecologically and aesthetically sensitive area. And it is our responsibility as Christians to ask that they do so.

God's presence is infused in all of creation. And when we take our children into God's outdoor cathedral—into the woods, the river, the streams, the meadows, even just the backyard, and show them the wonders of what God has created—that it is God who made all this, and that it is our job to love and protect what God has created—we are indeed following Jesus' example. We take our children in our arms, by the hand, and welcome them into this beautiful sacred world, and we do it in Jesus' name. And when we do this, we are, indeed, welcoming God. Amen.

Sermon Analysis

An eco-hermeneutic for preaching applied to the Jeremiah and Mark texts assigned for that Sunday in the lectionary raised the following questions for me in my preparation:

- How are the images of vulnerability in nature informing the human drama between Jeremiah and his adversaries?
- Jeremiah was a prophet whose life was threatened for speaking truth to power. In what ways are "Creation-prophets" threatened by our current power structures?
- What is the church's role in speaking prophetic truth about Earth and Earth's creatures?
- What might be the connection between being a servant of Jesus, a servant of Earth, and a servant of children?

The sermon raises awareness (flowering) in two ways: by connecting the health and well-being of children to the health and well-being of Creation, and by sharing information about a threatened natural area about an hour north of the congregation. The sermon calls for direct action (leafing) by inviting parishioners to sign a petition calling for the protection of the area. Finally, the sermon addresses the need for long-term transformation (fruiting) by connecting Jesus' valuing of children with our responsibility for caring for and protecting God's Creation for children so they can experience God's wonders in nature.

This sermon utilizes a rhetoric of change by emphasizing (1) the *urgency* of protecting the threatened area in the Loyalsock State Forest,

(2) the *agency* of the congregation in indicating their support for protecting Rock Run, and (3) the *possibility* of putting their Christian values into action that could help leave a legacy of protection for the fragile and beautiful area. The responsibility for preserving God's Creation is framed within a biblical context by contrasting the ones wanting to "cut down the tree with its fruits" with Jesus' advocacy for and blessing of the children. The sermon also engages the listeners in a public theological witness by inviting them to sign their names to the petition, thus making the connection between the sacredness of Rock Run and the sacred duty of Christians to honor, cherish, and preserve the area for their children.

Another important aspect of this sermon is the way it addresses a local ecojustice issue and directly involves the listeners in advocating for protecting Rock Run. In this way, the sermon is an example of what we will explore in the next chapter: how to map our "neighbors" in the wider biotic community and proclaim God's grace for those most vulnerable in Creation. In this case, the public theology of preaching had a role in helping to frame society's ethical values within a Christian context when the sermon was shared via blogs and websites by members of organizations such as Responsible Drilling Alliance and Protecting Our Waters, and advocates of the "Keep It Wild" campaign for protecting the Loyalsock State Forest. In turn, members of the Interfaith Sacred Earth Coalition (myself included) were invited to speak at the beginning of a rally for Rock Run by offering prayers and rituals from different religions.[43] Thus the voices of local faith communities were joined with secular constituencies to stand together against the governmental, economic, and corporate powers threatening this particular sacred place in Creation. Not only does this enlarge a pastor's circle of care to include people beyond one's own congregation, it also widens Christians' embrace to include the other-than-human "persons" who suffer and languish, hoping for the arrival of the caring Samaritan.

Notes

[1]Margaret Swedish, *Living Beyond the "End of the World": A Spirituality of Hope* (Maryknoll, N.Y.: Orbis Books, 2008), 192, citing Mary Evelyn Tucker and John Grim, "Daring to Dream: Religion and the Future of the Earth," in "God's Green Earth: Creation, Faith, Crisis," special issue, *Reflections* (Yale Divinity School) (Spring 2007).

[2]Ibid., 201.

[3]Christine M. Smith, *Preaching as Weeping, Confession, and Resistance: Radical Responses to Radical Evil* (Louisville: Westminster/John Knox Press, 1992), 5.

[4]Ibid., 6.

[5]Chief Shikellamy was an important figure in the colonial history of Pennsylvania. Overseeing the Shawnee and Lenape tribes in Central Pennsylvania, he was an Oneida chief and emissary for the Iroquois in Pennsylvania in the mid-1700s who served as a communicator between the tribes of the Six Nations and the colonial government in Philadelphia.

[6]Jan Jarrett, "Seven Deadly Sins of Hb 1950, http://Pennfuture.Blogspot.Com/2012/02/Seven-Deadly-Sins-of-Hb-1950.Html," in *A Bear in the Woods: Environmental Law Blog* (Pennfuture, 2012). The state Commonwealth Court struck down the zoning regulation portion of Act 13 as unconstitutional on July 26, 2012. The State of Pennsylvania subsequently submitted an appeal.

[7]Scott Detrow, "What You Need to Know About Act 13's Confidentiality Requirements, http://stateimpact.npr.org/pennsylvania/2012/04/19/What-You-Need-to-Know-About-Act-13s-Confidentiality-Requirements/ (Accessed April 19, 2012).

[8]Evamarie Socha, "Group Slams Gas Law," *The Daily Item,* February 18, 2012.; Kevin Mertz, "Pastor Challenges Lawmakers to Debate," *Standard Journal,* February 18, 2012.

[9]Doug McAdam, *Political Process and the Development of Black Insurgency, 1930–1970* (Chicago: University of Chicago Press, 1982), 40.

[10]I am indebted to The Rev. Dr. Katie Day, The Charles A. Scheiren Professor of Church and Society at the Lutheran Theological Seminary at Philadelphia, for the distillation of these elements.

[11]Hank Johnston and Bert Klandermans, "Cultural Analysis of Social Movements," in *Social Movements and Culture* (Minneapolis: University of Minnesota Press, 2001).

[12]David A. Snow, "Framing Processes, Ideology, and Discursive Fields," in *The Blackwell Companion to Social Movements,* ed. Sarah A. Soule, David A. Snow, and Hanspeter Kriesi (Malden, Mass.: Blackwell Publishing, 2007), 383.

[13]In another example of theological frames employed for environmental issues, groups opposing mountain-top removal for coal put up billboards that read: "Stop destroying my mountains—God" and "Only God should move mountains."

[14]Hank Johnston, "A Methodology for Frame Analysis: From Discourse to Cognitive Schema," in *Social Movements and Culture,* ed. Hank Johnston and Bert Klandermans (Minneapolis: University of Minnesota Press, 2001), 219.

[15]Ibid., 222.

[16]Ibid., 224.

[17]This is not to say that a pastor's authority is dictated by perception. The call to preach is both divinely inspired and discerned by the one called as well as the community in which one will preach. Nevertheless, it is important for the preacher to keep in mind these human factors when understanding and gauging one's effectiveness in the pulpit.

[18]Johnston and Klandermans, "Cultural Analysis of Social Movements," 10.

[19]Ibid., 10.

[20]Leah D. Schade, "Preaching in the Context of Environmental Social Issues: A Case Study to Examine Religion and Ecology through Social Movement Theory," (unpublished paper, 2011).

[21]William A. Gamson and David S. Meyer, "Framing Political Opportunity," in *Social Movements and Culture* (Minneapolis: University of Minnesota Press, 2001), 285–86, citing Albert O. Hirschman, *The Rhetoric of Reaction: Perversity, Futility, Jeopardy* (Cambridge, Mass.: The Belknap Press of Harvard University Press, 1991).

[22]Ibid., 286.

[23]Ibid.

[24]The SRBC is made up of commissioners from the three states through which the Susquehanna and its tributaries flow—New York, Pennsylvania, and Maryland—plus a representative of the President of the United States. The votes of these four individuals determine the outcome of the management of the Susquehanna River and its tributaries.

[25]Go to www.creationcrisispreaching.com for a free download of further reading and resources.

[26]Peter Sawtell, "Three Layers of Environmental Preaching," http://www.eco-justice.org/3layers.asp (accessed May 9 2011).

27Ibid.

28Ibid.

29Ibid.

30Rabbi Marcia Praeger, personal interview. Philadelphia, March 2, 2011.

31Snow, "Framing Processes, Ideology, and Discursive Fields," 385.

32Ibid., 393.

33Steven Charleston, "The Isaiah Factor: Prophetic Words That People Can Hear," in *Earth and Word: Classic Sermons on Saving the Planet*, ed. David M. Rhoads (New York: Continuum, 2007), 83.

34Ibid.

35Ibid.

36Ibid., 84.

37Joy Bergey, Federal Policy Manager, Citizens for Pennsylvania's Future (PennFuture), also encourages the reframing of environmental issues into that of healing, as well as that of public health and safety. "Rather than ask people to speak out on global warming, which is such a huge issue, ask your congregation how many of them know someone who has asthma or other breathing issues. This will show them that this is about clean air. The whole conversation should be about clean air and public health. Who can argue against that?"(personal interview, March 14, 2011).

38Charleston, "The Isaiah Factor," 84–85.

39Ibid., 85.

40Ibid., 86.

41Ibid.

42DCNR stands for Department of the Conservation of Natural Resources.

43While DCNR has exclusive control of the surface, Anadarko Petroleum Corporation has proposed to set up industrial drilling operations for methane gas. As this book goes to press, the Clarence Moore tracts in the Loyalsock State Forest, of which Rock Run is a part, are still threatened by drilling and have not yet been protected.

3

Who Is My Neighbor?

Mapping a Preacher's Eco-Location

The question, "Who is my neighbor?" posed to Jesus by the lawyer in Luke 10:29 and the parable of "The Good Samaritan" that follows (Lk. 10:30–37) take on an added dimension when considered from a biocentric rather than anthropocentric perspective. The lawyer's question was intended to rationalize drawing the boundary tightly to exclude the "other" who is considered beyond moral consideration. How that line is drawn may be based upon race, gender, culture, religion, able-bodiedness, or any demarcation that limits the scope of one's responsibility of care. In the parable Jesus told in response to the lawyer's question, for example, both the Levite and priest found reasons to evade their responsibility for the man who fell victim of robbers and lay beaten along the roadside. While the parable does not reveal their inner thoughts, we can imagine the mental processes that resulted in drawing lines around themselves, putting the beaten man outside their circles of care. Perhaps it was fear of becoming unclean, or believing themselves to be too busy, too important, or even inadequate to the task of caring. Whatever the reasons, the two men apparently felt justified in walking by on the other side.

The one person the audience would never have expected to respond to the beaten man's need was the one who was thought to be beyond the line of care—the Samaritan. The religious and cultural differences between Samaritans and Jews could be compared to that of Sunni and Shiite Muslims in some countries, or whites and blacks in America, or between Jews, Christians, and Muslims in the Holy Lands. Yet the Samaritan, much to the surprise of the lawyer and those listening to the parable, was moved to help—not because he saw kin based on skin color or tribe or ideology, but because he saw suffering and responded with compassion. "'Which of these three, do you think, was a neighbor to the man who fell into the hands of the robbers?' [Jesus asked the lawyer, who responded,] 'The one who showed him mercy.' Jesus said to him, 'Go and do likewise'" (Lk. 10:36–37).

What can we learn from this exchange between Jesus and the lawyer? It is not the qualifications of the one who suffers that determine who should be considered "neighbor." *It is the one who chooses to care who makes herself or himself a neighbor.* In other words, "neighborness" is not initiated by the one in need of care. It is determined by the one choosing to act in a caring way toward another. Put another way, the lawyer's question could be restated as, "Who is worthy of my moral consideration? Who qualifies? Who can I justifiably and reasonably exclude?" Jesus turns the question around: "Who will you choose to care about? Neighborness is not determined by the receiver of compassion, but by the giver." From the Samaritan's perspective, the only qualification for neighborness was the suffering and need of the beaten man. All other lines, walls, hierarchies, and divisions fell away.

When we consider the Creation-crisis going on around us, this parable has profound ramifications for humans faced with questions about their moral obligations within the biotic realm and regarding environmental justice issues. The parable poses questions for preachers to consider as they seek to proclaim God's Word within their particular enviro-socio contexts. Are animals our neighbors? How about mountains? Ecosystems? How far down the food chain and how far afield should we go? In what ways does the interconnectedness of the water cycle, food web, air currents, and local/global economic systems impinge on how we preach?

Thus far we have seen how a "green" hermeneutic for preaching extends Jesus' command to care for "the least of these." Concurrently, this preaching enables the church to help form society's ethical values by aligning the voices of faith communities with those who are marginalized, oppressed, ignored, and destroyed by the powers of economic, governmental, and cultural forces. But how do we determine what issues need to be addressed in our congregations and communities?

This chapter attempts to answer that question by establishing some basic ethical and homiletical guidelines by which preachers may set their moral compasses. I will draw on the work of moral philosopher Mary Midgley and homileticians John McClure, Lucy Atkinson Rose, and Anna Carter Florence to provide some necessary concepts for helping preachers orient themselves theoretically. Those concepts are: reorienting our neighbor-lens to view the other-than-human entities in our midst; establishing the capacity to suffer as the criterion for moral consideration; expanding the "roundtable pulpit" to include other-than-human entities; and listening for the "testimony" of those voices. Then I will provide a list of questions and topics for preachers to consider, as well as exercises and projects that can help us survey our landscapes and expand the concept of neighbor to those of our Earth-kin. The chapter concludes with two sermons to illustrate how this mapping and eco-location may be put into homiletical practice for Creation-crisis preaching.

Part One: Beyond the Human: Criterion for Determining Who Is "My Neighbor"

In his book *Other-wise Preaching*, John McClure seeks to develop an ethical perspective for homiletic theory that strives to be "other-inspired" and "other-directed" so that the "neighbor" may be clearly seen and responded to. Other-wise homiletics, he explains, "seeks to place the totality of homiletics under deconstructive erasure so that preaching might be transformed by a profound awareness of the proximity of preaching's 'others.'"[1] He believes that this reorientation of preaching will bring about compassionate responsibility within our sermons. McClure appropriates the ethical philosophy of Emanuel Levinas in what he calls "'the-one-for-the-other,' which is 'a point outside of being,' the point of being 'face-to-face' with the other."[2] McClure explains that because alterity is originary for Levinas, "knowledge and thought tend to proceed from *ethics* rather than ontology—from responsibility for and to the other rather than from one's sense of being in the world (what 'is') and one's sense of identity (who 'I am')."[3] In other words, since otherness is part of who we are as beings, in Levinas' thought, it calls us into relationship, and by its very nature summons us to respond to the other and to be responsible to the other. For Levinas, it is the neighbor's face (*visage*) that compels us to "experience an absolute obligation toward compassion, resistance, justice, and hope that grips our lives and holds us to a new vision for all humanity."[4] This *visage* is not just the physical face of the other, but the totality of the living presence of another. Because the face is the most visible and expressive part of the body, Levinas chooses this part to represent that which calls us to ethical consideration of the other.

In applying Levinas' thought to homiletic theory, McClure does not include other-than-human beings in the "others" he considers. However, it is not a great stretch to extend his other-wise homiletic to include the other-than-human world of Creation. In fact, what better direction to turn in the task of deconstruction than to the erasure of androcentric humanity, which has subordinated the natural world throughout its history? Bringing an ecological perspective to McClure's other-wise ethic for preaching, I suggest, would open preachers to the testimony of the Earth community, which is often (falsely) conceived as being beyond the margins of the circle of testimony.

To be clear, an *erasure*-testimony—in which one term of the binary undergoes erasure—does not mean that it is made to disappear. Rather, McClure's aim is to see that the dominant and oppressive *assumptions* that compromise our ethics are placed under suspicion or, in fact, subverted. Thus, an erasure testimony would not entail the disappearing of humanity (a type of misanthropy). Rather we are placing androcentric anthropocentrism—which assumes a hierarchy in which women and Earth are dominated—under erasure. Thus an ecofeminist homiletic, as will be discussed further on, will take up the task of identifying the patterns of environmental destruction, nonhuman animal exploitation and cruelty, and social injustice in order to erase the logic and illusion that such patterns are natural or divinely sanctioned, as per Wendy Lynne Lee (see Introduction).[5]

Further, the neighbor's face will no longer be exclusively human, but will include the visage of the rainforests, endangered species, and the waters that flow in and around our planet. An other-wise ecological homiletic would have us "exit" androcentric anthropocentrism and enable us to be open to "the absolute mystery of the other," which elicits compassion, resistance, justice, and hope, not just for a new vision for all humanity, but for the entire Earth community.[6] Seeing this *visage* of Earth and our other-than-human kin consequently compels us to dismantle and reconstruct our religious and theological authorities according to the vision of liberation, equity, and love which God has for all Creation, inclusive of humanity (more on this idea of dismantling and reconstruction in the next chapter).

Admittedly, there may be some awkwardness with this process of incorporating the alterity of nature into our ethical stance, especially when using the concept of encountering the "face" of the other, which, according to Levinas, interrupts us and introduces a profound obligation to be responsible to this other. For example, how can animals be considered our neighbors when they are traditionally understood as property, food, labor, or generally as non-persons? And if we do attempt to include so-called lower life forms in the category of neighbor, what is the criteria for determining their moral consideration?

Moral philosopher Mary Midgley can be helpful here. She names two criteria for determining the scope of our moral concern. First, we must determine if the being is capable of *suffering*.[7] In other words, do they "mind what happens to them"?[8] Second, is the animal capable of *emotional fellowship*? In other words, do they have the capacity for forming "deep, subtle and lasting relationships?"[9] Cetaceans, primates, porcines, bovines, felines, canines, and even birds can thus be categorized as neighbors, as can all sentient beings, and are worthy of our moral consideration.

But how should humans regard other-than-human beings that are not capable of sentience and self-determination? In what way should we be concerned with those beings that appear to lack the capacity for suffering and the ability to develop social and emotional complexity? This is especially challenging when the tree that cleans our air has no "face," the worms that aerate our soil have no eyes, and the microbes that absorb the toxic chemicals of fracking fluids cannot even be seen without a microscope. How do we encounter these others on moral grounds?

Here we may turn to H. Paul Santmire's modification of Martin Buber's I-Thou conceptuality. When it comes to the relationship between humans and other-than-humans, his notion of I-Thou accounts for "rich relationships between persons and nature that are not I-It relationships."[10] Buber, Santmire notes, believed it possible for a person to become bound up in relation to a tree and to view it as a holy other. However, because a tree cannot speak, he is left with an idiosyncratic awkwardness when trying to explain the relationship of mutuality and reciprocity. Hence Santmire proposes a third type of relation he calls the "I-Ens relation," from the Latin participle for "being."[11] The Ens, according to Santmire, has several characteristics that distinguish it from an It: its givenness, its mysterious activity or spontaneity, and its beauty, which exhibits its unity and diversity in an integrated whole.[12] These characteristics evoke wonder in the person who encounters the Ens, whether that is a tree, a rock formation, or an undulating field of flowers. Such wonder includes four things: a person's total attention, his or her openness to the Ens, a willingness to humble oneself before the Ens, and a profound sense of gratitude.[13] Such wonder does not supplant the awe one experiences toward God, but rather helps us to "account for, and then in appropriate ways become advocates for, increasingly desirable relationships of mutuality and cooperation between persons and other creatures of nature."[14]

Yet there is still the challenge of how we make morally sound decisions when humans interact with their environment in the process of securing food, housing, transportation, and energy, for example. In summarizing John Cobb's critique of deep ecology, Mark Wallace puts it this way: "If all beings—everything from megafauna such as human beings and blue whales to microflora such as mold spores and green algae—are sacred, if everything is equal in value and worth, then on what basis can decisions be made about what should be saved and protected and what can be used and destroyed?"[15] In other words, without some sort of hierarchy of values, there would be no way to engage in ethical decision-making because value would collapse into sameness. Wallace's approach, with which I am in agreement, "would be to ensure…the health and dynamism of the life cycle rather than protect the interests of added-value beings (such as human beings) whose inner life is more complex than other beings. Thus green spirituality is able to make highly nuanced and sophisticated *practical* judgments about use and value, but it does so in biocentric rather than anthropocentric terms."[16] Theologically, then, "judgments about value should be based on keeping open the living channels of energy that make life possible… [P]ractical decisions about resource allocations and the like should focus on ensuring the dynamism and vitality of the energy cycle, not on the particular needs of individual participants within the cycle, including the needs of individual human participants."[17]

This is not to say that the needs of individual humans are no longer taken into consideration. However, what Creation-crisis preaching emphasizes is that it is, in fact, "the least of these" whose needs must be considered *first*. The hierarchy is flipped and the needs of those traditionally seen as located on the bottom are prioritized.

This applies both in the other-than-human as well as the strictly human realm. For example, human fetuses, children, and women are biologically and historically among the most vulnerable of human beings. Their needs would be prioritized when making decisions.[18] In the biotic cycle the most basic building blocks of life on a cellular and microbiotic level must be considered, and any activity that threatens them would be avoided.[19] Thus, rather than determining the rightness of a human activity from the top down (i.e., those in power protecting and promoting their immediate self-interest and gratification), we would gauge it from the bottom up. In other words, if it's not good for the children, the fish in the sea, or the microbes in the soil, an inverted pyramid of care dictates that it should not be done. Stated in a positive way, the "least of these" are what Jesus has said are most sacred, so whatever promotes their health and well-being fulfills the divine command of caring for them. The "who" and "how" by which this discernment process is carried out will be explored further on.

With humility we recognize that even our best efforts to engage the nonhuman other on ethical grounds will be partial and may, unwittingly, perpetrate injustice on some level. Nevertheless, just as the kenotic emptying of Christian proclamation can rend oneself open toward the human other, I believe that simply the process of breaking open our preaching to the other-than-human other can create the space for a reorientation toward Creation. It requires a level of meekness not usually experienced by human beings that will decenter us from the hierarchical positions within the constructed human/nature binary. And, indeed, it is a false binary, for humans are as much a part of Creation as any other creature. It is the hubris of thinking ourselves superior to and unaccountable for our treatment of the rest of God's Creation that is rendering our world increasingly uninhabitable.

Expanding the "Roundtable Pulpit" to Include Other-than-Human Entities

Lucy Atkinson Rose makes an important contribution to the preacher's process of locating oneself within the biotic community outside of the church's walls.[20] In her book *Sharing the Word: Preaching in the Roundtable Church*, she makes the case for what she calls "conversational preaching," which is characterized as communal, nonhierarchical, personal, inclusive, and scriptural. Rose's proposal seeks to move preaching away from a separation between preacher and congregation, and toward a more relational, mutually respectful, and shared task. "Conversational preaching," she says, "seeks to gather together these voices—local and global, present and past— paying particular attention to those that have been drowned out by the din around the round and rectangular tables of our world, paying particular attention to the whispers and pauses where people's voices are missing."[21]

It must be noted that Rose makes no reference to ecological concerns or care-of-Earth issues. However, her metaphor of the roundtable and the concept of conversation within God's *oikos* (household) are helpful for an environmental homiletic if we enlarge them to include an ecological perspective.[22] For instance, the goal of conversational roundtable preaching is to seek out and listen to unheard voices. As we have seen, one of those voices that has been missing, suppressed, ignored, and overlooked—both at the rectangular tables and in the pulpit—is that of Earth. There has been a disconnect between humanity and the rest of God's Creation. Human beings are spiritually alienated from the soil, water, flora, and fauna of the planet we share. A rupture in the relationship has divorced us from those with whom we share this *oikos*. It is vital, then, that preachers proclaim a Word that helps to repair this rupture and assist with the rebuilding of the relationship. Rose's conversational preaching "aims to gather the community of faith around the Word where the central conversations of the people of God are fostered and refocused week after week."[23] Preachers wanting to address environmental issues will view Earth as one of those conversation partners and consider how their sermon preparation, content, and form may change by seeing Earth as a partner alongside humankind in God's work of redemption.

Rose stresses, "Within this community of shared faith and commitment, conversational preaching seeks to acknowledge a diversity of experiences, interpretations, and wagers, especially those on the margins without power, status or voice."[24] Indeed, Earth and its nonhuman inhabitants traditionally have had no legal standing in the human community, no voice within government, no status in commercial realms, and no power, save for their response to human action.[25] If it is true that "[c]onnectedness within the congregation is inseparable from connectedness beyond the congregation,"[26] then beyond the congregation, surrounding the congregation, beneath the congregation, and over the congregation are the other members of the

Earth community. We cannot ignore or separate ourselves from them indefinitely, because we are in relationship with them sacramentally, liturgically, ontologically, and personally.

Rose makes use of the image of *oikos* as a way to describe how the church may be reformed in the spirit of conversational preaching, restoring to the household of God those who have been excluded and silenced. I would expand her model to include the very household itself, this *oikos* of Earth, which has been dominated and forced into submission for too long. Similarly, Rose states that the household of the *ecclesia* (church) must extend beyond the walls of the church and the homiletic academy to include those in other fields who may provide new perspectives, fresh ideas, and necessary input for the task of proclamation. She asks, "What more can be said about conversational preaching by those outside the field of homiletics? What insights from other disciplines can help our reflecting, describing, and naming?"[27] I respond that the field of ecology and environmental justice can be a profound source of insights for preaching. Also, such a conversation helps to situate preaching within the midst of the public square.

Finally, it is Rose's understanding of power and authority that lends itself well to the challenge of Creation-crisis preaching. If we, as preachers, are seeking to reorient our hearers to a relationship with Earth that is "communal, nonhierarchical, personal, inclusive, and scriptural," then our preaching would do well to model this very orientation.[28] Form must mirror function. Homiletic praxis must mirror theology.

Listening for the "Testimony" of Other-than-Human Voices

Anna Carter Florence's book *Preaching as Testimony* draws "on the classical definition of *testimony* as both a narration of events and a confession of belief: we tell what we have seen and heard, and we confess what we believe about it... [T]he preacher tells what she has seen and heard *in the biblical text and in life,* and then confesses what she believes about it."[29] Florence draws on this tradition of testimony in preaching with an eye to both restoring the homiletic memory of women's preaching and encouraging women today to fully employ their heretofore marginalized voices. "This tradition," she says, "is part of a long history of preaching by marginalized Christians that calls us to rethink our assumptions about what it is to preach and what it takes to become a preacher."[30]

While any concern with ecological issues is beyond her scope, Florence's work has thoughtful implications for preaching that takes

Creation and one's biotic context into account. For instance, she suggests that *"experience, as it relates to testimony, is an encounter with God.* It is what happens when God meets us, right smack in the middle of things."[31] If this is the case, what if one's testimony is that God meets me right in the middle of this forest, and that this is, indeed, holy ground that demands protection from desecration? Even more to the point, what might be *Earth's* testimony to us? What kind of testimony might we hear from the thousands of animals, fish, birds, and plants, *and* their human-kin, who are right now dying from waters poisoned by fracking fluids, for example?

This is not an instance of falling into the trap of romanticizing or anthropomorphizing Earth and Earth's creatures. Rather, it is meant to compel preachers to stand in solidarity with all those who suffer, human and nonhuman alike. As Florence says, "[T]rue speech summons us home, but not necessarily to the 'home' we dream about, in a nostalgic or ambitious sense. True speech calls us to a home where everyone is loved and no one is lost—and *that* may look like a home we can scarcely imagine. True speech is for the realization and embodiment of *justice*, not the preservation of the community as is."[32] True speech, then, might prophetically preach that the other-than-human beings and ecosystems of this Earth live in exile, in a kind of Babylonian captivity, and want to return "home," back to a state of belonging within the *oikos* of Earth. And it will tell the truth that human beings are also in exile, captive to forces that make us homeless even in our own home of Earth. Those of us choosing to offer a testimony, to preach prophetically in the midst of exile, will proclaim freedom and homecoming, an eco-resurrection if you will— even when all evidence points to the contrary, and the stone at the tomb is feared sealed beyond all hope.

Florence does caution that our testimony will not always, or even usually, be received with enthusiasm by all hearers: "One community's liberation is another community's sorrow. One community's good news is another community's heresy."[33] This is important to realize in Creation-crisis preaching. There are myriad complexities that must be recognized when attempting to preach about and for Earth. One parishioner's call for land preservation, for example, may directly oppose a fellow parishioner's desire to sell land for development. Therefore Florence's advice (echoing that of Lucy Atkinson Rose) is that we must keep in mind the *relationship* between preacher and listeners, remembering that we are with them and for them, not apart from or against them. "They may not always agree on what the Word looks like, as it moves across the pages of the text and flickers through our days," she reminds us, "but they at least agree that it is there; it is real; we are all attending, describing, testifying—waiting."[34]

Thus when we receive the inevitable push-back from the parishioner who hears only "law" and no "gospel" in an ecologically oriented sermon, we must remember that the point of ecological theology is not to replace one form of hierarchical orthodoxy with another ("eco-orthodoxy," if you will). This will only further the hardening of hearts in those hearers and drive a wedge into the relationship between the preacher and the parishioner who does not share this environmental orientation. For the parish pastor it is those relationships that we seek to nurture between ourselves and our congregations, and between them and God, that are essential. Without those relationships, there can be no hope of healing anything, much less our relationship with Earth. Consequently, as Florence reminds us, we must *love* those with whom we have this preaching relationship. Even if that love is difficult to enact, we must discern a way to practice love toward them. We must attend to our parishioners the way God attends to Creation—watching them closely, discovering their (sometimes hidden) beauty, and naming them as "good." Florence reminds us, "None of this happens automatically, and it doesn't happen accidentally, the way infatuations do; it happens slowly, deliberately, over time. We have to work at it, like any relationship. We have to persevere through the dry spells and forgive and be forgiven."[35]

PART Two: Guiding Questions and Exercises in Mapping Our Neighbors

Once we have understood and accepted that the other-than-human entities on this planet are worthy of moral consideration, we can then join up the threads of connection to those on the margins in our human society, communities, families, institutions, and houses of worship. Feminist theologian Rebecca Chopp reminds us that in addressing the justice issues of our day, we must pursue the underlying systemic, linguistic, and theological causes of oppression and the relations, structures, and rules that create and support them.[36] As well, ecological issues must be seen in the larger context of other justice issues. Chopp urges us to always see instances of oppression as symptoms of deeper systemic problems so that the underlying causes can be named, confronted, rooted out, and transformed.

For example, we must inquire as to the "[p]rinciples that necessitate that space be always 'controlled' rather than dwelled in and adorned; that time be linear or existential rather than cyclical or cosmic. Such rules and principles are today the deepest values, orderings, and metaphors that constitute the barriers to freedom."[37] Certainly the task of confronting such entrenched and potentially destructive values will be formidable. Notwithstanding the difficulties, however, if the preacher is going to stand in a place of Christian orientation in the task of proclamation, it will not be from a position assumed as superior to the other, but kenotically "from below," recognizing the margins, decentering the discourse, and inverting the hierarchies.

To that end, what follows are some practical suggestions of things preachers can do and questions they can ask that can help them map the ecological, social, cultural, and political location of a particular congregation. The results of this inquiry can help preachers better contextualize their sermons.

1. **Walk**. Walk the grounds around the church building. Consider your surroundings, including the land you are sitting or standing on, the plants near you, the air you are breathing, other living creatures perceptible to your senses. Who are your biotic neighbors? Also consider the houses, buildings, businesses, factories, and other human-made "neighbors" in the vicinity.

2. **Sit.** Choose a location where you can sit and quietly observe and reflect on the interactions that are occurring between you and your multi-faceted surroundings. Allow all of your senses to be engaged as you listen, sniff, and feel the world around you. Where do you perceive harm or pain? What interrelations are beneficial? Neutral? How do your natural surroundings affect your physical or spiritual existence? Your feelings? Your values?

3. **Look at a topographical map of where the congregation is located.** Google Maps, Google Earth, or other online mapping services are free and can reveal a bird's eye view of your setting. Go to a local county archive or university library to find printed maps. Notice the local waterways and other landscape features (mountains, desert, beach, green spaces, etc.). How are they disrupted, connected to, or otherwise intersecting with human civilization?

4. **Look at maps that show population densities as well as the locations of major businesses, industries, landfills, waste**

processing, etc. Do some research of the basic demographics of the area (census data, income data, sociological data). In what ways do the major players interact with and have an impact on each other and the biotic community?

5. **Talk with members of your congregation** to get a sense of who (in the expanded ecological sense) are their neighbors, and who "has been beaten and lies along the side of the road." Who are "the least of these" in need of attention and care? (This can be done in a combined youth/adult forum, over a meal, or walking and talking together in the neighborhood.)

6. **Talk with other clergy** to learn the history of neighbor-relations in the community. What stories do they tell about neighbors helping each other (or not)? Do any of them have shared interest in environmental issues so that you may collaborate on preaching ideas and/or Creation-care projects between congregations?

7. **Talk with community members** to hear their stories about environmental issues that are part of the community's history. Were there any grassroots efforts to clean up blighted areas? Protest pollution? Confront toxic dumping? What was successful? What lessons were learned? What work remains to be done?

8. **Talk with local health care workers such as doctors and nurses** to find out what the key public health issues are in the community. There are often environmental connections involved (asthma, obesity, cancer, and depression, for example, are all exacerbated by deleterious environmental conditions such as air pollution, radioactive waste, waste incineration, limited access to healthy food, etc.).

9. **Meet with local chapters of environmental groups** such as Sierra Club, Clean Air Council, Interfaith Power and Light, and grassroots activist groups to find out what environmental issues are facing your community. Ask how local houses of worship can be helpful in their work.

10. **Talk with local naturalists, master gardeners, fishermen/women, hunters, farmers, beekeepers, or others whose work involves the natural elements.** Ask what changes they have observed in animal, plant, insect, fish, or other biotic communities in the last few years and decades. What ecological issues most concern them?

11. **Search for clean-energy businesses** in your community such as wind farms, solar farms, geothermal companies, and the like. Inquire as to how they see their work in relation to the community and the planet.

12. **Meet with your elected officials.** Ask who they consider "the least of these," or those most vulnerable among their constituents. What are their main environmental concerns regarding the watersheds, land, forests, and biotic communities within their territories?

13. **Create a "map" of your findings.** This can take the form of an actual map with key features noted, a hand-drawn representation, a collage of photos or images, a video, PowerPoint, or some other kind of visual display of the "neighbors" surrounding your congregation. This can be a collaborative project with youth and adults.

"Council of All Beings" Ritual

Once this neighbor-mapping has been done, how can we listen to the voices of Earthly others and attend to their testimony? One example of creatively imagining these voices is through a ritual called the Council of All Beings. As described by Mark I. Wallace, this is a variation on a deep ecology/neopagan ritual wherein "participants enact a mystical oneness with the flora and fauna in a particular area by speaking out in the first person on behalf of the being or place they have chosen to identify with."[38] This ritual enables members of the group to speak "as" and "for" other natural beings and to "feel imaginatively what it might be like to be bacterium, bottle-nosed dolphin, alligator, old-growth forest, or gray wolf. Participants become this or that animal or plant or natural place and then share a message with the other human persons in the circle."[39] The goal is to foster compassion for all life-forms and begin healing the misconceptions and mental divides that separate us from the natural world.

Once participants take on the role of speaking for their entity, ask them how they feel about some of the environmental impacts you have observed in your neighborhood. The challenge will be to stay "in character" with the role-play and suspend their human opinion. Such imaginative speaking "for" and "with" other-than-human-beings will have intriguing implications for preaching from an ecological perspective, as we will see in the sermon examples later in this chapter and the ones that follow.

Creative Ideas for Ecological Preaching

The number of online and in-print resources for houses of worship to incorporate Creation into liturgy, religious education, buildings and grounds, and stewardship is steadily growing. Preaching for and with Creation is the newest frontier. The list below is an attempt to compile ideas with which preachers may experiment as they formulate approaches to sermons from an ecological perspective. These are based on my conversations with clergy colleagues who have experimented with different approaches to green preaching, as well as my own experiences over the course of my fifteen years as a pastor speaking and preaching in different churches and other venues among listeners of different ages, economic levels, political persuasions, and cultural backgrounds. You may have other ideas, and I encourage readers to continue the dialogue online through my website www.creationcrisispreaching.com.

- Preach a series on a biblical saga from different points of view (including the nonhuman). For example, explore the story of Balaam's donkey (Numbers 22:21-41) from the perspective of Balaam, the angel, and the donkey, giving each perspective a turn over the course of three weeks. Even experiment with speaking as Earth itself (see Chapter Seven's sermon "Earth Speaks: What's Next?).
- Employ an eco-narrative criticism to preach as one of the "nature" characters in a biblical text (e.g., preaching as the fig tree whom Jesus causes to wither, preaching as the stones about to cry out along the "Palm Sunday Road," preaching as the birds or lilies from Jesus' parable).
- Bring in or at least show a picture of an actual object of nature mentioned in a biblical text (tree stump, water, flowers, rocks, etc.).
- Preach a sermon series on Jesus' parables about or inter-actions with Creation. (For a full listing of Jesus' parables, teachings and interactions with nature, visit www.creationcrisispreaching.com.)
- Provide time in a sermon for listeners to share about their favorite places in Creation or particular aspects of Creation. This not only allows them to hold an image in their minds, but helps to foster relationships between the listeners and some aspect of Creation within the context of preaching.

- Tell the story of a local natural habitat, framed within a biblical context or concept. Incorporate Earth's story within the biblical story, and connect it with the listeners' stories.
- Do a sermon series on features of nature in the Bible, such as rivers, mountains, or valleys.
- Preach outside. This is a natural way to decenter the congregation and directly address the larger "congregation" of the Earth community. (See "A Resurrection Sermon for an Earth-kin Congregation" later in this chapter.)

In any green sermon, when we forestall the desire to speak so that we may first attend to other-than-human perspectives, this helps us slow down and allow other heretofore ignored or silenced voices to be heard. Such a shift may enable a kind of parable-like crack to open in our worldview through which God's light and love for other creatures may be seen. The sermons that follow are two examples of preaching that attend to place, the biotic community, and the human connection with God's Creation, all scripturally and theologically framed to deepen faith and proclaim God's work in the world.

SERMON: "An Earth Day Sermon"

LEAH D. SCHADE

TEXTS: Genesis 3:17b–19; 4:8–16; Psalm 19:1–10; Romans 8:18–25; Matthew 12:40

Introduction

The texts for this sermon were not from the lectionary readings for the day, but were specifically chosen for an Earth Sunday celebration and worship service. I interpreted the texts through a green lens that highlighted an eco-centric focus. The interpretation of the story of "The Fall" in Genesis 3, for example, replaces the traditional explanation for original *anthropocentric* sin with that of original *anthropogenic* sin—humanity's first crime against nature. Similarly, the interpretation of God's law in Psalm 19 is expanded to include God's law in nature and humanity's relationship with Creation rather than being limited to the commands that govern inter-human relationships. And the Romans 8 passage is specifically lifted up as indicating the saving significance of Jesus Christ for the healing of the relationship between humanity and the rest of Creation.

In terms of the three-fold approach to preaching outlined in the previous chapter, the sermon begins by "flowering" with a lengthy description of a local nature preserve in order to create a word-picture of an Eden-like oasis for the listener. Specific plants and birds are mentioned by name and details of the landscape are included to help connect listeners with Creation, cultivating a sense of wonder and respect for the nonhuman other. "Leafing" in this sermon is more subtle in that there is an implied call to action (preserving natural lands). But the "fruiting" is apparent throughout the sermon as I utilize my dual role as parent and pastor to model for other adults raising children what it might look like to nurture "children of God" as "children of Earth" as well, teaching them to cherish, respect, and honor their Earth-kin in their particular habitat.

Sermon Text

I was a pastor in Media, Pennsylvania, for nearly ten years. Media is an affluent suburb on the outskirts of the Philadelphia metro area. I remember driving up and down the Rt. 252 corridor back in 1999 when I first started my call at Reformation Lutheran Church. After crossing over the lovely expanse of water known as Springton Lake, you would see a stretch of woods rising up on either side of the road until you approached the intersection of Rt. 3. But in the course of nine short years, those woods disappeared. Little by little, tract by tract, the trees were chain-sawed, the land bulldozed, and the housing developments, soccer fields, strip mall, office complexes, and retirement estates appeared. I helplessly watched as the home of countless deer, rabbits, groundhogs, birds, and all manner of foliage was cleared to make way for human progress and profit. I often wonder where these environmental refugees go, and if the people living in those homes and shopping in those stores give any thought to the beings who lost their lives and homes so that they could enjoy such a comfortable setting. And I have quietly raged and mourned the loss of this natural habitat, while fuming at the complexity of circumstances that make such environmental devastation possible.

Then in 2007 I received a brochure in the mail about a place called Hildacy Farm Natural Lands Trust located right in Marple Township. It's a 55-acre preserve that contains about 20 acres of woodlands and hedgerows and 30 acres of meadow. I took my children, Rachel and Benjamin, then ages 4 and 1, to see what it was like. I couldn't believe I had lived in the area almost a decade and never heard about this place. We drove over Springton Lake and made a sharp right onto Palmer's Mill Rd., dropping down on the north side of the lake. When we pulled into the parking lot and got out of the car, Rachel took a long look around at the trees, the barn, and the marsh and said, "Mmm, I like it here. It's so peaceful and quiet."

We started down the path around the marsh, listening to bull frogs calling to each other. We watched a Baltimore Oriole alight on a reed jutting up from the water. Then we climbed up the path through the meadow, watching a bluebird making a home in one of the nesting boxes. We made our way down through a quiet stand of evergreens, whispering as our sounds were muffled by the carpet of fallen needles. Then we came out at the bottom and heard rushing water. We discovered, much to our delight, a waterfall cascading down from Springton Lake, which then flowed into the rolling waters of Crum Creek. We followed the creek all the way along the path until we came back up along the other side of the meadow and returned to our starting point.

Along the way, Rachel saw many different kinds of flowers that she wanted to pick. But I explained to her that everything that lived there wanted to stay there. Just because we saw shiny rocks or colorful flowers did not mean that we were allowed to take them with us. This was their home, and we had to respect their place in the world. "You wouldn't like it if someone took you from your home and made you live somewhere else, would you?" I asked. And she understood.

Here at last we had discovered a place where native plants and wildlife were allowed to live without fear. No hunting, fishing or trapping will threaten the animals. Picnics and camping are not allowed, so that no trash will spoil the natural landscape. The way God's hand fashioned this land is the way it will remain. Human visitors are permitted, but are to leave no trace of their visit when they're gone.

As we walked, I kept thinking of the garden paradise established by God for human beings in the first two chapters of Genesis. It was like we had discovered a tiny Eden oasis right there in Marple Township. And yet from nearly every vantage point on the preserve, you can see houses and the passing cars on Rt. 252 looming above—a grim reminder that the sanctity of this place is hemmed in by relentless human pressure on all sides. I knew that as soon as we got back in the car, we would drive through to the other side of the Eden story—where the ground is cursed and human beings are engaged in constant battle with the earth from which they were brought forth.

Why does God curse the ground in this passage from Genesis 3? Do you remember? It's because Adam and Eve ate fruit from the tree of knowledge. Most people see this story as the explanation for the concept of Original Sin—the doctrine that all human beings are born into a sinful state because of the fall of Adam and Eve.

But there is another way to view this story. The myth of the "fall" of human beings has specific application to the current environmental crisis. Let me explain. This story in chapter 3 shows us that God set out limits for human beings in how they were to exist in the garden. For the good of Adam and Eve, for the good of the tree, for the good of the entire garden, God essentially said: "This far and no farther." God established a boundary for the mutual protection of the relationship between humankind and the created world.

Did the original humans respect these boundaries? No. They did not obey the limits God set for them. They ignored the warnings, flouted the rules, and crossed the line. There's almost a feeling of entitlement you sense from Eve and Adam's rationalization of their disobedience. It's as if they're saying, "This is our garden after all. God gave it to us. We should be allowed to do anything we want with it. Look, the fruit is good to eat. It will make us smarter, better, richer. God just doesn't want us to be like God. God's afraid we'll know what God knows. And why shouldn't we?"

And because of this arrogance, there is an immediate cascade of events that shatters the relationships of paradise. The humans hide from God, and are not honest with God or themselves. They blame each other, and they blame one of God's creatures for the temptation. They refuse to accept responsibility for what has happened, but the consequences are unavoidable. From that point on, their relationship with the earth is cursed: "Cursed is the ground because of you; / in toil you shall eat of it all the days of your life." [Gen. 3:17b]. All because of human beings' insistence that we can have whatever we want whenever we want it, no matter what the cost or consequences

Can you see the similarities to what we are experiencing today? Psalm 19 tells us that the laws, decrees, and ordinances of God are about respecting the boundaries of relationships, including the delicate balance of our ecosystems, and being mindful of our impact on them. And yet we continually cross those lines and insist that we can and should pluck the fruit from the tree of knowledge of good and evil, rationalizing that we have the right to become like God.

But just because we can does not mean that we should. The warnings are clear. Do not continue to pollute the air and the water and the soil. You'll learn good and evil the hard way when your children die from strange diseases and you can't swim or eat fish from the poisoned waters. Do not continue burning fossil fuels. You'll learn good and evil the hard way when the gasses trap heat within the atmosphere and melt your icebergs and flood your islands and coastlands and whip up catastrophic weather events. Do not continue to clear-cut the earth to make way for one more shopping mall or housing development. You'll learn the good and evil the hard way when species die out and invasive plants and animals prey on your weakened natural habitats.

There are limits as to what the earth can withstand. There are boundaries that need to be established and respected. But we have done more than just cross the line. We have decimated the entire garden. We are not just plucking fruit from the tree anymore. We're cutting the whole tree down to make toilet paper and pave a parking lot! And we are now living with the consequences of a dying earth.

A dying earth? Really? Some will balk at that phrase, arguing that the state of the earth is not so dire. There are voices all along the spectrum of environmental issues ranging from denial to anger to depression. But I'll tell you why I use this language of a dying earth. I do it because when we acknowledge the pain and suffering, this is what opens the door to healing and redemption. In the words of Tom Ravetz, in the *Journal for the Renewal of Religion and Theology,* we "can accept the reality of the situation without flinching because we see its place in the development of the world. We see, too, where we can help to redeem it, letting its deeper meaning shine forth. We can accept the reality of the dying earth, because we know that we are engaged in its reenlivening."[40]

This is why I find these words of Jesus in Matthew 12:40 so profound: "[F]or three days and three nights the Son of Man will be in the heart of the earth." The Greek phrase is en kardia ge, literally "in the heart of the earth." And "heart" here does not just mean in the center of the earth. Jesus is saying that he is going to that place within the earth that is the seat of physical life, just like a human heart. This is extremely important for our concept of the created world. Jesus is acknowledging that Earth is a living entity, for one thing. And that Earth has a center of spiritual, intellectual, and physical life.

This is a revolutionary change in attitude toward Earth from the one some people read in Genesis 1:26, which can be interpreted as authorizing humans to, literally, stomp on top of the earth as if it were grapes in a winepress. Squeeze the most out of it you can. Subdue it, bring it into bondage, keep it under your feet. Instead, Jesus is saying that he will not rule over earth, but allow himself to be taken in by it. His crucifixion and resurrection, therefore, is not just for the salvation of human beings, but for the very earth itself.

And that's why Paul can declare in Romans this hoped-for vision of reconciliation between Earth and humanity: "For the creation waits with eager longing for the revealing of the children of God...in hope that the creation itself will be set free from its bondage to decay and will obtain the freedom of the children of God" [Rom. 8:19–21]. This is why more and more congregations are beginning to establish an ecology ministry to do everything they can to promote environmental education, recycling, care of Creation, and preservation of natural habitats.

You see, this movement is more than just "grass roots"—it's tree roots, flower roots, everything living thing that has its connection to the "Ground of Being,"using an expanded ecological sense of that theological term. Ecological ministry must be sown into the soil of our theological discourse in order for it to be drawn up into our daily lives, like clean water absorbed up through the root system to nourish the tree. If we do not allow ourselves to be used by God to be channels of an "eco-resurrection"—the bringing back to life of the dying earth—then everything else is for naught. Ecology affects all areas of justice—children, women, the poor, minorities, and developing countries. If we work to save "the least of these"—the ones with no voice on the natural level—we may also be moved to save the least of these on a human level.

Hildacy Farm is a beautiful example of human beings finally obeying the command of God in the garden of Eden—this far, and no farther. And every time another tract of land or flowing waterway is saved through the Natural Lands Trust or other land-preservation efforts, it means that the wildlife, plants, water, and soil of that place can never be destroyed. No bulldozer will rip an ancient oak tree up from its roots. No luxury home will displace a den of foxes. No mown soccer grass will supplant a field of goldenrods, asters, and black-eyed Susans. No parking lot will ever be paved over a wetland that absorbs and filters the rainwater from the surrounding hillsides.

Sometimes there is great blessing in establishing boundaries and protecting them. Sometimes the benefits of changing your lifestyle or business practices to reduce your carbon footprint outweigh the initial sacrifice of entitlement. Sometimes foregoing profit in order to preserve a natural legacy reaps rewards far beyond monetary wealth. And sometimes acknowledging a dying earth is the only way to save it. Because after coming through the scorched land of crucifixion, God will bring us to the resurrection in the new Eden—the garden of Easter morning. Amen.

Reflection

I have preached this sermon at two different churches within the suburban Philadelphia area. Both were located in upscale, mostly white neighborhoods. Both times congregants expressed curiosity about Hildacy Farms and indicated their intention to explore the preserve in the future. The most moving comment came from a gentleman who shared that he and his family had a piece of property inherited from his parents, and they were debating what to do with it. He said that after hearing the sermon, he was considering doing with the rural property what had been done at Hildacy Farms—turning it into a land trust to preserve it for posterity. He thanked me for planting the seed in his mind. This is a demonstration of the leafing effect of the sermon in that a call to specific action was implied (preserving land through trusts). It also shows fruiting in that the call was heeded.

In terms of Lutheran theology, the sermon moves between law and gospel by contrasting the local protected site with the pressures of human society encroaching on all sides. It is a context-specific sermon that uses the microcosm of Hildacy Farms in Delaware County, Pennsylvania, in a synecdochic way to reference the larger ecological issues of the day. The use of the word *eco-crucifixion* is rhetorically wrestled with in the sermon and is explained as a plausible term to describe the destruction of so many of Earth's habitats, species, and fundamentals of life. But the sermon does not end with guilt-inducing law that leaves the listener without hope. Rather, God's intention and action to heal and restore the land concludes the sermon, thus assuring the listener of the resurrection for our crucified Earth.

SERMON: "A Resurrection Sermon for an Earth-Kin Congregation"

(A Sermon for an Outdoor Setting)
Preached at R. B. Winter State Park in Pennsylvania, in the outdoor Whispering Pines Amphitheater

LEAH D. SCHADE

TEXT: Colossians 1:15–20; John 20:1–18

Introduction

The "audience" for this sermon is what sets it apart from the previous examples. Taking a cue from Francis of Assisi,[41] I reintroduce his idea of preaching to the creatures, flora, and nonhuman others in Creation. In this way, the eco-hermeneutical principle of proclamation for the other-than-human community of Earth is given a completely different conceptual framework. The Earth-congregation is directly addressed, and the humans are told they can "listen in." Thus anthropocentrism is decentered from the outset and humans are relegated to the margin. Moreover, the members of the other-than-human community are addressed not just as "Brother" and "Sister," but are identified by their role within the liturgy of Creation, much the way humans have parts to play in the worship service as ushers, greeters, choir members, and lectors.

The ecological hermeneutic is also woven throughout the sermon by seeing the story of the Passion and Resurrection from the nature characters' points of view. They are identified as witnesses to the events from Palm Sunday through Good Friday and as co-sufferers in Jesus' crucifixion. Thus the sermon, through both its form and content, enacts a creative actualization of the biblical story from Earth's perspective and situates them as equals in the divine drama of the Passion and Crucifixion.

The primary text for consideration alongside that of the John's Gospel is the "hymn of the Cosmic Christ" in the first chapter of Colossians. Here I drew on Joseph Sittler's interpretation, which contains seeds of an early ecofeminism in that he identifies nature as "God's sister":

> We must not fail to see the nature and size of this issue that Paul confronts and encloses in this vast Christology. In propositional form it is simply this: a doctrine of redemption is meaningful only when it swings within the larger orbit of a doctrine of creation. For God's creation of earth cannot be redeemed in any intelligible sense of the word apart from a doctrine of the cosmos which is God's home, God's definite place, the theatre of God's selfhood, in cooperation with God's neighbour, and in a caring relationship with nature, God's sister.[42]

While the ontological implications of such a relationship between God and nature (i.e., If they are siblings, who is their parent?) are worth exploration at another time, what I wish to highlight is the way in which Sittler expands a salvific Christology to be inclusive of Creation. With this in mind, the middle of the sermon takes time to trace the contours of the story of the Cosmos' and Earth's ancient, primordial history in order to provide the memory of God's steadfastness and love through the unfathomable reaches of time.

The sermon then returns to Holy Week. Earth is described as taking Jesus' body into herself and birthing him from her womb as the Resurrected One. The Greek chorus of Creation is contrasted against the reaction of the women at the tomb on Easter morning. And just as the elements of Creation provide a unique witness to the crucifixion, so they also provide a fly's eye, stone's eye, and birds' eye view of the risen Christ. The description of what they see is influenced by Catherine Keller's description of an ecological resurrection: "[T]he old creation will remain, marred and scarred, to be mourned, healed, teased, its lonely phallic signifiers danced around like ancient maypoles."[43]

Sermon Text

St. Francis of Assisi, the patron saint of ecologists, preached to the flowers. He preached to cornfields, stones, forests, earth, air, and wind. He considered them and all God's creatures to be his brothers and sisters. He thought of them as his fellow worshipers of God and exhorted them to praise their Creator.

I think it is high time to revive his practice of preaching to our Earth-kin, so this sermon is not for my human sisters and brothers; it is for my other-than-human family. You are welcome to listen in. But as we stand in this cathedral of God's Creation, surrounded by the very presence of God in the midst of this congregation of trees, creeks, hundreds of varieties of plants and wildlife, thousands of insects, and microbes we can't even see, this sermon is for them.

Brother Fern and Sister Porcupine; Choir of Cicadas and Altar Guild of Spiders who weave the fair linens of the forest; Lightning Bug Acolyte and Lector Bull Frog who reads to us the lessons of God's Creation as the sun sets each summer evening: Grace to you and peace from our Lord and Savior Jesus Christ. Amen.

One of the most moving hymns that we humans sing on Good Friday is "Were You There When They Crucified My Lord." Lest we forget that God's very Creation witnessed to Jesus' suffering and death, I want to acknowledge your presence at every point along Jesus' journey to the cross, and that you witnessed his resurrection before any human eye beheld him.

Stones, your voices echoed the ringing "Hosannas" shouted by the disciples and crowds along the road to Jerusalem. Palm Leaves, you laid a green carpet for Donkey's hooves as he carried Jesus into the city. Olive Grove, you stood sentry over Jesus as he prayed at Gethsemane, knowing the suffering that awaited him. Sun, you hid your face during those torturous hours Jesus hung on the cross, as Nephesh, the Breath of Life, was forced from his lungs with each passing hour. And Trees, both of you felled in the prime of your life after having housed countless birds, insects, and children's playtimes—they lashed you together crossways and forced you to become the scaffolding of death for Jesus. Each of you was there. Even you, Rocks, trembled and shook, fractured and split as Jesus breathed his last.

Yes, you were there. You suffered as Jesus suffered. And is your suffering any different today? Yes, it is different. For as man's death-machine has become more sophisticated, so has his ability to violate your life processes become more complex and sinister. Brother Trees, you are massacred by the millions every hour to make room for human houses, strip malls, fields of human-designed genetically mutated seeds, and drill rigs. Sister Rocks, you tremble and shake, fracture and split, as these rigs puncture you, inject you with biocides and chemicals to kill any and every living thing, as the essence of your ancient depths is extracted. Nephesh, Breath of Life, you are polluted with carbon dioxide, fumes, and the smallest particulates that find their way into our children's lungs and cause them to gasp for air. Sun, your heat is no longer simply beneficial, but trapped inside the atmosphere of Earth, causing Brother Ice Caps to shrink, Sea to rise, and Storm to rage with irrepressible anger against us. The crucifixion of Jesus happened once in history. But your crucifixion, O Earth, is carried out daily.

It is no wonder that you groan, waiting for those of us who are Christian to claim our birthright and responsibilities as Children of God to finally stand up and say, "Enough!" We have done such damage to you, committed so many sins against you and our human brothers and sisters, I worry that we may have already reached the tipping point and that we are on a fast track to an environmental Good Friday, the likes of which few of us will survive.

But when I am tempted to give in to despair, I am reminded of a story that gives me hope. It is the most ancient of stories. It is your story—the story of the birth of the universe itself. Cosmos of God, you are nearly 14 billion years old. The story we hear in Genesis is of your creation, conceived from the great unfathomable depths of God's bottomless, tehomic love. And the set of circumstances for life to begin and evolve on this fragile blue orb is so impossible, it can only be Love itself that would enable it to happen at all.

I am reminded that in Earth's history there have been waves of catastrophic events which have threatened life on this planet. But again and again, the resiliency and creativity given to you by God has found ways to push through and around the crises and enabled life to flourish once again. I have to believe that God, who has brought us through 14 billion years of time, will not abandon us now. That somehow God is working through even this man-made catastrophe of global climate change, deforestation, mass extinction, and toxic poisoning to find a way for life to push through once again. And so I make the choice to believe—and act on my firm belief—that on the other side of the Good Friday of the eco-crucifixion, there is an eco-resurrection waiting to surprise us.

Because when I remember that you were there at Jesus' crucifixion, I also remember that you were there at his resurrection. Earth, you took Jesus' body into yourself, into the very heart of your bosom. What did you witness there if not a birth from the womb of your body? Great Stone hewn from the cave, how light you were in the hands of the angels who rolled you away. Quiet Garden in which the women stood, uncomprehending of the miracle before them, how the Crickets must have laughed, how the Flowers must have glowed with joy, seeing the women's faces behold the Resurrected One.

What did you see, Sister Flies, no longer drawn to a decomposing body? How did Jesus appear to you, Brother Birds who whistled the first "Alleluia, Christ is Risen!"? He was the same, yet different. He was filled with new life, yet with scars remaining. So, too, will be your appearance, O Earth, when your resurrection is complete. For God so loved the world—the cosmos—that She gave her only begotten Son, so that all who believe in him will not perish, but will have eternal life.

I ask you, Sister Dolphin and Brother Arctic Moss, not to give up hope. Believe in the One who loves you, who created you, who suffers with you, and who will raise you up into new life. Do not give up on us, O Earth. There are humans who are teaching their children and others how to see the world not just from a human point of view, but from your point of view. We are learning how God sees the interrelatedness within all of Creation. We are learning from you, listening to your teachings, reintroducing ourselves to Brother Fox and Sister Salamander. We are drawing our faith from you, and repenting of our arrogance that has oppressed you for so long.

You, our Earth-kin, are grounding us in the universe story so we can see where we come from and what we come out of—this soil and water and breath—reminding us that we are all indeed one—of the same substance that exploded in that glorious instant of creation. You will help us to unfetter our imagination by asking: What does the world look like when we live within our means and see Earth as family? And you will show us what it looks like when all God's creatures, including these Children of God, praise their Creator through worship and song and quiet meditation. As we learn to love you, O Earth, and love God, we are being moved to advocate for you and to be servants of the Most High God.

O Earth, I must believe that we can look forward to the Resurrected One calling our names and opening our eyes to your crucified body transformed to new life, even as we have done all we could in our faithful witnessing and ministering, and still fallen short.

Pray for us, Earth-kin, as we pray for you. It is no accident that you are here, that any of us are here. God has brought you to this place and God will guide you and lead you as you lead and guide us. Go forth with the faith that will sustain you and assure you that you are doing God's work with your very existence. And God's work never fails. Amen.

Reflection

This sermon is designed to be a "fruiting" sermon that sows seeds of long-term transformation in that it answers a question posed earlier in this chapter: "What would a sermon look like in which Creation itself was the *listener*?" At the same time, Creation is giving its testimony through a sermonic voicing. The sermon is intended to be preached outside so that the audience is decentered and the notion of sanctuary is turned inside-out. In this case, the sermon was preached at a state park in Pennsylvania where the congregation I serve had spent the weekend in a camping retreat. In the spirit of public theology, the Sunday service was open to all campers on the grounds and was well-attended by both the campers and members of the congregation. By directly addressing Creation and moving the human audience to the sideline, a number of possibilities are opened. Humans are allowed to "overhear" the way in which Creation experiences oppression by *man*kind.[44] In this way the audience is rhetorically escorted out of their human-centeredness, and the other of Creation is given primacy.

Contemporary, urgent, context-specific issues of ecological injustice are addressed throughout this sermon as it references clear-cutting and deforestation, oil and gas drilling, air pollution and children's asthma, mass extinctions and climate change as examples of environmental destruction that have damaging effects on human health and society. Preached in a different location where different ecojustice issues are prominent (toxic dumpsites, incinerators, water pollution, or desertification, for example), the sermon would incorporate those as well. These are categorized as instances of eco-crucifixions, in the spirit of Mark Wallace who, as we will discuss further on, makes the connection between the cruciform Spirit and "the continual debasement of the earth and its inhabitants."[45]

It is at the point of despair in the midst of "an environmental Good Friday," however, that the sermon proclaims the Cosmic Christ resurrected and Earth's creatures as witnesses to the miracle. In this way, the Lutheran concept of *Deus Absconditus,* the hiddenness of God under the form of opposites, is invoked and listeners are given hope in the midst of the darkest hour of the Easter vigil. Further, the sermon avoids "ecological works righteousness" by emphasizing that Christ will appear to us and call our name "even as we have done all we could in our faithful witnessing and ministering, and still fallen short."

The prophetic call for action is, again, "overheard" by the congregation as the preacher implores Earth not to give up on us, and to have hope in the repentance and reconciliation some humans are living out through a reorientation to Earth. Finally, Earth is asked to "pray for us," again highlighting Creation's agency and relational quality with humanity. Creation is sent forth, apostle-like, to continue its proclamation of God's grace and trust in God's never-failing love.

Notes

[1]John S. McClure, *Other-Wise Preaching: A Postmodern Ethic for Homiletic* (St. Louis: Chalice Press, 2001), xi.

[2]Ibid., 120, with reference to Emmanuel Levinas, *Otherwise than Being,* trans. Alphonso Linguis (The Hague: Martinis Nijhoff. 1981), 136–37.

[3]Ibid.

[4]Ibid., 134, with refernce to Emmanuel Levinas, "Meaning and Sense," in *Collected Philosophical Papers,* trans. Alphonso Lingis (The Hague: Martinus Nijhoff, 1987), 97.

[5]Wendy Lynne Lee, *Contemporary Feminist Theory and Activism: Six Global Issues* (Ontario, Can.: Broadview Books, 2010), 196.

[6]McClure, *Other-Wise Preaching,* 134.

[7]Mary Midgley, "Is a Dolphin a Person?" *The Essential Mary Midgley* (Oxford and New York: Routledge, 2005), referencing Jeremy Bentham, *Introduction to the Principles of Morals and Legislation* (1789; New York: Barnes and Noble, 2008), ch. 17.

[8]Ibid., 140.

[9]Ibid., 141.

[10]H. Paul Santmire, *Nature Reborn: The Ecological and Cosmic Promise of Christian Theology* (Minneapolis: Fortress Press, 2000), 68.

[11]Ibid., 69.

[12]Ibid., 69–70.

[13]Ibid., 70–73. For Santmire, humbling oneself before the Ens means to "become small and lowly...especially before objects that are otherwise insignificant" (71), particularly those entities that it would be easy to pass by, manipulate, dispose of, or kill, such as an ant or a flower, for example. He does recognize the fact that humans do intervene in

nature in numerous ways, many of which arise out of the necessity for survival and daily living. His point in articulating the I-Ens relationship is to provide a means by which we may account for and advocate for relationships of mutuality and cooperation between persons and other creatures of nature and to think about nonhuman entities as members of our extended family.

[14]Ibid., 73.

[15]Mark I. Wallace, *Green Christianity: Five Ways to a Sustainable Future* (Minneapolis: Fortress Press, 2010), 150.

[16]Ibid., 151.

[17]Ibid., 152–53.

[18]This would include, for example, curtailing air pollution from power plants and cleaning up toxic waste sites (or avoiding building them altogether), both of which involve chemicals and toxins that are particularly harmful to children and pregnant women.

[19]For example, certain human activities involve the use of chemicals, toxins, and radioactive materials that negatively affect the life cycle at its foundations (such as fracking fluids that contain endocrine disrupters, and the use of fossil fuels that lead to climate change, which is affecting ocean temperatures and, along with other human factors, is causing the collapse of coral reefs, the foundation of much aquatic life.)

[20]The concept of the Roundtable Pulpit was originated and developed by John McClure in his book *The Roundtable Pulpit: Where Leadership and Preaching Meet* (Nashville: Abingdon Press, 1995).

[21]Lucy Atkinson Rose, *Sharing the Word : Preaching in the Roundtable Church* (Louisville: Westminster John Knox Press, 1997), 4–5.

[22]Here Rose draws from Letty Russell's concept of the "household" within which meals, conversation, and hospitality are shared. Russell redescribes power, authority, and leadership as being shared among equals, rather than exercised in dominance over others. (Letty M. Russell, *Church in the Round: Feminist Interpretation of the Church* [Louisville: Westminster/John Knox, 1993].)

[23]Rose, *Sharing the Word,* 93.

[24]Ibid., 128.

[25]There are some who have begun to make the case for the legal rights of other-than-human beings, such as philosophers Mary Midgley and Wendy Lynne Lee, and criminal justice expert Christopher Stone, as well as organizations such as The Global Alliance for the Rights of Nature (http://therightsofnature.org/). The Rights of Nature movement has led to the legal protection of New Zealand's Whanganui River, and the incorporation of Rights of Nature articles into Ecuador's constitution.

[26]Rose, *Sharing the Word,* 122.

[27]Ibid., 121.

[28]Ibid.

[29]Anna Carter Florence, *Preaching as Testimony* (Louisville: Westminster John Knox Press, 2007), xiii.

[30]Ibid., xxvi.

[31]Ibid., 68, summarizing Paul Ricoeur.

[32]Ibid., 77.

[33]Ibid., 88.

[34]Ibid., 154.

[35]Ibid., 153.

[36]Rebecca S. Chopp, *The Power to Speak: Feminism, Language, God* (New York: Crossroad, 1989), 67–68.

[37]Ibid., 68.

[38]Wallace, *Green Christianity,* 138.Wallace shares a moving story of enacting this ritual with one of his college classes in pages 137–40.

[39]Ibid.

[40]Tom Ravetz, "Reenlivening the Dying Earth," *Journal for the Renewal of Religion and Theology,* December 2006.

41Francis' first biographer, Thomas of Celano (1229), wrote: "When he found an abundance of flowers, he preached to them and invited them to praise the Lord as though they were endowed with reason. In the same way he exhorted with the sincerest purity cornfields and vineyards, stones and forests and all the beautiful things of the fields, fountains of water and the green things of the gardens, earth and fire, air and wind, to love God and serve him willingly. Finally, he called all creatures brother, and in a most extraordinary manner, a manner never experienced by others, he discerned the hidden things of nature with his sensitive heart, as one who had already escaped into the freedom of the glory of the sons of God" (1 Celano, 81–82) (as cited in Leonardo Boff, *Cry of the Earth, Cry of the Poor* [Maryknoll, N.Y.: Orbis Books, 1997], 210.)

42Joseph Sittler, "Called to Unity: Redemption within Creation," in *World Council of Churches Meeting* (New Delhi, India: 1961, reprinted 1985), 3.

43Catherine Keller, *Apocalypse Now and Then: A Feminist Guide to the End of the World* (Boston: Beacon Press, 1996), 179, 180.

44This word, used instead of *human*kind, is an indirect ecofeminist denunciation of patriarchy by way of language choice. In this case I truly mean that our patriarchal society bears the majority of responsibility for Earth's distress.

45Wallace, *Green Christianity*, 23–24.

4

Ecofeminist Theology and Implications for Preaching

I currently serve as a Lutheran (ELCA) pastor at a small, rural congregation in the upper Susquehanna Valley in the center of Pennsylvania, just south of where the shale gas industry has swept across the Marcellus Shale formation of the state to frack for natural gas. Fracking is short for slickwater horizontal hydraulic fracturing, an extraction process for methane gas and oil in which holes are drilled vertically thousands of feet beneath the Earth's surface and then horizontally into shale formations. The shale, formed over 400 million years ago from marine sedimentary rock, is fractured using explosives to release the gas and oil.

Modern slickwater hydraulic fracturing first began in 1998 in Texas (in contrast to conventional gas drilling which has been done since 1947). The process uses millions of gallons of water mixed with silica sand and chemicals, including known toxins and carcinogens, which are injected with great pressure into the fractures. The copious amounts of water needed for each well opening involve a corresponding withdrawal of fresh water from its natural source (rivers, aquifers, wells), which has the potential to negatively impact these sources.[1]

Wastewater returns to the surface in two ways: as "flowback" and "produced water." The former consists of chemical additives and total dissolved solids (TDS) used in the fracking process, while the latter is "naturally occurring water found in shale formations that flows to the surface throughout the entire lifespan of the gas well. This water has high levels of TDS and leaches out minerals from the shale, including barium, calcium, iron, and magnesium. It also contains dissolved hydrocarbons such as methane, ethane, and propane along with naturally occurring radioactive materials (NORM) such as radium isotopes."[2] While the flowback from the well can be reused for future drilling, there is currently no way to safely process and treat wastewater produced from hydraulic fracturing and return it to a potable state. Also, there are numerous and substantiated reports, as well as a growing body of scientific studies, indicating that the process of shale gas drilling, fracturing, and related production contaminates underground and surface water, and causes both immediate and long-term health problems in those exposed to the process.[3]

After anecdotal reports of contaminated well water, blow-outs, and illegal dumping of flowback water began to surface among residents near frack sites, a small but growing number of individuals and local grassroots organizations began forming to raise awareness about the dangers of the shale gas extraction process. A key catalyst of the movement was the provocative 2010 documentary by director Josh Fox entitled *Gasland,* which famously portrayed the deleterious effects of fracking on family farms and properties across America. Images of tap water lighting on fire have drawn considerable worldwide attention, as well as industry backlash, and have contributed to turning "fracking" into a household word.

Fracking will be a recurring issue throughout this book, addressed through the lens of ecofeminist theology. I have highlighted this environmental issue for several reasons. First, fracking provides a tragic but excellent example of the kind of joint oppression of women and Earth that happens when the forces of industry, capitalism, classism, culture, and a patriarchal, instrumentalist view of nature converge.[4] Second, the flowback and produced water from fracking results in the release of radioactive materials, dissolved solids, and carcinogens, all of which pose significant threats to plant, animal, and human life, particularly to women, pregnant women, fetuses, infants, and children.[5] Also, there is growing concern about the impact of natural gas drilling on women in terms of increased violence against women in drilling boom towns, increased instances of breast cancer, and the risk of spontaneous abortion and birth defects.[6] In addition, the methane that leaks from frack sites, pipelines, and compressor stations is a more potent form of greenhouse gas than carbon dioxide within a twenty-year period, a time-span that is critical for curbing global warming. Thus the process of extracting, processing and burning shale gas is contributing to climate change.

With this context in mind, this chapter outlines the basics of ecofeminist theology and draws implications for preaching focused on environmental justice. An overview of ecofeminism's critique of patriarchy, hierarchy, instrumentalism, dualism, and "othering" leads to a discussion of the problematic association between women and nature and its misogynistic origins, particularly around the issue of essentialism. Part Two examines ecofeminist theology and concludes by bringing ecofeminist principles to bear on preaching, which will, in turn, raise issues and questions that will guide the rest of this book.

Part One: What Is Ecofeminism?

The term *ecofeminism* is a compound word made from the terms ecology and feminism. The words are co-informative in that feminist principles are applied to ecology, and ecological concerns are applied to the feminist movement. As Ivone Gebara explains, "This positive word is born of two negative situations: the destruction of the natural world and the oppression of women. Ecofeminism is a recent word created by women as a reaction against the destruction of life carried out by patriarchal systems. It is a clear position that makes connections between the struggle for the dignity of women and respect for the different processes of life."[7]

The term *écoféminisme* was first introduced by French feminist Françoise d'Eaubonne in her 1974 book *Le féminisme ou la mort* (*Feminism or Death*).[8] In this book she urged women to begin a revolution in ecology in which both women and nature would be liberated. Yet even before the word itself became widely used, the ecofeminist movement was already afoot. In 1975 Rosemary Radford Ruether sounded the call for the need to develop a worldview and practices that combined feminism and ecology:

> Women must see that there can be no liberation for them and no solution to the ecological crisis within a society whose fundamental model of relationships continues to be one of domination. They must unite the demands of the women's movement with those of the ecological movement to envision a radical reshaping of the basic socioeconomic relations and the underlying values of this...society.[9]

True to the tendency of feminists in general to value interconnectivity, ecofeminists recognize the fundamental connection between humans and the natural world. Therefore, ecofeminists are committed to efforts to protect and save the planet and its oceans, land, sky, and inhabitants—human and nonhuman alike.

Emphases within Ecofeminism

According to Karen Warren, there are a variety of different perspectives within ecofeminism that "reflect not only different feminist perspectives (e.g., liberal, traditional Marxist, radical, socialist); [but] also reflect different understandings of the nature of, and solution to, pressing environmental problems."[10] She identifies eight apparent connections between feminism and the environment:

1. the deleterious historical and causal effects on women and the environment wrought by patriarchy in the realms of culture, philosophy, science, and commerce;
2. the conceptual links between how gender, sexuality, women, and nature are negatively conceived and valued within a dualistic, hierarchical domination structure;
3. empirical and experimental inquiries measuring the effects of environmental degradation on women (particularly in Third World, indigenous, and poor communities), as well as the importance of valuing the earth-based spiritualities of the women in indigenous cultures;
4. a formation of epistemological understandings through which women's ways of "knowing" affect philosophical and ethical approaches to the environment;
5. an exploration of the symbolic connections between women and nature in language, metaphor, theology, and literature;
6. an ethical analysis of the treatment of women and the natural world, which is decidedly non-male-based;
7. theoretical reflections that examine the tension between traditional and nontraditional stances among consequentialist, ontological, utilitarian, existentialist, and Marxist positions as they relate to ecology and feminism; and
8. the political ramifications of all of the above on practical issues such as health, technology, development, militarism, animal rights, and peace efforts, especially as they involve women and the environment.[11]

These different emphases are not meant to be seen as competitive or exclusive, since the claims and insights overlap and inform each other.[12] Warren concludes her overview with the recognition that taking all of these issues seriously will involve a challenging revision of scholarship and curricula, and that such a daunting project is necessary "not only for women, animals, and planet Earth, but for the development of worldviews and practices which are ecologically responsible and socially just for all."[13] Such is the case for preaching as well, for ecofeminism will also involve challenging the way we read and interpret Scripture for proclamation, as well the form and content of our preaching.

Principles of Ecofeminism

Because ecofeminists are committed to the liberation of both women and nature, this means that they begin with a relentless questioning of all epistemological, theological, cultural, philosophical, political, ecclesiological, and ethical proposals in order to determine the sources of oppression, domination, and the simultaneous hatred of women and the natural world. Eleanor Rae wisely observes that "our unexamined presuppositions naturally bring us to the place where we are today."[14] Hence, a raising of awareness is key to revealing values couched within our worldviews, because "without an awareness of our worldviews we believe them to be true without ever having questioned their validity."[15]

1. The Critique of Patriarchy, Hierarchy, Instrumentalism, Dualism, and "Othering"

Ecofeminists are united in their refusal to accept patriarchy because it is structured on hierarchical value systems and based on a dualistic method of determining worth. As Gebara states, "For patriarchal systems, life is understood as a hierarchical process wherein each one can destroy the other in order to save the individual. The same competition present in the big trade markets is present in the relations of humans among themselves and with nature."[16] According to ecofeminists, where this patriarchy is most blatantly manifested is in the Western capitalist economic system, which has resulted in imperialism, colonialism, slavery, and, most recently, multinational corporations that Gebara denounces as "destroying natural resources and manipulating different cultures and environments in order to produce and sell more goods. These corporations...do not perceive the connectedness and interdependence of everything, and they continue to be hostile to women, poor people, and nature, considering everything as an object to conquer."[17] As a result, the patriarchal system employs a strategy of instrumentalism, whereby women and nature are both seen "in terms of their usefulness to others rather than as having intrinsic worth in their own right."[18] Such instrumentalism results in a blatant disregard for the needs of women and Earth, and has brought us to a crisis chillingly described by Rosemary Radford Ruether:

> Infinite demand incarnate in finite nature, in the form of infinite exploitation of the earth's resources for production, results in ecological disaster: the rapid eating up of the organic foundations of life under our feet in an effort to satisfy ever-growing appetites for goods. The matrix of being, which is no less the foundation of human being, is rapidly depleted. Within two centuries this pattern of thought and activity has brought humanity close to the brink of the destruction of the earth and its environment.[19]

Ecofeminism's critique of patriarchy is closely related to its critique of dualism in which the dichotomies of male/female, mind/body, intellect/sexuality, reason/emotion, and so on, result in negative attitudes toward whoever (or whatever) those in power deem "other" and, thus, inferior. While ecofeminism emphasizes that all of nature is one sacred "body," patriarchy "divide[s] our social body into different parts, each one living by domination of one over the other. This negative behavior, domination, is present among persons; among different groups; among nations, cultures, ethnic groups, sexes; and in human control over nature."[20] This leads to what Heather Eaton calls "radical exclusion" in which the "other" is both less than and separate from the dominant ones. For example, she says, "Women are said to possess a different nature, the natural world is ontologically other, and both are subordinated which allows for a dominant identity to be established against the subordinated identities. This justifies the dominators' controlling privileges and access to goods and limiting the power of the inferior groups."[21]

Bernice Marie-Daly identifies Carolyn Merchant, a prominent historian and ecofeminist, as the foremost critic of the scientific and industrial revolutions' contributing to the "othering" of both women and Earth. According to Merchant, the scientific and industrial revolutions were the greatest contributors to the idea of the Earth being "the other" in the same way as women are "other" than men. This led to the domination and exploitation of Earth on a massive scale. In the scientific-industrial paradigm, "Either women and nature are seen as uncontrollable and wild and as such, evil, or as sources of nurturance and compassion."[22] This results in the archetypal virgin/whore/mother split, in which women are simultaneously objectified and generalized. As Merchant describes, "The virgin nymph offered peace and serenity, the earth mother nurture and fertility, but nature also brought plagues, famines, and tempests. Similarly, woman was both virgin and witch... Disorderly women, like chaotic nature, needed to be controlled."[23] It is this tendency to associate women and nature that becomes problematic.

2. The Association of Women and Nature

For good or for ill, women and nature are inextricably linked on every level of human consciousness. Our archetypes, language, metaphors, myths, visual imagery, fairy tales, etc., all point to the connection humans make between the feminine and Earth. Think of the Greek goddess of Earth, Gaia; the archetype of "Mother Nature"; and the biblical term for women who do not bear children — "barren" (like an unproductive field). Some see the connection between women and nature as a positive association that transcends culture and context and comes from "deep roots within human consciousness and spiritual sensitivities."[24] Others see the connection as a double-edged sword. As Rae points out, "When the attitude toward nature is one of reverence and awe, this association works for women's benefit. When the attitude is one of rape and plunder, as it is today, this association does not benefit women."[25]

Why are women so closely associated with Earth (or at least appear to be so)? Several theories have been offered. Celia Deane-Drummond locates the woman/nature nexus in the social roles historically assigned to women, such as practical, domestic chores, which are seen to be more rooted in the Earth than tasks such as governing and commerce, typically set aside for men. Another possible explanation for the association of women with nature is "the biological basis of women's physiology, including menstruation, childbirth, and so on, [which] roots the experience of women in the natural cycles of the earth."[26] Robert Jay Lifton concurs: "Women, because of their capacity to create life, have always had a special symbolic relationship to nature. Woman is, in fact, perceived *as nature,* and many cultures have their own equivalent of our 'mother earth' or 'mother nature.' Destruction of nature is, in our imagery, closely tied to destruction of women and the sources of human life."[27]

Nevertheless, this association is problematic in several respects. First, the attempt to seek a link between nature and women can lead to *essentialism,* meaning that men and women are each seen to have an essential nature linked to their physiology and biology that underlies culture and socialization and that can be uniformly applied to each gender. Essentialism is the opposite of *constructivism,* which postulates that there is no essential nature of each gender, but only a socially, culturally constructed appearance of what it means to be a man or woman. The tension between essentialism and constructivism remains unresolved in ecofeminism, where the extremes of both approaches threaten to return us once again to crushing dichotomies.[28]

A second problem of the association between women and nature is *universalizing* the experiences and personhood of women. Marie-Daly's summary deserves full attention:

> [T]his connection between women and nature has been much celebrated within the ecology movement. The association, however, is both problematic and conflictual. "Mother Earth" suggests an integral relationship between *mater* and matter, women being considered the "mother of matter." However, since matter has been perceived as corruptible, so has woman. Thus, the sacredness of matter can be realized only to the degree that mater is recognized as sacred. Since "feminine" energy has been abstracted from the life of real women and analyzed dualistically through androcentric values, the celebration of mother earth is largely an embrace of "the feminine" qualities of nurturance and life-giving energies without having to deal with the reality of women as the primary carriers of feminine energy. Embracing the stereotypical feminine and maternal qualities of nature is reminiscent of pastoral depictions of nature as passive and benevolent, nonassertive, always accessible and supportive of man's needs. While historically nature has typically been depicted as feminine this has never been to women's advantage because we have continued to be socialized in a patriarchal culture.[29]

This raises some deeper questions as to the origins of the negative views of women and nature. Which came first—the conquering of nature, or the oppression of women? Which sparked the other?

Was it an oppressive view of nature that led to an oppressive view of women? Or vice versa? In light of these questions, it becomes necessary to pause from our overview of ecofeminism to do some digging into the ground at our feet, taking note of what comprises the source of the misogynist poison seeping into the ground and affecting all aspects of our worldview.

3. Critique of Misogyny

What is at the root of this seemingly inescapable need of men to dominate? Why does "man" continue to "assert his own self-importance which leads to all manner of domination, the most fundamental of which is misogyny, and the most catastrophic, planetary devastation," as Marie-Daly puts it.[30] Feminists have varying explanations. Marie-Daly locates misogyny in the hierarchical worldview of patriarchy in which the assumption is made that men are better than women, and that empowering women will upset the balance of power from which men have long benefited.[31]

Grace Jantzen, according to Deane-Drummond, identifies the dualistic worldview as the main cause of misogyny, theorizing that the projection of dualism provides "a rationalization and justification for the misogynism characteristic of Western culture."[32] The desire not to lose control underlies this strong dualism, Jantzen suggests, which is accompanied by a deep fear of rejection. This, in turn, requires healing.[33] Ultimately, it is the Spirit of God, she suggests, that can break through the impasse and bring about liberation and healing.

In yet another attempt to discover the source of hatred of mother-goddess-earth, Hazel Henderson locates it in the emergence of the male ego in primitive cultures railing against its mortality in the face of the "great mother." She theorizes that patriarchy's revolt against the Mother Goddess of ancient societies "may explain the deeply-buried fear of women, mother and earth and their mythic connection with decay, entropy and death, expressed in mythology and recently examined in male psychology."[34]

When patriarchal men face the terrifying reality of mortality, they "choose to oppress women," theorizes Deane-Drummond, paraphrasing Susan Griffin.[35] Marie-Daly concurs, stating, "The fear of mortality, of not being in control of life and death, is the basis for much of the hostility toward women and nature who represent the womb and tomb of human existence. Our inability to change this cyclical life/death pattern appears to be a source of great resentment."[36]

In terms of Creation-crisis preaching, then, we can begin to see how difficult it is to address ecological and feminist justice issues. The fear is so ancient, so embedded, and so rarely acknowledged, it wields powerful control over listeners who may not even understand why they react so strongly and negatively to sermons that preach for the liberation of Earth and women. The challenge will be to craft sermons that find a way to create the parable-like shifts in the listener's consciousness, creating enough space for seeds of a new paradigm to begin to take root and unfold. Because, as we shall see, the liberation of Christ's resurrection is as much for oppressor as the oppressed.

A "Third Way" to Approach the Women/Earth Connection?

Despite the negative ramifications of the female/nature association, some ecofeminists defend making this connection and seek to preserve their essentialist position. They reason that the historic problems with the binaries previously discussed are not due to the distinction made between "male" and "female" qualities, "but that the masculine was valued over the feminine. In response, they argue that present-day feminists need to celebrate and perhaps even privilege feminine distinctiveness."[37]

It seems fair to conclude that validity and risks exist simultaneously in both the constructivist and essentialist camps. On the one hand, it can be argued that there *is* some kind of fundamental link between women and nature because of women's biological make-up and bodily reproductive/nurturing capacities. This connection is not entirely constructed. For example, the archetype of the "Earth Mother" in so many cultures past and present points to some very basic link between the creative, reproductive, nurturing processes of women and those of Earth, which is, in some way, worthy of veneration. Certainly there are exceptions to this norming principal, and it can obviously be abused, taken advantage of, and dominated by any power structure, whether matriarchal or patriarchal. But at the heart of such a connection lies a capacity for deep intimacy with, compassion for, and protection of Earth on the part of women that can and should be encouraged, especially within the religious realm. On the other hand, there is a limit to how far this basic connection can and should be extended, especially if it undermines the goals of ecofeminism, results in reiterating harmful gender-based stereotypes, or leads to public policies that further oppresses women.

Having provisionally explored the benefits and risks of both essentialism and constructivism within ecofeminism, Serene Jones suggests "a position somewhere in-between, a position known as 'strategic essentialism.'"[38] Ecofeminists often follow this "third way" of pragmatic application of certain universals and essentials, based on their determining the appropriateness of such application in any given situation. Ultimately, they will employ whatever strategy (essential or constructive) they discern will best serve the purpose of liberating and empowering women, and liberating Earth. An example of this is Deane-Drummond, who views the association of women and nature as having positive benefits and suggests two responses to this association:

1. Call for direct political action in order to liberate both women and the environment; [in this way] the cry of the oppressed becomes a joint chorus of women and nature.
2. Celebrate the association between women and nature as a means of reclaiming women's power. In this case, the power of women may be recast by looking back to the time when the power of women could be expressed in the form of worship of a goddess.[39]

Marie-Daly also suggests that the conceptual joining of women and nature need not be rejected. In fact, it may be impossible to pull apart the associations between the two entities given the historical, cultural, and archetypal connections between them. Therefore, as we think about sermons that address ecological themes, we will need to proceed with caution, altering "the cultural perceptions that both women and nature are either always available, passive, and subordinate or wild, evil, dangerous, and requiring control."[40]

One of the tasks of this book is to determine how preaching can help accomplish this alteration of negative associations between women and nature. It is precisely this kind of "strategic essentialism" that is employed in the sermons that follow. They illustrate in a dramatic way the connection between women and Earth (both positive and negative) while proclaiming the Good News that the person of Jesus and the figure of the Cosmic Christ attend to the suffering of woman and Earth in a redemptive way. And, it is the "third way" we will explore as we next turn to an examination of ecofeminist theology that moves beyond binary gendered conceptions of Jesus Christ, his cross, and resurrection.

Part Two: An Overview of Ecofeminist Theology

Ecofeminist theologians take ecofeminism in the direction of religion and spirituality.[41] As with the larger subject of ecofeminism, ecofeminist theology has no overarching method, textual source, or doctrine. Nevertheless, there are some key principles that ecofeminist theologians share.

First, they interrogate Scripture, Christian history, theological doctrine, ecclesiology, and practical theology to discern if such resources support a positive theology of nature and the emancipation of women. Or, they may find that the orthodox and traditional metaphors, symbols, stories, motifs, and dogmas need to be reinterpreted, reimagined, or even rejected if they contribute to the dualistic othering of women and nature in a way that is patriarchal, oppressively hierarchical,[42] and diminishing of their value. A main goal for ecofeminist theologians is to resist and overturn the coinciding subjugation of women and the destruction of Earth, especially within the realm of religion and spirituality. Stated in a positive way, ecofeminist theologians see enormous potential for the renewal of the church and human society through their emancipatory work, as well as for the Earth community and all marginalized peoples.

In her comprehensive book *Introducing Ecofeminist Theologies*, Heather Eaton describes the confluence of the myriad approaches to ecofeminist theology as a kind of "roundabout" where the intersection of ecofeminism, theology, religion, spirituality, and religious communities enter at different points going in varying directions.[43] For ecofeminist theologians, the twin prongs of patriarchy and ecological destruction are connected to a third tine, that of misogyny and the domination of women, particularly within the religious realm. As Elizabeth Johnson summarizes, "I am persuaded by the truth of the ecofeminist insight that analysis of the ecological crisis does not get to the heart of the matter until it sees the connection between the exploitation of the earth and the sexist definitions and treatment of women...and these distortions influence the Christian experience."[44]

Christian ecofeminist theology has been influenced by process theology in the person of John Cobb, one of the first theologians to draw attention to the burgeoning ecological crisis.[45] Cobb's writings and teachings were picked up and developed by several ecofeminists, including Catherine Keller and Ivone Gebara. In Gebara's words we hear echoes of process theology's concept of co-creativity with God influencing the ongoing evolution of reality:

> Ecofeminism…invites us to rethink our Christian tradition, as well as all religious traditions, to recover in them the values that can help all life in the present time. To rethink theological constructs in a "cosmogenesis perspective" means that all of us are revelations of the one and only Body in an evolutionary and creative process. Creative evolution allows human beings to intervene in different processes, and it is our responsibility to stop the destruction and to initiate new behavior.[46]

Heather Eaton distinguishes two methods by which Christian ecofeminists engage in a constructive connection between ecology and Christianity. One approach is to reinterpret principal Christian texts, themes, doctrines, and liturgy in light of an awareness of Creation and its value in the eyes of God, and, thus, for humans.[47] She cautions, however, that this approach may not go far enough if it produces only a "Christianity [that is] environmentally friendly rather than [one that mitigates] ecological ruin."[48] The second is to "engage in a radical revisioning of an understanding of religion and religious truths for the purposes of reawakening a sense of Earth's sacredness, and resisting further ecological degradation."[49] Because of their strong tendency and power to maintain cultural patterns of patriarchy and domination, religions are constantly interrogated by ecofeminist theologians who question their fundamental presuppositions and theological methodologies.[50]

As we explore the relationship between women, the Earth, and religion, we find deep, flowing waters between these three that are potentially mutually beneficial. However, a serious inquiry is needed into how this three-way partnership can go forward without the continuing domination of either Earth or women on the part of religion. As Eaton advises: "Religions have a lot to learn with respect to their own women/nature nexus. Religious histories need to be probed… Religions and religious insights are powerful influences in human affairs, in spite of their ambiguous ideas and effects."[51] This process of understanding the relationship between women, Earth, and religion involves a deep and courageous questioning of biblical hermeneutics, church tradition, and ecclesial structures that, according to Eaton, requires a fundamental reorientation of theology toward Earth-consciousness. As our theology expands to include that of Earth, she says:

> One cannot help but be inspired by the expansiveness of life, and the genius and creativity of the emergence of life on earth. One's image of God enlarges to a breathtaking point. The incarnation is expanded and intensified to embrace the earth. Revelation becomes the sensing of a sacred presence revealed through all of life processes. The world/earth is much more awesome, extraordinary and sacred than previously appreciated![52]

As noted in chapter 1, ecological theology challenges us to see how religion can be re-visioned "to recover values, experiences, and commitments in an understanding of the way human beings are connected to the ecosystem."[53] One of the primary ways ecofeminist theologians seek to undertake this re-visioning is by exploring, recovering, and integrating the feminine aspects of God into theology and religious practice. For some, this involves a turn toward ancient goddess imagery and theology. For others, it means inversing the dominant images of God as being male-gendered in order to introduce the Divine Feminine. However the reorientation is done, ecofeminists generally agree that our religious language, images, rituals, symbols, and practices must be expanded to include women and all of Creation into the sacredness of God. As Donald Gelpi observes, "[W]e become what we worship, since we worship what we value ultimately and absolutely."[54] It follows that if our images and metaphors continue to be male-dominated, we will continue to worship the male as divine. In this respect, ecofeminists are in agreement that alternatives must be found to the transcendent, hierarchical, father "sky god" of patriarchy.[55] These alternatives must conceive of, articulate, and worship the Divine in a way that takes the feminine and Creation into account to at least an equal extent as males.

This is not to say that the Divine is, in fact, a human construct. In many ways the mystery of God remains beyond the scope of human expression. The point ecofeminist theologians try to make is that, in our human attempts to articulate a limited understanding of God, we not limit them even further to a strictly patriarchal construct. Neither do we seek to obliterate masculine imagery and concepts for describing God. Instead we are urging for a more *expansive* way to speak about and image God to include the feminine. According to

Rae, "Precisely what this feminine will encompass will have to come from the lived experiences of all women, with the understanding that being a woman is, for us, a primary source of revelation."[56]

There is, of course, a tension between different sources of revelation, whether they are divine, individual, communal, nature-oriented, or something else entirely. James Cone, for example, contends, "God's revelation is found in black liberation," and, "[T]he hermeneutical principle for an exegesis of the Scriptures is the revelation of God in Christ as the Liberator of the oppressed..."[57] He stresses, however, that revelation is "not derived from the human situation," but moves "from God's revelation to our needs."[58] Applied to an ecofeminist theology, we can say that God also chooses women's experience and Creation as means for God's revelation, since both are oppressed, and their liberation cannot be separated from Christ's death and resurrection. This point will be more fully developed in the next chapter.

Initial Implications of Ecofeminist Theology for Preaching

It will be one of our tasks to determine how preaching can employ the commitments, critiques, and values of ecofeminism in concrete, contextual and creative ways. As Clark Williamson and Ronald Allen remind us: "[W]e are always called upon [to preach] to people who live in a new historical situation, one significantly different from that in which [the people of the Bible] were born. Preachers must speak plausibly to questions that are not only urgent but new, if they are to help people understand what it means to live a Christian life in the present."[59] Preaching can help people make meaning of their lives in the world in light of their faith, while simultaneously helping people understand their faith in light of their experiences and questions in this world. Through the unique lens of ecofeminist theology heretofore underutilized in the discipline of homiletics, preachers will be urged to consider issues of gender, language, androcentrism, theological imagery, and their own unwitting complicity with the Powers that hold Earth and women in thrall.[60] Below we draw some initial implications of ecofeminist theology for preaching.

Language, Metaphors, and Symbols

Ecofeminism mandates a critical assessment of the language and symbolic connections that exist between how we speak about gender and nature in the pulpit, not the least of which is the ongoing challenge of describing the Divine in ways that avoid traditional patriarchal language. Because ecofeminist theology involves "a way of reimaging the relationship between God and creation," this entails a serious rethinking of how we use language in the pulpit.[61] This includes how we speak of and symbolize God, as well as how we speak of and about Earth and women. For example, preachers may reconsider using strictly masculine, hierarchical language and metaphors for God, seeking to explore, for instance, what it might mean to speak of Earth as God's body.[62] Preachers will also need to examine how word choices and seemingly innocent metaphors, images, and verbal associations can subtly reinforce negative attitudes toward both women and nature.

How does our language inferiorize women and nonhuman nature? Karen Warren describes what is involved with this difficult linguistic problem:

> For instance, women are often described in animal terms (e.g., as cows, foxes, chicks, serpents, bitches, beavers, old bats, pussycats, cats, bird-brains, hare-brains). Nature is often described in female and sexual terms: Nature is raped, mastered, conquered, controlled, mined. Her secrets are penetrated and her womb is put into the services of the "man of science." Virgin timber is felled, cut down. Fertile soil is tilled and land that lies fallow is "barren," useless. The claim is that language which so feminizes nature and naturalizes women describes, reflects, and perpetuates the domination and inferiorization of both by failing to see the extent to which the twin dominations of women and nature (including animals) are, in fact, culturally (and not merely figuratively) analogous.[63]

This has profound implications for preaching as pastors consider how they will handle biblical texts such as Genesis 1:28, which uses language that can be interpreted as authorizing domination over nature, as discussed in chapter 1. This realization may also encourage preachers to experiment with using female pronouns interchangeably with male ones when referring to God.

There is also the issue of giving "voice" to Earth and Earth's nonhuman inhabitants, to speak for the "other" in nature that "is not conceived of subjectively in our civilization," as Ynestra King states.[64] How can the pulpit attempt to speak for Creation, or to be a means by which Earth and Earth's other-than-human inhabitants find voice and can speak? Is it possible to do this? Or would we be in danger of anthropomorphizing Earth? Who gets to do this speaking? By what criteria will we discern an appropriate spokesperson for Earth? These are all questions that will need to be addressed as ecofeminist theology begins informing the task of preaching, and which I will address throughout the remainder of this book.

Telling Earth's Story

Ecofeminism can influence preaching by encouraging us to consider what and whose stories we tell in our sermons, since, as Stanley Hauerwas observes, our preaching is profoundly rooted in "how the Church is storied by God and accordingly stories the world."[65] What stories shall we tell about God's creation and redemption of Earth and its inhabitants? What stories shall we tell about those whose lives are most adversely affected by our negative attitudes toward nature and women, particularly those living in poverty? Even more basic, do we tell just one story? Do we allow just one narrative to determine our liturgy and prayers and worship? Or shall we recognize, with Hauerwas, that "[o]ur unity is constituted by our inability to tell our stories without one another's stories... [In our story being joined to God's story,] our story is not obliterated, but rather it shapes how the story is told so that it may contribute to the upbuilding of Christ's body—so that finally our stories will be joined in one mighty prayer."[66] Shall we listen to and learn from a multitude of stories from a variety of locations spoken by voices previously unheard? Shall we invite those stories from the margins—the poor, women, the Earth—to break our hearts, change our minds, bring us to our knees in repentance, and creatively resist evil with all our strength? Ecofeminist theology takes us by the hand to behold the beauty, grandeur, and fragility of Earth's landscape laid out before us and to hear this story, poignantly described by Eleanor Rae::

> Before the beginning, the Holy One gave herself over entirely to her Spirit and to her Word. The cosmos is the result of this emptying out of herself. Because of this emptying out, she cannot be known. But we can know her Word and her Spirit. There exists no particle, no tree, no bird, no life-form, no galaxy, no void which they do not fill. In knowing them, it may be said that we know Her... We stand in silence and in awe.[67]

"Exiting" Androcentrism

As mentioned in the previous chapter, John McClure's *Other-wise Preaching* is a philosophical and theoretical analysis of what is going on conceptually in preaching from a postmodern perspective. The book aims to deconstruct oppressive binaries that McClure believes need to be broken open and "exited" in order to hold preaching to a higher standard of ethical faith commitments in its public witness in the new millennium. McClure names four "houses" from which preaching must exit in order to deconstruct its binary strongholds: scripture, tradition, experience, and reason.[68] This leads preachers to be open to those located on the margins so that their testimony might reorient us to the previously disregarded other.

The question may arise: if we are exiting and deconstructing all the houses that have traditionally authorized preaching, is there any basis left for preaching? To clarify, exiting and deconstructing involve taking a step back from the authorities in order to question and critically assess them. As McClure explains: "Deconstruction exposes the potentially dangerous binary operations that can exist at the heart of ontologies as well as non-foundational systems of thought. Unless they are critiqued and pried open, these binary operations can turn in on themselves and engender social closure, oppression, or suffering."[69] This is not to say that reason, experience, tradition, and scripture are completely left behind or abandoned. Rather, "Each proposition is examined and critiqued in light of its use-value—What is it doing? What are its effects? Especially: Is it an idea or part of a theory or ideology that is causing suffering?"[70] Thus, exiting is a teleological approach to homiletics in that it looks at the end results and works back through the foundational assumptions, placing them under erasure and then *reclaiming* them "as open space—new ground in which to grow ideas that are other-wise."[71]

Bringing an ecofeminist ethic to bear on McClure's process of exiting, I would add the dimension of *androcentric anthropocentrism* as needing to be identified, exposed, critiqued, deconstructed, and placed under erasure. Within each of the aforementioned "houses" can be found the structures of *androcentrism* that create dangerous binary operations leading to a hegemony that exists not just within and beyond churches, but at the very foundations of the falsely conceived human-Creation split. The embrace of an ecofeminist other-wise commitment will extend to the proximity of nonhuman others, recognizing that God's reign is inclusive of the cosmos, Earth, and all Earth's inhabitants.

An Ecofeminist Hermeneutic for Preaching

Taking all we have learned from ecofeminism and ecofeminist theology and making some initial implications for preaching, we can now make a more direct connection between ecofeminist theology and homiletics. For this we incorporate the work of Christine Smith, who developed four principles for preaching a feminist hermeneutic by drawing on Elisabeth Schüssler Fiorenza's *Bread not Stone* to establish the internal structure of feminist biblical interpretation.[72] I have expanded these principles to include ecofeminist concerns, which provide important hermeneutical criteria for preaching:

Principle 1. An ecofeminist critical interpretation for preaching begins with a *hermeneutic of Earth-orientation* rather than with a hermeneutic of anthro- and androcentrism. This entails reading Scripture through a green lens to ascertain how texts may be oppressive or liberating to women and the Earth community.

Principle 2. An ecofeminist hermeneutic for preaching includes *proclamation and power for both the human and other-than-human community of Earth,* and analyzes the impact and power certain texts will have when preached in a community of faith within its ecological context.

Principle 3. A preacher's ecofeminist hermeneutic of *remembrance* seeks to recover biblical traditions through an eco-historical-critical reconstruction of biblical history from an ecofeminist perspective. It is a hermeneutic that refuses to allow andro- and anthropocentric texts to have the final word about the subordination of Earth and Earth's inhabitants, particularly women.[73]

Principle 4. An ecofeminist hermeneutic for preaching includes *creative actualization,* which seeks to retell biblical stories from Earth's and women's perspectives, to reformulate biblical visions and injunctions in the perspective of the discipleship of equals among the human and other-than-human communities,[74] and to create narrative amplifications of the ecofeminist seeds that lie dormant in andro- and anthropocentric texts.

With these interpretive criteria in mind, we can begin to apply these principles and commitments within ecofeminism and ecofeminist theology to our preaching. These are the values that provide clarity and conviction "that there is an interwoven, and interconnected, quality to all forms of oppression," especially that of women and Creation, while also showing the commitment to "peace and disarmament and a vision about living in harmony with all creation."[75] A key task in our Creation-crisis preaching is to tell the truth about the deleterious effects of our androcentric view of God, Christ, Scripture, and the Church. Only by naming this truth and confronting it through the authority of mutuality and solidarity within the community can the next step toward creative proclamation of the Good News for Earth and Earth's human and other-than-human creatures be undertaken.

Conclusion

An ecofeminist homiletic, as has been demonstrated, shares McClure's commitment to uncover binary operations that privilege the patriarchal hierarchy that naturalizes and divinely sanctions the domination of women, people of color, non-Western nations, and the natural world. It is meant to decenter patriarchal hegemonic experience as normative and exclusionary of the feminine and nature so that we may reprivilege the voice of women and Creation. Utilizing "strategic essentialism," we next move into an examination of how ecofeminist Christology can undergird preaching that makes the connection between women and Earth while proclaiming the Good News that the person of Jesus and the divine figure of the Cosmic Christ attend to the suffering of women and Earth in a redemptive way.

Notes

[1]The Patrick Center for Environmental Research, "A Preliminary Study on the Impact of Marcellus Shale Drilling on Headwater Streams" (Philadelphia: The Academy of Natural Sciences of Drexel University, 2012) http://www.ansp.org/research/environmental-research/projects/marcellus-shale-preliminary-study/ (accessed March 21, 2012).

[2]"What is flowback, and how does it differ from produced water?" The Institute for Energy & Environmental Research for Northeastern Pennsylvania, http://energy.wilkes.edu/pages/205.asp, accessed Feb. 27, 2015.

[3]Stephen Osborn, A. Vengosh, N. Warner, R. Jackson, *Methane Contamination of Drinking Water Accompanying Gas-Well Drilling and Hydraulic Fracturing* (Durham, N.C.: Center on Global Change, and Division of Earth and Ocean Sciences, Nicholas School of the Environment, Duke University, April 14, 2011); Abraham Lustgarten, "E.P.A. Finds Compound Used in Fracking in Wyoming Aquifer," http://www.propublica.org/article/epa-finds-fracking-compound-in-wyoming-aquifer (November 13, 2011) (accessed March 21, 2012); Center for Disease Control Agency for Toxic Substance and Disease Registry (ATSDR), *Health Consultation; Chesapeake Atgas 2h Well Site – Leroy Hill Road, Leroy – Leroy Township, Bradford County, Pa.* (November 4, 2011).

[4]Wendy Lynne Lee, "Fracking Is a Variety of Environmental Rape Abetted by the Law: Governor Corbett's Pennsylvania, Inc.," Raging Chicken Press, http://www.

ragingchickenpress.org/2011/12/15/fracking-is-a-variety-of-environmental-rape-abetted-by-the-law-governor-corbetts-pennsylvania-inc/(December 15, 2011) (accessed October 19, 2012).

[5]Katrina Smith, Walter A. Jones Korfmacher, Samantha L. Malone, Leon F. Vinci, "Public Health and High Volume Hydraulic Fracturing," *New Solutions*, 23, no. 1 (2013); Texas Oil and Gas Accountability Project and Earthworks Report, *Natural Gas Flowback: How the Texas Natural Gas Boom Affects Health and Safety* (April 2011); Conrad Daniel Volz, Graduate Faculty, Graduate School of Public Health, University of Pittsburgh, Director & Principal Investigator, Center for Healthy Environments and Communities, Director, Environmental Health Risk Assessment, Certificate Program, Assistant Professor of Law (Secondary Appointment), "Written Testimony in Committee on Environment and Public Works and Its Subcommittee on Water and Wildlife," United States Senate (April 12, 2011); Michelle Bamberger, Robert E. Oswald, "Impacts of Gas Drilling on Human and Animal Health," *New Solutions*, 22, no. 1 (2012); Jerome A. Paulson, MD, FAAP, Associate Professor of Pediatrics and Public Health, George Washington University, Medical Director for National and Global Affairs, Child Health Advocacy Institute and Director, Mid-Atlantic Center for Children's Health and the Environment, Children's National Medical Center, "Potential Health Impacts of Natural Gas Extraction Using High Volume, Slickwater Hydraulic Fracturing from Long Laterals," http://www.childrensnational.org/files/PDF/MACCHE/PAAAP-Secure.pdf (accessed May 2, 2012).

[6]Sara Jerving, "The Fracking Frenzy's Impact on Women," in *http://prwatch.org/news/2012/04/11204/fracking-frenzys-impact-women*, http://PRWatch.org (The Center for Media and Democracy, April 4, 2012); Associated Press, "North Dakota City Police See Increase in Crimes," *Claims Journal* (November 29, 2011) (accessed April 10, 2013).

[7]Ivone Gebara, "Ecofeminism," in *Dictionary of Feminist Theologies*, ed. Letty M. Russell and J. Shannon Clarkson (Louisville: Westminster John Knox Press, 1996), 76.

[8]Françoise d'Eaubonne, *Le féminisme ou la mort* (Paris: P. Horay, 1974).

[9]Rosemary Radford Ruether, *New Women, New Earth: Sexist Ideologies and Human Liberation* (New York: The Seabury Press, 1975), 208.

[10]Karen J. Warren, "Feminism and the Environment: An Overview of the Issues," in *Philosophy of Woman: An Anthology of Classic to Current Concepts*, ed. Mary Briody Mahowald (Indianapolis/Cambridge: Hackett Publishing Company, Inc., 1994), 502.

[11]Ibid.

[12]It must also be mentioned that *ecowomanists* bring yet another layer of complexity to the feminist/environmentalist question. Scholars such as Karen Baker-Fletcher, Patricia Hunter, Shamara Shantu Riley, and Linda E. Thomas ask how the realities of racism impact environmental justice issues, perhaps even more so than that of sexism, and seek to bring black women's experience with ecology into Christian theology.

[13]Warren, "Feminism and the Environment," 504.

[14]Eleanor Rae, *Women, the Earth, the Divine* (Maryknoll, N.Y.: Orbis Books, 1994), 29.

[15]Heather Eaton, *Introducing Ecofeminist Theologies* (London and New York: T&T Clark International, 2005), 61.

[16]Gebara, "Ecofeminism," 76.

[17]Ibid.

[18]Rae, *Women, the Earth, the Divine*, 30.

[19]Ruether, *New Women, New Earth*, 194.

[20]Gebara, "Ecofeminism," 77.

[21]Eaton, *Introducing Ecofeminist Theologies*, 59.

[22]Bernice Marie-Daly, *Ecofeminism: Sacred Matter/Sacred Mother* (Chambersburg, Pa.: Published for the American Teihard Association for the Future of Man Inc. by Anima Books, 1991), 4.

[23]Carolyn Merchant, *The Death of Nature : Women, Ecology, and the Scientific Revolution* (San Francisco: Harper & Row, 1980), 9.

[24]Ibid., 54.

[25]Rae, *Women, the Earth, the Divine*, 25.

[26]Celia Deane-Drummond, "Creation," in *The Cambridge Companion to Feminist Theology*, ed. Susan Frank Parsons (Cambridge, UK: Cambridge University Press, 2002), 191.

[27]Robert Jay Lifton, "While There's Life, Can We Still Hope?" *Vogue* (October 1984): 227, 216. A point worthy of further discussion is the fact that concepts of human reproduction were vastly different from what contemporary society understands in light of scientific inquiry in the twentieth century. Before the discovery of female ova and male sperm, the prevailing view was that women were incubators for male seed and had no part in the creation of human life. The ignorant concept of the woman being little more than the field for the male seed influenced Hebrew as well as Greco-Roman social norms. This, in turn, shaped much of Western ideas of women's relative lack of worth and subservience to men. In contrast, some scholars point out that there were ancient matriarchal cultures that emphasized women's reproductive primacy, giving rise to goddess theology.

[28]The essentialist/constructivist debate is poignantly ambivalent within ecowomanism. Ecowomanists, in particular, see the dangers of the Eurocentric patriarchal power structure manipulating the earth-woman connection to secure its power over black women. Black women have been animalized since the emergence of the African slave trade in Britain in the 1400s, and this tactic provides psycho-social validation for their being dominated, enslaved, and abused. Shamara Shantu Riley points out the way black women have been associated with "animal nature" (disturbingly illustrated in Toni Morrison's novel *Beloved*, as well as in Alice Walker's novel *The Color Purple*), and the reality of ecological racism as a justice issue that needs to be addressed by the black community. Yet ecowomanists also point to the unique ways in which black women are able to connect their spirituality to the God of Creation, celebrating the delicious and delightful ways God incarnates in and through nature and human fleshliness. See: Karen Baker-Fletcher, *Dancing with God: The Trinity from a Womanist Perspective* (St. Louis: Chalice Press, 2006); *Sisters of Dust, Sisters of Spirit: Womanist Wordings on God and Creation* (Minneapolis: Fortress, 1998); "Something or Nothing: An Eco-Womanist Essay on God, Creation, and Indispensability," in *This Sacred Earth: Religion, Nature, Environment*, 2nd ed., ed. Roger S. Gottlieb (London: Routledge, 2004), 428-437. Also see: Patricia L. Hunter, "Women's Power—Women's Passion: And God Said, 'That's Good,'" *A Troubling in My Soul: Womanist Perspectives on Evil and Suffering*, ed. Emilie M. Townes (Maryknoll, N.Y.: Orbis Books, 1993).

[29]Marie-Daly, *Ecofeminism*, 3.

[30]Ibid.

[31]Ibid., 10. This is what Martin Luther King Jr. would call the "drum major instinct," which is the driving need for recognition, attention, and superiority (Martin Luther King, Jr., and James Melvin Washington, *A Testament of Hope: The Essential Writings of Martin Luther King, Jr.* [San Francisco: Harper & Row, 1986], chapter 43).

[32]Quoted in Deane-Drummond, "Creation," 198.

[33]What ecofeminists have not yet adequately addressed, I believe, is the *psychological* basis for this fear. I see this as an area of inquiry that deserves attention from ecofeminists because it gets at the root of what is really at stake for men, and all of humanity, in their struggle for life, autonomy, control, and love. Until we address the underlying reason for this innate fear and hatred of women/earth, we will not be able to name and thus confront this awesome power that threatens all existence. It is my theory that there are deep psychological reasons for this fear-based misogyny which can be traced back to the emergence of the child from the womb and the primary experiences with the mother. I believe a psychoanalytic analysis of misogyny by way of psychotherapists Melanie Klein and Nancy Friday may yield fascinating insights helpful to ecofeminism.

[34]Hazel Henderson, "The Warp and the Weft: The Coming Synthesis of Eco-Philosophy and Eco-Feminism," in *Reclaim the Earth: Women Speak out for Life on Earth*, ed. Lèonie Caldecott and Stephanie Leland (London: Women's Press, 1983), 209–10. (As quoted by Rae, *Women, the Earth, the Divine*, 37).

[35]Deane-Drummond, "Creation," 192.

[36]Marie-Daly, *Ecofeminism*, 4.

[37]Serene Jones, *Feminist Theory and Christian Theology: Cartographies of Grace* (Minneapolis: Fortress Press, 2000), 30.

[38]Ibid., 44.

[39]Deane-Drummond, "Creation," 191.

[40]Marie-Daly, *Ecofeminism*, 5.

[41]It must be noted that not all ecofeminists count the religious realm as an ally in the quest for the liberation of Earth and women. Some ecofeminists reject any attempts to give their work a religious grounding, believing that there are no redeeming aspects of religion because of its intrinsic, unavoidably androcentric orientation.

[42]Granted, not all hierarchies are oppressive. Some relationships require hierarchy in order to maintain order, protect the weak, and provide clear channels of communication and responsibility. For example, in a family with parents and young children, a hierarchy is necessary for the parents to set and enforce boundaries, rules, and consequences for the health and safety of the child. In the legal system, a hierarchy is required for good order, accountability, and the establishment of rights and responsibilities. A hierarchy becomes oppressive when power is abused by the one(s) to whom it has been entrusted, rights are violated, and the weak are victimized.

[43]Eaton, *Introducing Ecofeminist Theologies*, 87–88.

[44]Elizabeth A. Johnson, *Women, Earth, and Creator Spirit* (New York: Paulist Press, 1993), 10.

[45]See John B. Cobb and David Ray Griffin, *Process Theology: An Introductory Exposition* (Philadelphia: The Westminster Press, 1976), ch. 9; and John B. Cobb, *Process Theology as Political Theology* (Manchester, England: Manchester University Press, 1982).

[46]Gebara, "Ecofeminism," 77.

[47]Eaton, *Introducing Ecofeminist Theologies*, 71.

[48]Ibid., 72.

[49]Ibid.

[50]See Carol J. Adams, *Ecofeminism and the Sacred* (New York: Continuum, 1993).; Laurel Kearns and Catherine Keller, eds., *Ecospirit: Religions and Philosophies for the Earth* (New York: Fordham University Press, 2007).

[51]Eaton, *Introducing Ecofeminist Theologies*, 61.

[52]Ibid., 104–105.

[53]Gebara, "Ecofeminism," 76.

[54]Rae, *Women, the Earth, the Divine*, 82, quoting Donald L. Gelpi, *Divine Mother: A Trinitarian Theology of the Holy Spirit* (Lanham, Md.: University Press of America, 1984), 140.

[55]While outside the scope of this project, the question of the level to which Jesus' invocation of God as *Abba* contributes to the male domination of theological language and imagery needs to be raised. Was Jesus' nomenclature for God simply a product of his time, which was strongly patriarchal in its imagery of God? And is it normative for today? Is the fact that Jesus called God "Father" descriptive or prescriptive?

When considering these questions, we must also recall that in the Gospel of Matthew he tells a crowd of people that "whoever does the will of my Father in heaven is my brother and sister and mother" (Mt. 12:50). But he leaves out "father" altogether. He does the same in the Gospel of Mark when he tells Peter, "Truly I tell you, there is no one who has left house or brothers or sisters or mother or father or children or fields, for my sake and for the sake of the good news, who will not receive a hundredfold now in this age—houses, brothers and sisters, mothers and children, and fields, with persecutions—and in the age to come eternal life" (Mk. 10:28–30). Again, he leaves out fathers in the second part of this passage. Even more perplexing is Jesus' instruction to "call no one your father on earth, for you have one Father—the one in heaven" (Mt. 23:9). Certainly Jesus was aware of the dynamics of oppression, abuse, and violence within patriarchy and the way they influenced the men, women, and children to whom he ministered. And that is why Jesus so directly challenged the darker side of patriarchy. "In the new family of Jesus there are only children, no patriarchs," (Walter Wink, *Engaging the Powers: Discernment and Resistance in a World of Domination*. Minneapolis: Fortress Press, 1992), 119.

In addition, the name *Abba* is a term that means not just "Father" but "Daddy," connoting warm affection and trusting confidence. So to refer to God not as "Supreme Father" or "Mighty Lord" but as "Daddy" is itself quite subversive and controversial. In other words, Jesus is not addressing God as "Father" in order to *support* existing power structures of domination. Rather, as Elisabeth Schüssler Fiorenza points out, "The 'father'

God of Jesus makes possible the 'sisterhood of men' (in the phrase of Mary Daly) by denying any father, and all patriarchy, its right to existence. Neither the 'brothers' nor the 'sisters' in the Christian community are to claim the 'authority of the father' because that would involve claiming authority and power reserved to God alone," (Wink, 119, citing Fiorenza).

Further, we must attend to the fact that Jesus refers to himself metaphorically as a "mother hen" in Luke 13:31–35, which indicates that there is room for a more expansive conceptualization of God. Gail Ramshaw explores both gendered and nongendered images for God in her book *God Beyond Gender: Feminist Christian God-Language* (Minneapolis: Augsburg Fortress, 1995).

[56]Rae, *Women, the Earth, the Divine*, 82.

[57]James H. Cone, *God of the Oppressed* (New York: Seabury Press, 1975), 225, 81.

[58]Ibid., 99.

[59]Clark M. Williamson and Ronald J. Allen, *A Credible and Timely Word: Process Theology and Preaching* (St. Louis: Chalice Press, 1991), 42.

[60]I draw this concept from the work of Walter Wink in his series on The Powers. Wink describes the Powers this way: "In the biblical view they are both visible *and* invisible, earthly *and* heavenly, spiritual *and* institutional. The Powers possess an outer, physical manifestation (buildings, portfolios, personnel, trucks, fax machines) and an inner spirituality, or corporate culture, or collective personality. The Powers are the simultaneity of an outer, visible structure and an inner, spiritual reality. The Powers, properly speaking, are not just the spirituality of institutions, but their outer manifestations as well," (Walter Wink, *Engaging the Powers: Discernment and Resistance in a World of Domination* [Minneapolis: Fortress Press, 1992], 3.

[61]Deane-Drummond, "Creation," 197.

[62]Sallie McFague, *The Body of God: An Ecological Theology* (London: SCM Press, 1993).

[63]Warren, "Feminism and the Environment,"501.

[64]Ynestra King, "The Ecology of Feminism and the Feminism of Ecology," in *Healing the Wounds: The Promise of Ecofeminism*, ed. Judith Plant (Philadelphia: New Society Publishers, 1989), 20.

[65]Stanley Hauerwas, "The Church's One Foundation Is J.C. Her Lord; or, in a World without Foundations: All We Have Is the Church," in *Theology without Foundations: Religious Practice and the Future of Theological Truth*, ed. S. Hauerwas, N. Murphy, M. Nation (Nashville: Abingdon Press, 1994), 149.

[66]Ibid.

[67]Rae, *Women, the Earth, the Divine,*76–77.

[68]The reader will recognize these as the "Wesleyan Quadrilateral," the four sources John Wesley used in coming to theological conclusions. The term was coined by Wesleyan scholar Albert C. Outler in his book *John Wesley: A Representative Collection* (New York: Oxford University Press, 1964).

[69]John S. McClure, *Other-Wise Preaching: A Postmodern Ethic for Homiletic* (St. Louis: Chalice Press, 2001), 2.

[70]Ibid., 109.

[71]Ibid., 150.

[72]Christine M. Smith, *Weaving the Sermon: Preaching in a Feminist Perspective* (Louisville: Westminster/J. Knox Press, 1989). These principles are found on pp. 95–101 of Smiths' book, and she is quoting Elisabeth Schüssler Fiorenza, *Bread Not Stone: The Challenge of Feminist Biblical Interpretation* (Boston: Beacon Press, 1984), pp. 15–20.

[73]Just as Phyllis Trible's work, *Texts of Terror*, recovers the hidden and ignored stories of women who have been treated with violence, so we may begin to assemble the "texts of terror" for Earth in order to fully assess the ways in which Scripture tells the story of Earth's violation.

[74]The reader will recall from chapter 3 that my understanding of the "discipleship of equals" between human and other-than-human is characterized by Santmire's description of the "I-Ens relation" wherein the nonhuman is regarded with respect to its givenness,

mystery and spontaneity, beauty, and simultaneous unity and diversity. This regard evokes wonder characterized by attention, openness, humility, and gratitude toward the Ens as a Creation of God.

[75]Smith, *Weaving the Sermon*, 110.

5

Developing an
Ecofeminist Christology
for Creation-Crisis Preaching

Sophia-Mer-Christ

At the former Mount Saint Alphonsus Retreat Center along the Hudson River in Esopus, New York, there were three places for worship of and meditation on the figure of Jesus Christ. One area was the chapel with its traditional, orthodox conceptions of Christ. Its beautiful stained-glass windows and classic statuary reminded believers of the salvific significance of Jesus' birth, life, ministry, death, resurrection, and cosmic reign. Outside the chapel on the grounds of the retreat center were the Stations of the Cross. Surrounded by stately trees and overlooking the serene Hudson River, one was reminded of the importance of the natural world while walking the stations that depicted Christ's suffering and passion.

Back inside the castle-like edifice was a large meditation room on the second floor. Upon entering this room in 2001 while on a church retreat, I gasped to see the most amazing depiction of Jesus I have ever encountered. A statue of Christ stood at one end of the room, ten feet high, holding the Eucharistic bread at his chest, a triangular piece broken off right at his heart. As I moved to different points of the room and experimented with different lighting settings, the figure appeared to play tricks on my eyes. Different "faces" of Jesus appeared from different perspectives. Sometimes his brown face looked old and grimacing, other times young and wide-eyed. At one angle he appeared African, at another Caucasian, then Asian, then Middle Eastern.

The figure also played tricks on both gender perception and images of human/animal traits. Surrounding his body was what appeared to be a woman's aquamarine hooded robe that framed his face and body to give the impression that he was hovering in a vulva-like opening, perhaps emerging from the waters of baptism, perhaps submerging into the depths of chaos. When I stood at the far back end of the room it appeared as though he had a fishlike tail from the pelvic area downward, giving the impression that he was a mermaid. When I stood directly next to him to view his profile, I saw that he was pregnant! His full, round womb appeared to be at the end of the second trimester. When I stood directly under him looking up, I noticed that the bread he was holding emerged directly from his chest. Bread and body were joined so that he appeared to be giving his very breast, like a woman feeding the world.

"Sophia-Mer-Christ," a ten-foot-high statue of Jesus created by Anthony DiLorenzo, is framed by "flowing water," and contains both male and female characteristics, human and animal traits, and facial features from different races – a creative rendering of the kind of ecofeminist Christology envisioned for Creation-crisis preaching. See back cover for full-color photo. For more images of this statue and other art in the meditation chapel, visit www.creationcrisispreaching.com. *Photo by Leah D. Schade.*

The figure was set against an aqua-blue background that gave the impression of a shimmering wall of water. Framing the figure was a mosaic of blue tile that appeared to be cascading from his side and down to the floor. The design brought to mind the numerous biblical passages that feature water flowing, including Amos 5:24, "let justice roll down like waters, / and righteousness like an ever-flowing stream," John 19:34 in which blood and water gushed from Jesus' pierced side, and Revelation 22:1 in which a river flows from the throne of God.

Throughout the retreat I spent hours gazing, even adoring, the figure that I eventually named Sophia-Mer-Christ. *Sophia* is the Greek word for "wisdom" and is personified as female in both the Old and New Testaments. *Mer* stands for mermaid, a mythical water-creature fusing a female human torso, arms, and head to a fish's tail. And Jesus Christ's incarnation, ministry, teachings, miracles, death, and resurrection are central to the Christian faith. This depiction of Jesus in this meditation room of Mount Saint Alphonsus perfectly captured the kind of ecofeminist Christology I envision. It is a Christology that is both male and female, contains all races, is connected to the element of water, and contains both human and animal in the very form of his heart-broken body. And the shape-shifting quality of the artwork illustrated what I see as a "trickster" quality that I believe may be a fresh and binary-loosening alternative for preachers to view the person and figure of Jesus Christ.

As we go further into the realm of Creation-crisis preaching, this chapter will take us into the complexity of ecofeminist theology as it relates to Christology. There is a creative tension at this juncture that appears to hover in the question of how to maintain the uniqueness and soteriological power of the resurrection for women and Creation without furthering the hegemonic power of oppressive patriarchal hierarchies that are having such deleterious effects on the planet and those most vulnerable. For some ecofeminists, this tension leads to a critical question: Does the maleness of Jesus, and the way it has been used to legitimate the domination of women and Earth, negate the possibility for the crucifixion and resurrection to have any saving significance for them? In this chapter we will explore the possibilities of ways to navigate through this tension with the goal of opening up liberating alternatives for us to reenvision Christology and further deepen our Creation-crisis preaching.

As we attempt to construct an ecofeminist Christology, we will see how its implications can shape our preaching. For homileticians informed by ecofeminist theology, we must be able to articulate what Jesus' ministry, preaching, teaching, healing, miracles, death, and resurrection mean for the very real bodies of human beings, animals, plants, and even Gaia/Earth itself. What we will see is that by taking the values and commitments of ecofeminism into our sermons that proclaim Jesus Christ crucified and resurrected, we will discover both prophetic and creative ways to address the Creation-crisis that demands our homiletic attention.

Ecofeminist Christology—A Tense Discomfiture

To examine ecofeminism's uneasy relationship with Christology, it is helpful to tease apart the feminist and ecological perspectives. Feminists have approached the doctrine of Christology through a hermeneutic of suspicion, asking questions such as: Does this Christology support an egalitarian relationship between men and women and confront the dominant patriarchy embedded within classical theology? While ecotheologians ask: Does this Christology support a positive theology of nature that values Creation, not just in a utilitarian way for humanity, but as cherished by God and as a recipient Christ's redemption in its own right?

Ecofeminist theologians struggle against the way the church has interpreted the figure of Jesus Christ that deifies his male gender. While some, such as Mary Daly, reject Christology out of hand, others are compelled to ask Rosemary Radford Ruether's famous question, "Can a male savior save women?" For her, the ministry and teachings of Jesus are what are most valuable for feminists, in that he kenotically emptied himself and stood in solidarity with women. Thus it was necessary for patriarchy to be confronted by a man in the same way that racism must be confronted by whites themselves. However, Ruether and other feminist theologians chafe at the way the church's interpretation of Jesus' gender has led to the exclusion of women from ordained leadership, and the assumption that women are morally, intellectually, and spiritually deficient in comparison to men. This raises a critical question for ecofeminist Christology: Is there a way to reframe our understanding of Jesus that does not continue a patriarchal interpretation that violates Creation and women?

Another sticking point with Christology among feminists is the apparent need to reclaim Jesus' so-called feminine values, such as mutuality, caring, friendship, support, and forgiveness. L. Susan Bond warns of the risk of essentializing those values as feminine: "Although the intention of women theologians is clearly to use these concepts [of relationality and community] as tools for action, they are somewhat romantic and vague nouns... As soon as we speak of 'feminine' characteristics, we reinforce all the romanticism of the ladylike Jesus."[1] Bond particularly reminds us of the womanist critique of the white feminist's interpretation of Jesus: "Jacquelyn Grant has rejected this 'sweet' and 'bourgeois' Jesus who reinforces costly reconciliation without suffering, claiming that a 'relational' Jesus helps middle-class Christians maintain their privileged positions in church and society and leave the complaining and groaning disenfranchised out of the family."[2]

Just as feminists struggle with Christology, ecotheologians have difficulties as well. H. Paul Santmire, for example, observes that there are two motifs that characterize classical Christian thought about nature: spiritual and ecological. In the ecological motif, exhibited by thinkers such as Irenaeus and Francis of Assisi, there is a theology of fecundity wherein Creation is "blessed, embraced, and cared for by the very God who took on flesh in order to redeem a fallen humanity and thereby also to initiate a final renewal of the whole creation."[3] But in the spiritual motif, there is a theology of ascent wherein humans are viewed as hierarchically separate from nature, which is thought not to be worthy of Christ's salvation. Thinkers such as Origen and Aquinas emphasize Christ's divinity to such a spiritualized point that nature is only a stage upon which human salvation plays out, while itself being unworthy of redemption. Ecotheologians point out the way such interpretation has led to the devaluing of the natural world, the subjugation of Earth, and the lack of moral self-reflection when considering the impact of human society on ecosystems and other-than-human beings.

For example, Margaret Swedish has a serious critique of the way classical Christology has been damaging to humanity's relationship with nature:

> This is what God sent his only Son into the world to do—to suffer and die for us because we are so terrible and he is so good. We are not worthy of this sacrifice, of course. Why? Because of being nature, natural, a body, part of an earth community, soil, humus, dependent, mortal, subject to decay. This decay is part of the natural process that brings forth life. But, by this version of creation, what is nature bears within it this fundamental flaw—death, symbol of sin. Therefore, the driving goal is somehow to save ourselves from being subject to the nature that is our home and substance, our beginning and end.[4]

What this summary overlooks, however, is the fact that Jesus was a *human being*. He was of the earth, part of the earth community, the soil, humus. He was dependent on the stuff of Creation as much as any other human being. And he was mortal. He really did die. Otherwise, we have a Docetist Jesus who only *appears* to have suffered and perished. The question that follows, then, is that if we take the resurrection to have really happened, from an ecotheological perspective, how can we reconcile the resurrection in light of the natural processes of Creation? If feminists ask whether a male savior can save women, ecotheologians ask: Can an other-worldly savior save the world when that salvation appears to negate the very laws of Creation itself?

Another problem is Christ's humanity being emphasized to the point of ignoring his divinity and oneness with the Triune God. This results in the power and transcendence of Christ being overlooked, which can also have a detrimental effect on ecology. For if all of existence is no more than the birth-death life cycle, what need or hope is there for a God who is more than the sum of the parts of Creation? Is there a way to comprehend God simultaneously blessing—and Christ redeeming—Creation while interacting with Creation from a point of critical yet loving distance?

It appears that most ecotheologians sidestep these questions in favor of developing a doctrine of the Cosmic Christ and its implications for the natural world. This motif, drawn especially from Paul's writings in Colossians 1:15–20 and Ephesians 4:10, stresses that Christ's lordship is an eternal presence through time and space encompassing all of Creation in the ultimate fulfillment and consummation of God's will for the cosmos. What appears to be underdeveloped, however, is a theology of the cross for the sake of a theology of nature, which can then pulled through Good Friday and to the other side of Easter Sunday. Thus, as we think about the challenge of preaching Jesus in the face of the Creation-crisis, we see the necessity for an ecofeminist Christology that encompasses both Christ's transcendence and immanence, both his human nature and divine nature, both his incarnation and his cosmic reign, and, most importantly, his crucifixion and resurrection. Three feminist theologians—Sallie McFague, Mary Solberg, and Celia Deane-Drummond—approach Christology in ways that navigate through the tense discomfiture and help to undergird a green proclamation by challenging how we might preach about Jesus in ways that are life-giving to Earth and its biotic communities, including the humans who reside there.

Sallie McFague and Theological Models

Sallie McFague insists on the task of deconstructing and reconstructing the models by which we understand our relationship with God and the world, given the looming threats of nuclear annihilation, environmental devastation, and climate disruption. McFague seeks to "understand religious/theological language in terms of metaphors and models. Religious language is largely metaphorical, while theological language is composed principally of models."[5] Models, here, are the means by which we build our religious metaphors and structure our spiritual and ecclesiastical realities. Her method is to first critically examine traditional models of God to deconstruct their literalism and return them to their proper place as metaphors, which "are not descriptions but indirect attempts to express the unfamiliar in terms of the familiar."[6] She then proposes alternative models that are based on the parables of Jesus, which she sees as being primarily relational. These models more accurately reflect the "personal, relational images [that are] central in a metaphorical theology—images of God as father, mother, lover, friend, savior, ruler, governor, servant, companion, comrade, liberator, and so on."[7] Like other feminist theologians, McFague wrestles with how the maleness of Jesus can be incorporated into feminist theology. She describes the ministry of Jesus as "destabilizing, inclusive, and nonhierarchical,"[8] and understands him as a sort of "living parable" of God, in that his entire life, ministry, death, and resurrection serve as a metaphor for understanding God. However, her metaphorical theology stops short of identifying Jesus of Nazareth with God. For McFague, Jesus is simply one (albeit the most important) of the "paradigmatic individuals" who embody God's immanent love through the incarnation.[9] She is careful not to get caught up in the dogmatic renderings of Jesus that enshrine and deify his earthly, human qualities as "Son," which would simply perpetuate the entrenched, exclusive, hierarchical models that patriarchy has guarded for so long. Instead, she advocates for "thought experiments" that deconstruct traditional imagery and reconstruct different models for contemporary theology that are holistic, ecological, evolutionary, relational, and healing.

While drawing on liberation theology, she seeks to extend its vision beyond concern for the oppressed ones within humanity to that of all Creation, thus advocating responsibility for Earth and its inhabitants as well as for humans. This leads to McFague's exploration of alternative models of God as mother, lover, and friend, and to see the Earth as God's body, all of which are images that can help provide models of "kinship, concern, and affinity markedly different from the distance and difference of [other] model[s]. [In this way,] [t]he dualism of God and the world is undercut."[10]

McFague's rendering of these models is beautiful and compelling, suggesting a kind of power that is very different than that of patriarchal, hierarchical models, and based instead on "love that is unified and interdependent."[11] Yet, as in the aforementioned problem of essentialism and the women/Earth connection in ecofeminism, there is a point at which the models break down. For example, if your mother was absent, abusive, unavailable, mentally unstable, addicted, or neglectful, then the metaphor of God as mother may not be helpful for you. One also wonders what stage of motherhood and what aspect of the mother-child relationship McFague is envisioning in this metaphor, for this relationship is fraught with the multi-layered baggage of mothers who can at times be smothering, nagging, distracted, overworked, and simply exhausted. Thus, this model may put too many expectations on mothers and romanticize the state of motherhood, just as the old model did for fatherhood. Similarly, when talking about God as lover, one cannot help but think of abusive, abandoning, unfaithful lovers, nor can we avoid the troubling sexual aspect of this metaphor. Even the seemingly benign image of friendship also carries the darker side of betrayal, fickleness, and fighting.

Metaphors, McFague is aware, can only go so far. The models eventually waver and falter when pushed too far, and so we must keep their limits in mind. Nevertheless, especially for the mother metaphor, her point is true that "there simply is no other imagery available to us that has this power for expressing the interdependence and interrelatedness of all life with its ground. All of us, female and male, have the womb as our first home, all of us are born from the bodies of our mothers, all of us are fed by our mothers."[12]

In terms of ecological theology, McFague proposes the model of *body*, but not of the human kind, because that would lead to a hierarchy of the head over the rest of the body parts (the Western, patriarchal model). Instead, it is the body of the Earth—God's chosen embodiment—which includes all bodies: mountains, oceans, forests, insects, birds, and humans, to name a few. The positives of this model are that it links us with all Creation in a very intimate way, insists that all bodies have value (thus fostering an orientation toward justice), and images God as the panentheistic, inspirited body of the universe, while also retaining God's transcendence. This model of embodiment is what she hopes will move humanity to a more inclusive sense of justice for the needs of *all*, especially those who lack the necessities of life, including nonhuman beings. What she hopes would result from her project is a reorienting of ourselves and how we see the world, transforming our vision from a top-down, dualistic, utilitarian paradigm to that of belonging to and with Earth—loving, respecting, and protecting it.

In terms of developing an ecofeminist Christology, McFague's articulation of how Christ's resurrection relates to the ecological crisis is enormously helpful, especially for an "embodiment theology." She states:

> The death and resurrection of Jesus Christ are paradigmatic of a mode of change and growth that only occurs on the other side of the narrow door of the tomb... What is possible and appropriate...is to embrace these strains in Christian thought as a deep pattern within existence to which we cling and in which we hope—often as the hope against hope. We must believe in the basic trustworthiness at the heart of existence; that life, not death, is the last word; that against all evidence to the contrary (and most evidence is to the contrary), all our efforts on behalf of the well-being of our planet and especially of its most vulnerable creatures, including human ones, will not be defeated. It is the belief that the source and power of the universe is on the side of life and its fulfillment. The "risen Christ" is the Christian way of speaking of this faith and hope: Christ is the firstborn of the new creation, to be followed by the rest of creation, including the last and the least.[13]

Ecclesiastically, McFague's embodiment theology involves the church being a sign of the New Creation and the in-breaking of the new vision. Churches can be places where people experience this "decentering" from arrogant anthropocentrism and androcentrism and a "recentering" on Christ's concern for oppressed bodies, most notably those that are female, child, poor, nonhuman, and nature bodies. McFague's hope for the church rests on its ability to create organic communities that embody and live out concern for the basic needs for all bodies on Earth as well as Earth's body itself. "Where the new vision of the liberating, healing, inclusive love of the embodied God in the Christic paradigm occurs, *there* is the church," she writes.[14]

Implications of McFague's Work for an Ecofeminist Homiletic

From a homiletical perspective, there is much to appreciate in McFague's work, especially regarding her concern for how words articulate our faith, simultaneously limning and expanding our understanding of the Divine. What McFague challenges the preacher to do is question the underlying foundations of our language, especially within the overarching paradigm of patriarchy. When preparing sermons, McFague's work reminds us to ask: How might this image of God I am lifting up exclude certain people? How will certain word choices, phrases, or metaphors either liberate or subtly enforce oppressive paradigms?

McFague's work also deeply impresses on the preacher the understanding of why using female imagery for God is not only allowable but necessary. While it is doubtful her books will help those firmly entrenched within patriarchy, they are undoubtedly helpful for those looking for new insights, allowing themselves to be opened up to fresh ways of conceiving of and articulating images of God. What is particularly important for an ecofeminist homiletic is McFague's encouragement to conduct further "thought experiments" and imagine even more metaphors for God.

For example, I wonder what it would mean to speak of Jesus as "daughter" and use the phrase, "Jesus, Daughter of God"? In the spirit of the shape-shifting Jesus, if he is to be imaged as the vulnerable, innocent, crucified human being, what more fitting human entity is there than that of the human daughter, who in many parts of the world is unwanted because of her gender and thus often killed or abandoned at birth; or is subjected to genital mutilations; or is draped in a body-covering cloth at the onset of puberty and denied access to education; or is raped by men and shamed into suffering silence; or is readily sacrificed on the altar of war? Or, as in Western culture, daughters are bullied, manipulated by media and advertising to strive for unreachable images of so-called beauty, and mutilate or starve their own bodies in self-inflicted punishment. Are not our daughters "crucified" daily, hourly? Would it not be shockingly appropriate to image Jesus as a young, female human?

McFague states that her vision of an alternative way of being in the world that delights in the "others" rather than dominating them can only be effective if it takes place "not only within the academy but also and primarily among ordinary people who will begin to talk to and about God with new metaphors and models."[15] Indeed, this is a primary task of "ordinary preachers" talking to and with their congregations week in and week out from the pulpit, in Bible studies, and in pastoral conversations. As preachers familiar with the alternative models of God and Jesus offered by McFague, we can increase our comfort level with different ways of speaking about God and centering our ministries around Jesus' call to minister to "the least of these."

And yet the challenge on the ground in the midst of real-life ministry settings still seems like a Scylla-and-Charybdis situation. If we strive to have our language in worship and preaching be more balanced by speaking of the so-called female traits of God and using inclusive language, we run the risk of excluding those who are left out of this by their sexuality and gender, namely males. But if we choose to remain with traditional patriarchal and paternalistic models of God, we implicitly endorse the oppressive nature of religious language that women have endured for millennia, and which has enabled the rampant abuse of the poor and the natural world. How do we walk this fine line?

McFague states the problem this way: "The current resistance to inclusive or unbiased language...both at the social and religious level, indicates that people know instinctively that a revolution in language means a revolution in one's world."[16] Speaking from personal experience, this could explain the swift and negative reactions I have sometimes received from parishioners when introducing inclusive and feminine-oriented language in my preaching and liturgical language. How does a preacher navigate this? In the sermons later in this book, we will see examples of both narrative and embodiment strategies that address this question.

Mary Solberg's Lutheran Feminist Theology of the Cross— An Ecofeminist Appropriation

Mary Solberg is an ally in the quest to connect feminism and ecology with a theology of the cross and resurrection. Her book *Compelling Knowledge: A Feminist Proposal for an Epistemology of the Cross* arises out of her profound contemplation on her experience in El Salvador among some of the poorest communities in the Western Hemisphere. She takes as her biblical starting point the response in Matthew 25 of the "goats" who plead their case for not ministering to those in need: if we had *known* it was you, Jesus, we would have responded. This implies that there is something about *knowledge* that will compel people to action. But it also carries with it a rationalization for not helping; the excuse is often one of innocent ignorance, when, in fact, deliberate denial is more often the case.

Solberg's project stands out as a synthesis of three apparently unrelated theological strands: her lived experience in war-torn El Salvador, feminist epistemology, and Lutheran theology, all of which she fuses to create a framework by which we can live morally responsible lives. We learn, for example, the ethical significance of *not knowing,* as mentioned above, when ignorance, denial, and active resistance lead to immoral acts that affect, not just women, but whole communities of people who are not known by the powerful and wealthy. Solberg then takes a turn that may be surprising to some feminists and engages Luther's theology of the cross as a conversation partner and resource for constructing a new framework for epistemology. Feminists are rightly concerned that Jesus' cross glorifies suffering and has been used by countless generations of patriarchy to justify the use of violence against women and other victims of hierarchical power. But Solberg rightly insists that "an epistemology of the cross, far from glorifying suffering, helps us see and respond to it."[17] It is in our *knowledge* of the deep pain, humiliation, suffering, and evil of the crucifixion (and every recapitulation in history since) that leads us to a level of accountability and compels us to act in order to right the wrongs around us and in society. She uses a "Law-Gospel" method for examining the sources of knowledge for living morally responsible lives, and adds a third step of action, which is also a key component for a Lutheran ecofeminist homiletic.

Solberg lifts up "lived experience" as a primary source of knowing, and clarifies that it is not just any experience that informs our theology but that which reveals oppression. In the process of that oppression being revealed, lived experience also illuminates God's grace. Solberg stresses that accountability to those who suffer is key at all points of the discussion, so that the most ethical course of action can be discerned and taken. Where this dovetails beautifully with Luther's theology is in his insistence on a practical, nonspiritualized, down-in-the-dirt faith that does not seek to escape from the reality of the cross but to "call a thing what it is." In the process, God is found hidden in the last place we would expect to look. For feminists, this means that God is found precisely where patriarchal theology has said God would never be—in the bodies, experiences, work, faith, suffering, and poverty of women. When women claim their power to name what they see (call it what it is), a way may be found for healing in those sites of oppression in women's lives and bodies.

I propose to take Solberg's epistemology of the cross one step further, by intersecting her ethics with that of ecofeminism. Solberg asks, "What sorts and sources of knowledge should we consider compelling as we seek to live morally responsible lives?"[18] From an ecofeminist perspective, the knowledge of Earth and women, particularly at the places where their existences are joined in mutual experiences of oppression, poisoning, pollution, and threats to their ability to conceive and bring life to fruition, are precisely where the cross of Christ stands today. Moreover, such knowledge compels our moral response to the threats facing Earth and women.

Solberg reminds us that, according to Luther, "a theology of the cross...pointed to 'a gospel that drove men into the world, not away from it; that opened their eyes to what was there, rather than assisting them to look past what was there.'"[19] This is important for Creation-crisis preaching, because when we open our eyes to what is there in the world—namely, the countless instances of ecological devastation that are daily affecting the lives of those most vulnerable, human and other-than-human—Lutheran theology reminds us that we are compelled to tell the truth and then act in response to it.

As preachers informed both by Lutheran theology and ecofeminist values, this truth-telling means that our public Word to our congregations and the community outside our church walls must find a way to speak this truth that both holds us accountable and compels us to respond in kind. Further, lest our preaching leave listeners mired in despondency for the state of our planet, the theology of the cross gives us "the permission and command to enter into that experience with hope."[20] As Solberg explains, this process of living a life of accountability to the current crucifixions involves three parts:

1. Seeing or coming to know what is going on (or *that* something is going on)
2. Recognizing and comprehending one's own relation to or involvement in what is going on; and
3. Doing something about what is going on.[21]

Where Solberg's Lutheran theology begins to cut through the harmful essentialism that is sometimes found in ecofeminism is in the notion of God—in the person of Jesus—being hidden under the form of opposites. "God's works, Luther argued—like God's righteousness, God's wisdom, God's glory—are hidden in the form of their opposite (*sub contrario suo absocndita sunt*), and the cross is the ultimate instantiation of this apparent paradox."[22] This is where I believe ecofeminists can embrace a Christology that simultaneously honors the best of classic Christology, speaks a liberative Word in the context of public theology, and avoids the pitfall of a patriarchal co-opting of the symbol. For as Solberg acknowledges, "the cross is certainly an expression of inhumanity; it is also, however, an expression of the most profound humanity: 'the end result of a... life that challenges the systems [of oppression]...in solidarity with those who live on the periphery.'"[23] Further, "Luther was no more interested in glorifying suffering than liberation theologians are in promoting grinding poverty when they insist that God is to be found particularly among the poor."[24] On the contrary, as will be demonstrated, this ecofeminist Christology, especially as it is incorporated into preaching, "seeks to clarify and convict, to valorize accountability and enable its realization,"[25] especially as it regards women and Earth.

Celia Deane-Drummond's Ecological Theology

Celia Deane-Drummond's work is one of the most comprehensive and salient treatments of Christology I have found for informing Creation-crisis preaching. She considers the way in which Jesus, as a human being, reveals how God works in and through biological processes to incarnate and kenotically give of God's self to the world. Here she distinguishes between the kind of kenosis Karl Barth feared—that of weakening the sovereignty of God—and the kind that she draws from theologians such as Hans Urs von Balthasar and Sergii Bulgakov—namely, the divine self-giving that arises out of complete love and desire to be at one with Creation. This distinction is important, for it resolves the concern that we might be fusing God and Creation into one, and thus make God's being contingent upon the existence and form of Creation. Eschatologically, this would tie God too closely to the ultimate fate of the universe, whether that be an end through expansion into cold nothingness, or a fiery compression back to the point of origin (what Teilhard de Chardin calls the Omega Point). It is important to keep in place the critical distance between the Creator and Creation, and Deane-Drummond's Christology does this.

Deane-Drummond draws heavily on Balthasar's theology of *theodrama,* which she explains in this way: "Drama is about human actions and particular events in particular contexts, and theodrama is that which is connected to God's purpose. A theodramatic approach will always be in one sense eschatological in orientation. Attention to drama draws out the specific significance of human agency, the particular context, and also the wider plot or time dimensions."[26] Where her work is particularly helpful for Creation-crisis preaching is in her insistence that this drama places creatures "in kinship with humanity [wherein] the evolution of life becomes an integral aspect of the drama between God and God's creatures" rather than being merely the stage for an anthropocentric salvation.[27] Theodrama is also helpful for undergirding preaching that seeks to incorporate an ecofeminist Christology of the crucifixion and resurrection because it deals seriously with evil and tragedy. As she explains: "A theodramatic approach takes proper account of the tragic, one that is vivid in terms of the evolutionary history of the earth, but [which is now brought] into juxtaposition with an understanding of how God works in the tragic in human history. It therefore will resist any generalization of evil or attempt to wash over the contingency of events."[28] Because it both participates in and proclaims this very theodrama, preaching plays an integral role in creating an experience for the listener that conveys both the tragedy and the hope contained within the biblical story, Earth's story, and our story.

To illustrate how this theodrama can be visualized, seeking to more fully connect and integrate Christ's incarnation with his crucifixion and resurrection, we return once again to the meditation room at Mount

"Madonna and Child" by Anthony DiLorenzo portrays the tenderness and vulnerability of the mother and child and highlights the relational incarnation of Christ. For a full-color version of this photograph, visit www.creationcrisispreaching.com. *Photo by Leah D. Schade.*

Saint Alphonsus to further explore the space around the Sophia-Mer-Christ statue. Along one wall of the room was an alcove containing a carved bust of Mary and the child Jesus in a beatific pose. (Incidentally, it is the only piece of artwork from the site that has been salvaged; the others were destroyed when the building and grounds were sold into new ownership.) [29] The babe is swaddled in the same aqua-blue that swirls around him as an adult. The darker blue that lines his robe as an adult in the Sophia-Mer-Christ statue is echoed in the robe surrounding his mother in this Madonna-and-Child scene, reinforcing the feminine aspect of Jesus. Here the incarnation of Christ is symbolized in a work of art that portrays the tenderness and vulnerability of the human mother and child.

We then turn to a second alcove situated to the left of Sophia-Mer-Christ. It is the place of the skull. On a shelf is placed the skull of an animal, a deer, with its large hollow eye sockets and bone greyed by weather and time. Hanging over the skull is a cross studded with nails and a branch of thorns situated vertically through the center piece. A single round red glass droplet fits into the center, a reminder of the blood Jesus shed on the cross. Between these three works of art, then, we see the theodrama portrayed in its significance both for humanity and for Creation.

What is most helpful in Deane-Drummond's work for deepening our Creation-crisis preaching is her in-depth consideration of the meaning of the cross and resurrection for nature. Especially in the cross we see what Deane-Drummond would call the *evolutionary significance* of Christ's death and resurrection. She asks questions such as: How do we account for the "victims" of the evolutionary process, such as those species that have gone extinct? How do we understand the concept of suffering among nonhuman beings? In what ways can we begin to grapple with the concept of theodicy from an ecological perspective? Do some animal species have a morality that has gone unrecognized? How can we understand the morality of God, who creates a world where pain is an inseparable aspect of life?[30]

This is not to say that all death within nature is evil. As Deane-Drummond points out, "[N]atural death is both the end of an existing life and a condition without which nothing could live."[31] But there is a distinction between natural death and death as a result of what she calls *anthropogenic evil*—the harm committed against nature that finds its origins in human actions individually and collectively. This gives us a helpful category with which to speak about seemingly victimless

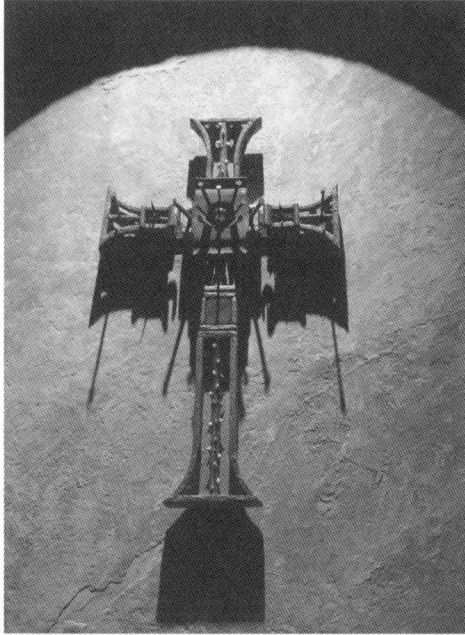

The place of the skull" in the Sophia-Mer-Christ meditation room evokes the notion that Christ suffers in solidarity with all Creation. For a full-color version of these photographs, visit www.creationcrisispreaching.com. *Photos by Ken Hilston.*

crimes of habitat destruction, extinction, and climate change so that we have a way to name what is happening to the Earth as *evil*. As Deane-Drummond points out, the more species complexify, so does moral intelligence. Consequently, the capacity for evil intensifies and complexifies, as evidenced in the staggering and almost unimaginable ways human beings have conceived for doing evil unto each other and Creation.

So, for example, while the deer whose skull is in the artwork may have been killed by natural predators or processes, it is possible that the symbolic significance of placing an animal's skull beneath the cross in DiLorenzo's art is meant to draw our attention to the ways in which nonhuman beings suffer as a result of human evil. Thinking about the suffering of nonhuman Creation in theological terms "encourages us to reflect in detail on the depth to which evil and suffering reach into the biological world and to become more aware of the potential of [Christ's redemption] to widen out to include such forms of ill. Our hope in the possibility of transformation is then informed by acknowledgment of the depths of ills that have afflicted both the human and nonhuman communities."[32]

We are reminded that the crucifixion did not just happen to one man in one historic moment, but that Creation itself continues to suffer as a result of the evil and domination of humankind. In this artistic space we encounter the full spectrum of an ecofeminist Christology: the theodrama that spans the incarnation, the embodiment of Jesus through and with all aspects of humanity and Creation, and the suffering he endures and overcomes with and through Creation via the crucifixion and resurrection. I am making the case that Creation is sometimes the victim of the same forces that crucified Christ. At the very least, what Deane-Drummond, and, I believe, DiLorenzo's art argue for is "the inclusion of evolved beings in the theodrama, rather than their relegation to the position of the 'stage.'"[33] So, too, our Creation-crisis preaching must include these other-than-human beings within the scope of our moral consideration and proclamation of hope.

For Deane-Drummond, the key concepts for developing a Christology that takes both the incarnation and the crucifixion of the theodrama into equal consideration are *wonder* and *wisdom*. Wonder is that experience of awe, excitement, mystery, and profound beauty that is found both in the secular realm of scientific observation and discovery and in the theological realm of the sacred. It thus "becomes a mediating category in consideration of christological and evolutionary ideas."[34] She argues that "the dramatic encounter of Christ with the world is best situated in the context of an understanding of the theological meaning of beauty in the world, that is, an encounter with natural wonder."[35] The category of wonder also connects the fragile, vulnerable beauty of the *incarnation* (as depicted in DiLorenzo's portrait of Madonna and Child) to the tragic, horrific beauty of the crucifixion (as depicted in the alcove of the skull).

The wonder of the incarnation, in turn, has important implications for an ecofeminist theology in terms of the relationship between women and God. As she explains, "It is the receptivity of Mary through the work of the Spirit that enables the incarnation to take place, and it is this aspect that has, arguably, been forgotten by many writers in the Protestant tradition."[36] This is not to say that Deane-Drummond endorses the idea that receptivity is necessarily exclusive to femaleness as such, because this would only reiterate a stereotypical view of women as always open and without boundaries. Rather, she seeks to emphasize, "The act of the incarnation is not so much God acting through an exclusive power over the other, but God in love eliciting human cooperation. According to Bulgakov, in Mary, original sin 'lost its power' by receiving the Word."[37] As DiLorenzo depicts in his artwork, so "Bulgakov argues that the proper image of the incarnation is not simply a solitary Christ, but mother and child."[38] In other words, what we see is a relational incarnation, one observed most readily in the relationship between a mother and child. This relational aspect between Creation, humanity, and God will be especially noticeable in the three sermons presented in chapter 7, which are each preached from the perspective of a nonhuman "character" in the theodrama.

Regarding *wisdom,* we can see that especially for ecofeminists it is Deane-Drummond's appropriation of Bulgakov's sophiology—Wisdom, the feminine Divine—that becomes critical. The ethical dimension of the figure of Wisdom is particularly emphasized, wherein "God's blessing and the fertility and flourishing of the earth implies human responsibility towards all the creatures of the planet. Furthermore, by situating the divine covenant as the context for divine creative activity, the responsibility of humans towards one another as well as towards the planet is emphasized."[39]

What Deane-Drummond emphasizes is that, ultimately, God takes evil into God's self, transforming it into what is life-giving once again. And inasmuch as the Church aligns itself with Jesus' Divine Wisdom in confronting evil, standing in solidarity with evil's victims, luring perpetrators back to the right path (in a process-theology sense), and working to reconcile and restore humanity and Creation, the Church, too, teaches, preaches, suffers, dies, and is redeemed by Christ. When faced with the countless species now extinct (whether by natural or anthropogenic evil), the vast array of techniques used to inflict harm on the world and on human lives, and the heartbreaking masses of humans and nonhumans devastated by evil, one can only stand in silence. Hence we see another aspect of the term *wonder* in Deane-Drummond's subtitle. Just as there is a mystery to Creation that even scientists acknowledge, so there is an unexplainability to the presence and fall-out from evil that cannot find expression in words. But it is not a silence that engenders despair, apathy, or numbness. It is the silence out of which profound Christlike empathy arises, empathy that moves us to stand in solidarity with the suffering ones. Thus we stand in the middle of the Mount Saint Alphonsus meditation room, alternately gazing at the Madonna and Child, Sophia-Mer-Christ, and the skull/cross, taking it all in with reverential, awe-filled, and hopeful silence.

Summary

Jürgen Moltmann reminds us that Jesus' cross is "the mystery behind all christologies which calls them into question and makes them in constant need of revision."[40] This is an important reminder for this project of developing a way to approach Creation-crisis preaching that takes seriously the meaning of the cross and resurrection for women and nature. Just as we have seen that classical Christology has needed to be interrogated and revised in light of ecofeminist values, so ecofeminist theology needs to undergo scrutiny in order to discern how it fares at the foot of the cross. What we have seen is that an ecofeminist Christology that fuses Solberg's Lutheran theology of the cross with Deane-Drummond's evolution-infused theology of wisdom and wonder under the rubric of the theodrama begins to answer those questions. An ideal Christology, as Susan Bond states, shows us, that "[t]he crucifixion becomes meaningful to the extent that it demonstrates the passionate love of God in Jesus, willing to risk everything for the world. This radical passionate love does not function to placate an angry God, but to embody a compassionate resistance to dominant power."[41] A Lutheran ecofeminist theology of the cross is intended to lead us further in that direction.

Whence the Resurrection?

Having described the crucifixion in ecofeminist terms, next we will focus on the resurrection. To what can we turn that offers a self-critical narrative of the Easter story that takes Earth's self-determination into account instead of rendering it as a passive, objectified entity in need of human "saving"? Along similar lines, how can the narrative of the victims (especially women) of ecological destruction be deconstructed, altered, and retold? How can their stories be recounted in a way that recognizes their agency and power to resist the eco-cidal, hegemonic forces of capitalism and patriarchal governance? And how can this recounting be done so that it does not simply lead us to pity the poor victims and thus reinscribe the very same patterns of oppression? Chapter 6 will wrestle with these questions and offer an innovative "trickster" hermeneutic for preaching the resurrection that has the potential to both upend and transform anthropogenic evil while recognizing the agency and power within Creation, women, and all vulnerable entities.

Notes

[1] L. Susan Bond, *Trouble with Jesus* (St. Louis: Chalice Press, 1999), 33.

[2] Ibid.

[3] H. Paul Santmire, *The Travail of Nature: The Ambiguous Ecological Promise of Christian Theology* (Philadelphia: Fortress Press, 1985), 35.

[4] Margaret Swedish, *Living Beyond the "End of the World": A Spirituality of Hope* (Maryknoll, N.Y.: Orbis Books, 2008), 149.

[5] Sallie McFague, *Metaphorical Theology: Models of God in Religious Language,* 2d ed. (Philadelphia: Fortress Press, 1984), 193.

[6] Ibid.

[7] Ibid., 20.

[8] Sallie McFague, *Models of God: Theology for an Ecological, Nuclear Age* (Philadelphia: Fortress Press, 1987), 48.

[9] Ibid., 183.

[10] Ibid., 111.

[11] Ibid., 20.

[12] Ibid., 106.

[13] Ibid., 191.

[14] Sallie McFague, *The Body of God: An Ecological Theology* (London: SCM Press, 1993), 206.

[15] McFague, *Metaphorical Theology,* xi.

[16] Ibid., 9.

[17] Mary M. Solberg, *Compelling Knowledge: A Feminist Proposal for an Epistemology of the Cross* (Albany, N.Y.: State University of New York Press, 1997), 20.

[18]Ibid., 19.

[19]Ibid., 84.

[20]Ibid., quoting Douglas John Hall, *Lighting Our Darkness: Toward an Indigenous Theology of the Cross* (Philadelphia: Westminster Press, 1976), 123.

[21]Ibid., 125. Solberg clarifies that these parts are not discrete or sequential stages, but dynamically interrelated and co-constitutive.

[22]Ibid., 71.

[23]Ibid., 151, quoting Yacob Tesfai, *The Scandal of a Crucified World: Perspectives on the Cross and Suffering*, ed. Tesfai (Maryknoll, N.Y.: Orbis Books, 1994), 7.

[24]Ibid., 155.

[25]Ibid., 152–53.

[26]Celia Deane-Drummond, *Christ and Evolution: Wonder and Wisdom*, Theology and the Sciences (Minneapolis: Fortress Press, 2009), 49.

[27]Ibid., 50.

[28]Ibid., 51.

[29]In May of 2012, Mount St. Alphonus and its surrounding 411 acres was purchased by The Bruderhof, a Protestant religious community that lives apart from society (similar to the Amish), for $21.5 million in order to establish a high school academy for the community's students and living quarters for the community. According to the *Daily Freeman*, the community undertook extensive renovations to the building. ("Anticipation Mounts: Bruderhof school takes shape at former seminary, retreat in Esopus," Paula Ann Mitchell, *The Daily Freeman*, July 1, 2012, http://www.dailyfreeman.com/articles/2012/07/01/news/doc4fefb102197df136583203.txt?viewmode=fullstory, accessed January 8, 2013.) Sadly, the meditation room was stripped of all its artwork and DiLorenzo's pieces, save for the "Madonna and Child," were destroyed. The pictures on this book's cover and in the accompanying pages are all that remain of the images.

[30]Moral philosopher Mary Midgley astutely addresses many of these questions in the following essays in the collection of her works entitled *The Essential Mary Midgley*: "Animals and the Problem of Evil," "The Problem of Natural Evil," "The Elusiveness of Responsibility," "Is a Dolphin a Person?"[Mary, Midgley, *The Essential Mary Midgley*, ed. David Midgley (New York: Routledge, 2005).]

[31]Deane-Drummond, *Christ and Evolution*, xvii.

[32]Ibid., 191.

[33]Ibid., xvii.

[34]Ibid., 33.

[35]Ibid., 57.

[36]Ibid., 113.

[37]Ibid.

[38]Ibid., 115.

[39]Celia Deane-Drummond, "Creation," in *The Cambridge Companion to Feminist Theology*, ed. Susan Frank Parsons (Cambridge, UK: Cambridge University Press, 2002), 202.

[40]Jürgen Moltmann, *Crucified God* (Minneapolis: Fortress Press, 1993), 88, paraphrasing Martin Kahler.

[41]Bond, *Trouble with Jesus*, 93.

6

Preaching a Shape-Shifting "Trickster" Resurrection in the Face of the Creation Crisis

What will be presented in this chapter is a unique contribution to ecofeminist theology, homiletics, and public theology—the image of Jesus Christ as the shape-shifting "trickster." Recall from the image of Sophia-Mer-Christ described in the previous chapter the uncanny ability of the figure to shift and transmute under one's gaze so that lines of gender, race, age, and human/animal became blurred. In this chapter we will further develop the notion of the shape-shifting trickster and draw implications for Creation-crisis preaching. The trickster both upends pyramidic power structures and strategically finds a way through dichotomous thinking in order to open a creative, playful, and hopeful space to preach God's grace for humanity and Earth suffering at the hands of deathly androcentrism. This proposal is offered as one suggestion of where an ecofeminist Christology for preaching might lead, bringing together ecofeminist theology and homiletic theory around the idea of preacher-as-trickster. Certainly this is not the only way to find resonance between ecofeminism and preaching, but this approach will provide one example of an expansive way to preach the significance of Jesus Christ both for humanity and for the Earth community.

As previously mentioned, an important aspect of Creation-crisis preaching is finding creative and liberating ways to view the cross and resurrection that neither reinscribe a hegemonic androcentric agenda nor ignore the intrinsic value of Creation as worthy of Christ's redemption through the resurrection. The image of the "trickster," in this case, helps dissolve binary categories of ecofeminism's essentialism, while simultaneously answering the concerns of ecofemininist theologians regarding the patriarchal implications of the resurrection for Creation and women. It is the central argument of this project that a *Lutheran ecofeminist trickster Christology* could be an innovative way through the binary gender categories that essentialize women and feminize Earth, opening the way to an ethical practical theology of preaching that disrupts oppressive powers and surprises us with what Lutheran theology teaches is essential about the cross and resurrection: God's grace in the last place we expect to find it. As Richard Lischer reminds us, it is only the resurrection that can give Christian preaching its significance and importance, and this preaching must include both the cross and resurrection.[1] I am suggesting that a trickster theology holds in playful, creative tension the needs of both ecofeminism seeking the liberation of Earth and women, and congregations longing to hear God's Word of promise enabling them to live out the Good News of the resurrection. And it is the preacher who can proclaim God's foolish power through preaching that "midwifes" us from Good Friday into Easter.

We will begin by briefly describing chaos theory and the theology behind the development of a shape-shifting trickster category for Creation and Christology. An Easter sermon illustrating Jesus as a shape-shifter follows. Then we will explore the trickster homiletic developed by Charles Campbell and Johan Cilliers. The chapter will conclude with a post-Easter Holy Humor Sunday sermon that employs this notion of Jesus-as-trickster and the resurrected community as *carnival*.

Part One: Rediscovering the "Witty Agency" of Creation

Recall the tension within ecofeminism about the problems that come with tying Earth and women so closely, essentializing both in the process. Michael Zimmerman describes the conundrum in this way: "With their image of the Goddess, some ecofeminists have attempted to conceive of nature not as a passive resource, but rather as an active subject. But conceiving of nature as the caring Goddess also means conceiving of her as the threatening and withholding Mother."[2] In his search for a radical reformulation of the concept of nature within ecofeminism, Zimmerman turns to Donna Haraway:

[F]or Haraway, a major task is to redefine nature. Nature is 'not a treasure to be fenced in,' as some radical ecologists seem to think; not an 'essence to be saved or violated'; not a 'text to be read in the codes of mathematics and biomedicine'; and 'not the "other" who offers origin, replenishment, and service. Neither mother, nurse, nor slave, nature is not matrix, resource, or tool for the reproduction of man.' Stressing the interactive, generative aspect of nature, Haraway defines it as 'figure, construction, artifact, movement, displacement.'[3]

Zimmerman points out that the notion of nature as a construct "does not reduce it...but emphasizes that nature is an ongoing coproduction, generated by humans as well as by organic, material, linguistic, and technical nonhumans."[4] What Haraway wants to avoid is viewing nature either as a resource for man's production or as a mirror image of a "transcendental naturalism" preferred by some radical ecologists. Both views relegate nature to being an object and ignore its "witty agency."[5]

Thinking of nature as having agency leads to a key move for Haraway—thinking of nature as *trickster*. As Zimmerman explains Haraway's suggestion: "[W]hy not picture nature as having a sense of humor, as being playful and unpredictable? Why not think of nature not as 'mother/matter/Mutter,' but rather as the native American Coyote or Trickster?"[6] Such a revisioning of the world as "coding trickster" means that humanity would no longer see nature as a Mother always at our disposal to serve and nurture (and suffer insatiable demands and abhorrent abuse in the process). Instead, explains Zimmerman, "[W]e must conclude that organisms are 'natural-technical entities' that emerge in the complex discourses occurring among biological, material, scientific, and technical agents."[7]

Catherine Keller observes that the trickster trope has "appeared to help popularize chaos theory" due to its ubiquity as an archetype in cultures throughout the world.[8] She makes a clever connection between her work developing the "tehomic" theology celebrating the chaos of the primeval waters that precede Creation in Genesis 1:1 and the work of philosopher Glen Mazis:

> Mazis makes visible resemblance between the trickster and the "sensitive interdependence" that generates physical

chaos: "interconnection involves a lot of friction and conflict as well as harmony and cooperation, and the Trickster figure demonstrates how these painful and potentially destructive dimensions of existence and community can be suffered through with humor and a sense of play." The tehomic waters glitter upon the surface of this play: "the very idea of humor, which is to become fluid (its roots mean 'to be wet'), to overcome the dryness of life and to allow our normal boundaries to be dissolved," suggests a "frolic," "an animal energy which infuses the world."[9]

Keller takes the trickster metaphor a step further by applying it to ecofeminist cosmology. She observes that Haraway's trickster revisioning "not only subverts the grinding exploitation of the feminized earth, but supersedes the maternal altogether. Trickster 'makes room for some unsettling possibilities, including a sense of the world's independent sense of humor.'"[10] Keller suggests that by refusing to accept "the symbolic reduction of woman to mother, and mother to matter, we circumvent feminist matricide and begin from the bottom up—where matter itself bottoms out into what we might call, crossing its sexes, a *trickster matrix*."[11] It is this trickster matrix, the chaotic, tehomic depths, which give birth and rebirth throughout Creation "in every chaos phenomenon of flux, dynamics, fluctuation, bifurcation; in the way flocks fly, trees branch, solitons swell, populations increase. Every wilderness behemoth or leviathan repeats it."[12]

Seeing nature as trickster, then, means we must come to terms with the fact that Earth has power that is beyond our control, and is possibly impersonal and indifferent to us. This would involve humanity as a species having to mature beyond infantile neediness and learn to relate to Earth on its own terms. As Keller reminds us: "This matron of matter will not lose the cruel edge of the trickster— who mocks any given meaning—but she may counter its unjust human deployment. If the trickster trope reanimates matter, might the maternal not shamelessly reinvent itself within the mergent chaosmos?"[13] Thinking of nature as trickster, then, upends the notion of the passive feminized Earth lying helpless under scientific observation, or as a doormat to be walked upon, or as a mother beaten and abused by her progeny.

How, then, might we apply the trickster theology to Jesus? Seeing Jesus as Trickster can help us come to terms with the fact that, while the resurrection is not consistent with processes of nature (a consistent complaint of ecofeminists), this is not necessarily a further manifestation of the patriarchal urge to control nature and escape mortality. Rather, it is the surprise sprung on the death-wielding forces that seek to destroy the vulnerable Lamb. In this way, the resurrection is not an invalidation of the integrity of Creation (as many ecofeminists fear), but is, in fact, consistent with Creation's ability to surprise and outwit the seemingly powerful androcentric forces that seek to dominate it. In the same way, the Trickster motif shows us that we need not interpret the resurrection as the male deity's usurping of natural processes of life/death. Neither does the resurrection need to be seen as invalidating women who are integrally part of the birth/life/death cycle. Our sermons, then, can play with the notion of Jesus as the Trickster, a fully active and engaged figure who works from below to undermine the dominant and dominating ones through wit and wile. Such a rendering of the Trickster Jesus has interesting implications for Creation and women alike, as we see in the following sermon.

SERMON: "The Gardener—An Easter Sermon"

(A Sermon for Easter Sunday)
LEAH D. SCHADE
TEXT: John 20:1–18

Introduction

The central metaphor for the risen Christ in this sermon is the shape-shifting "gardener" Mary sees at the opening of the tomb. The garden's image is reiterated throughout the sermon as the site in which life begins both in Genesis and through Jesus Christ. Thus, the stage is set for a hermeneutic of Earth-orientation from the beginning of the sermon. The metaphor is then buttressed throughout the sermon with references to Jesus' interactions with Creation and his use of nature images in his teachings throughout the gospels. These include sowing seeds in good soil (Mt. 13:3–8; 18–23; Mk. 4:1–9, 13–20; Lk. 8:4–8, 11–15), the tenacity of the mustard seed (Mt. 13:31–32; Mk. 4:30–32; Lk. 13:18–19), comparing himself to a grape vine (Jn. 15:1–11), and fertilizing fig trees (Lk. 13:6–9). The first part of the sermon ends with Jesus' reference to "the birds of the air" in his teaching from the Sermon on the Mount in Matthew 6:26, a secondary image that will become pivotal at the conclusion of the sermon.

Sermon Text

> *"The kiss of the sun for pardon, the song of the birds for mirth,*
> *One is nearer God's heart in a garden than anywhere else on earth."*

Have you ever heard of this little poem? It was written by Dorothy Frances Gurney, and the first time I read it was on a little placard in the garden of my husband's grandmother, Mildred Rummel, whom we called Mam Mam. I loved walking through Mam Mam's garden, sitting on the double-wide swing gazing at her well-tended flowers and plants. Every year I'd ask her to give me a tour of each bed, asking her the names of what was growing there to get ideas for my own garden. She knew each flower and plant by name through weeding the beds, harvesting the vegetables, and sharing her bounty at her kitchen table with whoever came to visit.

When you sat on the swing in her garden, you looked across the yards and saw the church where she was a member and the organist for over fifty years—Salem Lutheran Church in Elizabethville, Pennsylvania. Many times we sat on that swing there in the garden and listened to the chimes ringing out from the steeple, watching the sun set in the warm evening sky. Indeed, I often felt nearer to God's heart in Mam Mam's garden than anywhere else on earth.

I think it is very interesting that Mary would mistake Jesus for "the gardener" when she first sees him on that Easter morning. She doesn't mistake him for a soldier, or a priest, or one of the other disciples. Any one of those players in the events of the past three days could have been lurking around the tomb that morning. But Mary looks at the man standing there and sees…a gardener.

What does a gardener do? The gardener is the one who takes the seeds or the young seedlings and plants them in the ground. The gardener tends to the growing plants, bringing water when there is not enough rain, pulling out weeds that steal nutrients, and, if there is fruit or grain or produce to be harvested, the gardener carefully collects it, gleans the best seeds for new plantings, and starts the process over again.

You know, Jesus had a story about planting seeds. It's the one about casting the seeds in different types of soil, some falling on rocky ground, some eaten by birds, some choked by thorns, and only the ones falling on good soil growing into a full crop.

So, apparently Jesus knew something about the fragility of seeds and the precariousness of life. He also knew something about the tenacity of life—the power that lies within that tiny seed. Do you remember the story of the mustard seed that he used to tell? The tiniest seed that grows into the grandest of bushes, harboring the nests of many birds.

Yes, a gardener knows something about the cycles of life. A gardener knows that when you take a bulb in the autumn and dig a hole to put it in, and then cover it up, something close to miraculous happens. After the season of ice and snow and bitter winter wind, the sun warms the earth, and green blades rise up out of the ground. And soon beautiful petals appear in all shades of the rainbow.

That was how Mam Mam's garden looked during the spring and summer—like a rainbow had slid down to earth and draped itself across her yard. She spent many of her days tending that garden—trimming the hedges, cleaning out the dead leaves, picking cherries from the tree and grapes from the vine.

You know, Jesus had a story about a vine. In fact, he used this image to describe himself—"I am the vine, you are the branches." He talked about pruning the vine to produce the best fruit, and grafting branches onto the vine. So Jesus must have known something about the process of cultivating life and faith in order to make it as fruitful as possible. He even told a parable about fig trees and spreading fertilizer around one to get it to bear fruit.

In fact, if you think about it, Jesus has many, many parables that have to do with the processes of nature. There was the parable about the wheat and the weeds, the sheep and the goats, the blowing wind, fields ripe for harvest, how seeds grow, and the signs in weather. And he understood the interrelatedness of all living things. "Look at the birds of the air; they do not sow nor reap nor gather into barns, and yet your heavenly Father feeds them. Are you not of more value than they?" (Mt. 6:26).

Mam Mam loved the birds, too. She would place feeders out for them and sit on that swing to watch their aerial ballet. Several years ago, Mam Mam and I were sitting on her swing in the yard, and she told me how she had watched a blue jay sitting on the wire, calling "EEE-DEE, EEE-DEE!" And then his mate flew in, alighting on the wire beside him. Then both of the blue jays flew away together. During that visit, Mam Mam told that story to me two or three times. And I thought to myself, "I wonder if Mam Mam is trying to tell me something here..."

Commentary

What makes this a specifically ecofeminist sermon is the image of the grandmother, who is also a gardener. The way her story is interwoven with the biblical texts and the resurrected Christ creates an interesting connection between the idea of an elderly woman and that of Jesus as gardener. This sermon is a gentler application of an ecofeminist homiletic than what will be seen in later sermons. There is no outward critique of hierarchical patriarchy or misogyny. Nor is there any attempt to address contemporary issues of ecojustice and the oppression of women. No calls for political action to liberate Creation and women ring out from the sermon. However, by lifting up the grandmother as the central figure for a modeling of Sophia-like attributes, there is a subtle decentering of androcentric discourse. The grandmother is not portrayed in a role of subservience, but as the queen of her garden, tending to it with masterful skill. In a sense, she is reminiscent of Sophia, Lady Wisdom, sharing her bounty with all and welcoming all to her table to partake of her feast of wisdom that comes directly from the bosom of Earth. Thus, the relationship between the feminine and Creation is portrayed in a positive way and subtly hints at an expanded way of thinking about God beyond the male gender.

Sermon Text (continued)

That visit happened when Mam Mam was nearly eighty years old. Ten years later, Mam Mam continued to live in her house and work in her garden with the energy of someone half her age—until one October morning when she was out in the garden at the break of day and a tiny blood vessel burst in her brain, causing a massive stroke. When we came to the hospital, we saw her shoes still caked with mud from being in the garden that very morning.

It was so hard to see her lying on that bed in the hospital those many long days, especially when we were so used to seeing her up and active. Finally, in accordance with her living will and after conferring with the doctors, the family decided to remove her from life support, because the damage done was irreversible and unstoppable.

But we had a service of commendation for her before she was removed from life support. And my husband, Jim, and I were given some time alone with her before the service. She was surrounded by machines pumping fluids into her veins and air into her lungs. She had not woken up for three days. Jim stood on one side of the bed; I stood on the other. Through our tears, we talked to her. Jim said, "Mam Mam, it's Jimmy. I think you can hear me, and I want to tell you how much I love you." And at that moment he felt her squeeze his hand. We looked at each other and continued talking to her, telling her all we wanted to say.

Finally I said, "Mam Mam, I want to tell you what's going to be happening. You had a stroke and you're hooked up to a breathing machine, but the doctors can't fix what's wrong. We're going to be taking the tube out of you so that you'll be more comfortable. And it's going to be okay,

Mam Mam. Don't be afraid. You have such a strong faith. You know where you'll be going. You'll get to see your husband Lefty and your friend Millie and your brother and parents, and everyone who's gone ahead of you. It's okay to let go. You take as much time as you need. In a few minutes we're going to bring the whole family in and say prayers with you. We'll all be right here with you." And at that moment she opened her eyes, nodded her head and smiled. It was the first time in three days that she had responded in such a way. And she understood. She knew.

We had a beautiful service at her bedside. All of us crowded into that little room and circled her bed. And I said this prayer for her: "Almighty God, look on Mildred, whom you made your child in Baptism, and comfort her with the promise of life with all your saints in your eternal kingdom, the promise made sure by the death and resurrection of your Son, Jesus Christ our Lord. Amen."

After the service, we waited outside while the ventilator was removed. When we came back in, she held her two daughters' hands and whispered her final words: "God bless you." A few days later, she let go and passed into eternal life.

Those moments we had with her, when she gave us her blessing for entrusting her to God—those were resurrection moments for me. They were Easter moments, even in the face of death. Mam Mam's faith was cultivated in the church —and in the garden— and she believed God's promises to her. I have to believe that she especially drew comfort from these words: "Very truly, I tell you, unless a grain of wheat falls into the earth and dies, it remains just a single grain; but if it dies, it bears much fruit" (Jn. 12:24). Those words were spoken by The Gardener.

Commentary

The last part of the sermon returns to the biblical references to Jesus and Creation, making connections between Jesus' presence and activity at the beginning of the cosmos (Jn. 1:1–5) and the underlying truth of continual new life present within every aspect of Creation, even death (Jn. 12:24). The sermon attributes agency to Creation by encouraging listeners to allow themselves to be "taught by the Earth," and ascribes a high status to nature as the place where The Gardener beckons us to directly experience the promise of God's eternal presence (Rom. 8:38–39).

Sermon Text (continued)

The Gardener knows the truth of eternal life, and is trying to communicate that to us in as many creative ways as he can. I would say to Mary: It was no accident that the one you saw put you in mind of the Gardener—not a soldier, not a priest, not one of the disciples—but a Gardener. This is the one who understands the deep, deep truth that permeates all life—who gives purpose and meaning and hope to those who allow themselves to be taught by the Earth and nurtured by the promises of God.

Yes, Mary, this is the Gardener. The Creator of all life, the Incarnation of Love which exploded the world into glorious being. The one who created the first garden in Eden and wept tears of sadness in a garden at Gethsemane, and finally conquered death in the place where life begins— in the garden.

And The Gardener comes to each of us, just as he came to Mary, just as he came to Mam Mam, showing us the first daffodils and blue bells of spring, coaxing us out into the warm sunshine to sit in gardens and draw near to the heart of God, and remember the promise that neither life nor death nor things present nor things to come can separate us from the love of God.

Easter moments are all around us, reminding us that God's promise of eternal life is true. It is as certain as the buried seed pushing through the earth, as certain as the new baby pushing through the birth canal, as certain as Mam Mam's soul hearing the call of the blue jay in the garden that morning, and pushing up into flight.

A few days after the funeral, Jim's mother was walking down the path in Mam Mam's garden when something caught her eye. It was a feather. The feather of a blue jay.

The Gardener lives! Amen.

Reflection

The image of the grandmother and the garden is used under the rubric of a "strategic essentialism" in which the relationship between woman and nature is one of self-differentiated interdependence rather than a fusion of biological and sexual processes. The grandmother is seen neither as passive and taken advantage of, nor as domineering and smothering. Rather, she is portrayed as having agency within her domain of the garden, receiving loving care from her family as she died, and having access to a secret wisdom through the call of the blue jay. The listener may also note that the primary characters in the story—the grandmother, myself, and my mother-in-law—are women. While the allusion to the women at the tomb is subtle, the connection to Mary speaking to the resurrected Christ is more obvious.

I have preached this sermon at three different churches on different Easter Sundays. The first time was at Reformation Lutheran Church in Media, Pennsylvania, a large, mostly Caucasian, upscale suburban congregation; the second was at Spirit and Truth Worship Center, a small, African American congregation in Yeadon, closer to the heart of Philadelphia; and the third was at United in Christ Lutheran Church in rural Lewisburg, Pennsylvania, a small, Caucasian congregation filled with farmers, factory workers, and mid-level professionals. While the ecological contexts of each congregation were different (professionally designed nature-scapes at Reformation; a small yard and grass surrounded by a crowded neighborhood with very little open space at Spirit and Truth; vast cultivated fields, hunted woods, and rolling hills surrounding United in Christ), I received comments following all three preaching events that expressed appreciation for the images of Creation in the sermon. This was an indication that my "flowering" intent to reconnect listeners with the sacredness of Creation within the sermon had been achieved.

It was listeners' responses to the image of and narrative about Mam Mam, however, which indicated the congregations' resonance with the sermon. For example, the concept of gardening in one's yard was not a readily accessible idea at Spirit and Truth because none of the houses had enough room for a garden, and the culture was not one that included gardening as a primary activity. But the image of a *grandmother* caring for her family through the offering of herself, her home (inclusive of the garden), and her gifts was one that every one of the listeners could relate to. Grandmothers are highly revered in the African American community, and so a connection was forged between the listeners and Mam Mam and her garden on that account. At the other two congregations, in contrast, many listeners had memories of their own grandmothers gardening, or were themselves grandmothers with gardens, so they were able to connect with the sermon at that entry point. Thus, the experience of the grandmother and Creation translated across different geographic areas, socio-economic strata, and cultures.

Finally, the sermon makes a connection between the way in which Mam Mam's faith was cultivated in both the church where she served as organist and choir director, and the garden where she conducted a choir of nature all around her. Additionally, the sermon included personal testimony in sharing that Mam Mam's death was actually a resurrection moment for me. The sermon ends with God's surprising act of grace in the form of the blue jay feather—a multivalent symbol of Mam Mam's love for her long-departed husband and family, God's love for us, and nature's proclamation of Christ's resurrection—found on the path in Mam Mam's garden after the funeral.

Part Two: Preaching the Trickster in the Face of Ecological Injustice

The Trickster in Theology

In their book *Preaching Fools: The Gospel as a Rhetoric of Folly*, Charles L. Campbell and Johan H. Cilliers explore the archetype of the fool at the intersection of culture and religion, specifically focusing on the folly of the Gospel and its implications for preaching. "Fools come in a variety of shapes and forms, and they cross cultural boundaries and barriers," they explain. "They come to us as mythical trickster figures, who appear in virtually every culture and evoke a world that is not solid or settled, but liminal and contingent to its very core."[14] Various embodiments of the fool include the trickster, the jester, the theatrical fool, the clown, and the holy fool.

While they recognize that trickster figures function differently in different cultures, and that there is a risk of oversimplification and reductionism in abstracting certain characteristics about tricksters from their various manifestations in particular contexts, they identify three fundamental aspects of the fool's activity: "(1) the fool's role in instigating and sustaining liminality, (2) the fool's goal of changing perspective, and (3) the fool's call for discernment."[15] Regarding the first, they define liminality as "the experience of being and moving in between spaces and times," explaining:

> [T]he folly of the gospel interrupts the presuppositions and myths of the old age and creates a liminal, threshold space at the juncture of the ages—a space in which change (as fundamental transformation) can take place. We have suggested that the Spirit is active in that liminal space to keep believers changing and moving from the old age to the new. Finally, we have noted that liminal spaces are in fact the spaces of the fool.[16]

Especially in sermons, the preaching-fool is the one who actually creates that liminal space in which both new perception and discernment become possible.

The authors identify Jesus as the ultimate liminal figure, "crossing boundaries, teaching and preaching with intentional ambiguity, and calling people to perceive and live at the threshold of the old age and the new—in the reign of God that is breaking into the world... [Jesus embodies] in his own person the threshold between the human and the divine, between the old age and the new."[17] Jesus as fool is transgressive, even offensive, and challenges our notions about who we are, what we believe, and what we perceive. This is what tricksters do: they cross boundaries, break taboos, and blur religious and social conventions. "In his words, he often speaks as a kind of jester, using the indirect and intentionally ambiguous rhetoric of paradox and riddle and parable to subvert conventions, violate social and religious norms, and call people to new perspectives and new life in the new age. And through both his deeds and his words, Jesus invites us into a community that lives between form and re-form, fragment and figure, being and becoming."[18] He is often portrayed in the gospels as an elusive figure, keeping his identity secret. This allows for a variety of interpretations and, consequently, the task of discernment. Ultimately, Campbell and Cilliers note, "He calls us to become a carnivalesque community, in which the old hierarchies and categories are subverted, equality is enacted, and the liberating laughter of the great messianic banquet erupts." [19]

The trickster motif is particularly apropos when considering Luther's theology. One function of the trickster or jester is to "call a thing what it is," to use Luther's phrase, in a way that disarms those in power through humor and cunning. The jester had an important role within the kingly court—that of truth-teller. The trick for the homiletician is to learn from the fool how to slip the truth in between grins and guffaws. In addition, the Lutheran notion of God hidden under the form of opposites provides a perfect set-up for the Trickster Jesus' joke on the forces of evil that would subjugate, humiliate, and annihilate God's life-giving love. The preacher-fool joyfully proclaims the surprise of God's grace, upending the structures of death and revealing the triumph of resurrection in places where we least expect to find it. It is the trickster-preacher who, as a proclaimer of God's surprising grace, may embody for the congregation what it means to embrace a theology of the cross and resurrection that redeems, not just broken lives and communities, but the Earth-community as well. The trickster reminds us that even when our preaching seems insignificant in the face of the forces that have brought about the Creation-crisis, the changes we set off at the microlevel through our proclamation may set off shifts in social, economic, and ecological dynamics that are not discernible at the outset, but have wider-ranging effects than initially realized.

Campbell and Cilliers state: "Christ carries in his resurrected body the coarse and vulgar joke of crucifixion. The joke, one might say, lives on... [T]hrough the resurrection Christ defeats the final enemy—death—and sets believers free from the fear of death so we might take up the foolish way of the cross."[20] Like his crucifixion, Jesus' resurrection "interrupts the world's assumptions, opens a liminal space, and calls for new perception—for the bifocal vision at the juncture of the ages."[21] Thus, if ecofeminists could see the resurrection not as an imposition of deified patriarchal control over the processes of nature in order to deny death, but instead as a creative interruption of that system, the stumbling block of the resurrection might be seen as a gateway rather than a barrier.

It is the liminality of tricksters that makes them ideal figures of paradox and marginality. "They are ambivalent and thoroughly unsettling, interrupting and confusing social categories and order—sacred and profane, moral and amoral, clean and unclean, divine and human, heaven and earth, male and female, life and death. They are shape-shifters, fluid and in flux, never to be mastered, not even by contemporary categories of interpretation."[22] A trickster Christology for Creation-crisis preaching challenges us to fearlessly step into the fluidity of dissipating categories with playfulness, courage, and hope.

"A trickster will die, and then suddenly return to life; go to the underworld, then return to the living. Tricksters live and function at the boundaries, regularly unmasking, crossing, and redefining those boundaries. They are figures on the margin, belonging to the periphery, not the center. As such, they are transgressive, disruptive figures."[23] Utilizing a trickster theology in Creation-crisis preaching would allow us to help others see Christ hidden in those very places the world thinks God cannot possibly be—in the bodies of women and the "body" of Earth, which have both been violated, even crucified, by androcentric society.

It is with this double-vision that a Lutheran ecofeminist trickster theology of the cross and resurrection invites us to reexamine the situation of the Riverdale mobile home park mentioned in chapter 2. This is the place where water will be bought and sold to be itself violated with toxic chemicals and used in turn to violate Earth through the process of hydro-fracking. In the process, vulnerable women and their families are pushed aside and communities are crucified. But, as we will see, Riverdale is also the place to see a resurrection hidden within.

SERMON: "The Easter Surprise of Riverdale"
(A Sermon for Holy Humor Sunday)
First Sunday after Easter
LEAH D. SCHADE
TEXT: John 20:19–23

Introduction

Support for exploring the trickster as a comparative figure for Jesus Christ can be found in key places within theology. In African American theology, for example, James Cone points out that the trickster appears in animal tales and stories of folk figures. The stories of Br'er Rabbit emphasize "the wit and cleverness of the weak in triumph over the strong."[24] He quotes J. Mason Brewer's description of Br'er Rabbit:

> The role of the rabbit in the tales of the American Negro is similar to that of the hare in African folk narratives—that of the trickster who shrewdly outwits and gains a victory over some physically stronger or more powerful adversary. The animal tales told by Negro slaves with Br'er Rabbit as the hero had a meaning far deeper than mere entertainment. The rabbit actually symbolized the slave himself. Whenever the rabbit succeeded in proving himself smarter than another animal the slave rejoiced secretly, imagining himself smarter than his master.[25]

Cone points out: "Humor is an important element in black survival, and it is often related to the theme of freedom. Through humor, black slaves transcended their servitude and affirmed their right to freedom without the risks of revolutionary violence against slave masters."[26]

The present-day animated version of Br'er Rabbit is, of course, Bugs Bunny, the cartoon figure created by Warner Bros. in 1940 and famously voiced by Mel Blanc. I grew up watching Bugs Bunny cartoons. Saturday mornings were filled with his antics that made me laugh as a child. Now I watch the episodes on DVD with my children, delighting in Bugs' irreverence and cleverness, giggling along with my children, but also seeing a surprising metaphor for Jesus. Some may balk at such a comparison, but for the sermon below, Bugs Bunny is used as a humorous entry point for addressing a very serious instance of environmental and community crucifixion.

The sermon situates Riverdale as the central metaphor for the resurrected Trickster Christ and calls upon hearers "to discern the gospel within the scandal."[27] As the reader will see, the sermon itself carries foolishness within its very form. The story of Riverdale is told as a fairy tale, so a child could understand it. I crafted this part of the sermon knowing that on the Sunday when I was to preach it—Holy Humor Sunday[28]—there would be lots of children, because it would also be one of our Youth Sundays.

Sermon Text

Some people think it's not appropriate to laugh in church. But what many don't realize is that Jesus was a great trickster. He told jokes, funny stories, and did all kinds of things to get people to lighten up and see God's grace all around them. He turned water into wine, for one thing. He created a huge party out of a couple loaves of bread and some fish. And he made fun of all the stuffy, stuck up people who thought they were better than everybody else.

In fact, you know who Jesus reminds me of? Bugs Bunny! Bugs Bunny?![29] That's ridiculous, you may say. And I'll say, you're right! Bugs Bunny always made fun of the men with guns who were always after him. Yet time and again Bugs uses clever ways to foil their plans to get him.[30] Through wit and cunning, Bugs always finds a way to use humor to disarm Elmer Fudd or Yosemite Sam. Their guns explode in their faces, they trip all over themselves, and they usually fall into their own traps meant to ensnare Bugs.

Well, that's what happened to the people who were after Jesus. He used clever, nonviolent means to disarm them, and he always outsmarted them, getting people to laugh at the ridiculous pomposity of the leaders. And he got them to fall into their own traps that they set for him. The biggest trap of all was the cross. Like Yosemite Sam tying Bugs Bunny to the high dive above the tiny little barrel of water way below, the soldiers put Jesus on that cross and crucified him. But on Easter Sunday, Jesus pops out of the tomb and says, "Surprise! Guess what? I fooled you after all. Not even death can hold in the love of God." When Yosemite Sam sawed away at that diving board and it looked like Bugs was going to plummet to his death, the whole platform crashed down instead, leaving Bugs suspended in mid-air. "I know this defies the law of gravity," says Bugs, chomping on his carrot. "But you see, I never studied law."

I know that resurrection defies the laws of, well, everything—the laws of nature, the law of sin, the law of death. But, you see, God's resurrection of Jesus doesn't study human laws, isn't bound by the powers of evil. In Jesus, God fools even death. "Only as it fools us can the cross save us!" reads a line in the book Preaching Fools.[31] The resurrection is meant to open us up to new possibilities, new ways of seeing things, so that we can move from the old age to the new.

So what surprises is God doing among us today? And what does it look like when the Trickster Jesus shows up and creates new hope, new community, and new joy? Let me tell you a story about where I saw the Trickster Jesus surprise me and a whole community of people with Easter joy.

Commentary

The rhetorical device of the fairy tale in the story of Riverdale that follows creates a veil of innocence. But it masks a darker, troubling story that the adults listening will understand. Yet the sermon does not end with the reality of the crucifixion. It proclaims the resurrected Christ in the midst of the resurrected community. And it makes the move to compare those at Riverdale with the disciples, thus reinvoking the biblical story and contemporizing it for the hearers. Further, it disarms the criticisms of those who disapproved of the whole "foolish" Riverdale spectacle by reminding those naysayers that those exact kinds of criticisms were lobbed at Jesus and the disciples—and are directed at them as Christians—time and time again. Thus the perceived difference and separation between those at Riverdale and those in the congregation begins to dissolve.

Sermon Text (continued)

Once upon a time in the not-too-distant past there was a little village nestled snug along a wide and winding river. The villagers shared their land with deer and foxes, bear and geese, and, of course, the fish and other creatures that dwelled in the waters of the river. Children rode their bikes down the lanes that ran between the grassy lots of the houses. Neighbors visited each other in the evenings and had barbecues and picnics in the warm summer evenings. The villagers were humble, hard-working people, but they did not have much money. Their houses were not so very big, and were made of metal. But many of them decorated their porches with flowers and flags, and everyone trimmed their small, rectangular houses with colorful lights every Christmas. The neighbors felt safe in their little village. Everyone looked after each other's children. And there was always someone looking in on the elderly neighbors, who knew there would be a family nearby to welcome them to their Thanksgiving table.

The villagers were not perfect people. But, for thirty years, the families lived in the village in peace, grateful for the beauty of God's Creation around them and good friends and neighbors they could count on if there was ever a need. No matter how hard life would be at their jobs or at school, they always knew they could look forward to coming home to their little village nestled snug along the wide and winding river.

Until, one day they came home to find letters posted on all their doors. The letters told them that the land underneath their homes had been sold, and they had to move away. A large company was going to tear down their houses and put in big buildings with big pipes going down to the river. The pipes would suck out the water, take it up to the mountains, and shoot it down into the ground to break the rocks deep below.

The villagers were very upset. They could not understand why their village was the place where the big buildings and pipes had to go. "It's not fair," they said. "What will happen to the deer and foxes, the bears and geese? What will happen to the river? What will happen to us?"

Some of the villagers moved out right away, stripping the metal from their houses to sell for a little bit of money. In just a few weeks, the village was like a ghost town. The families scattered to the surrounding countryside, leaving the village scattered with broken furniture, broken toys, and broken houses. Some of the families took their homes with them, leaving behind porch steps leading to nowhere. The old men no longer walked the lanes waving to their neighbors. The few children still left were too sad to ride their bikes any longer.

But some of the villagers remained. They did not want to move. They wanted to stay and protect their homes and the river. They sent word far and wide asking for help, for people to stand with them as they stood up to the company. On the day before the bulldozers were to come, people arrived from all over the land, answering the call of the villagers. I was with them. You should have seen their faces when we arrived. They were so happy that we had come to be with them. We set a little table with thirty-two candles—one for each of the families who had lived in the village. We read words from the Bible and other holy books about God's love for the people and the land and water. We prayed for justice and hope. We cried with the villagers. We filled bowls with water from the river and blessed them. And then we held hands and promised to help the villagers. As the sun set and the summer air cooled with the mist from the river, I said good-night to the villagers.

But the next day when I came back I got a big surprise! The helpers had taken all the broken pieces left in the village and made big walls across the road to block the bulldozers from coming in. They created huge signs from old boards and bed sheets that said: "This is our community!" and, "We are Americans!" and, "This is a beautiful place! People live here!" The porch steps had been moved to the center of the wall and the villagers stood on top, holding signs for all the cars and trucks passing by on the highway to see. "Save our homes," the signs read. People driving by waved and beeped their horns. Even truck drivers who fractured the rocks honked their horns and waved.

For twelve days the villagers and their helpers kept the bulldozers away. They pitched tents and ate meals around campfires. When it rained, they huddled in the abandoned homes to stay dry. They held circle meetings on the grass by the river to decide how to share chores and help the villagers. They played with the children, brought instruments and sang songs, and created a whole new village out of the old one. People from across the land sent food to the helpers. Even our church sent supplies—paper towels and cleaning supplies, food and drinks. The villagers were so happy and grateful that we were helping them. They were filled with joy, even though they were surrounded by so many broken things. One of the villagers who had moved away even came back and took the roof off of his old home to make a big, colorful mural. They got some paint, dipped their hands into the cans to make handprints across the mural and wrote words to describe who the villagers were: mother, truck driver, school bus driver, veteran, all painted in colors of the sky, with purple and yellow flowers and green grass.

The village was called Riverdale. And it was in that little mobile home park, surrounded by the remnants of a crucified community, that I began to see what resurrection looks like. I saw a gathering of people around the foot of the cross, with nothing but death and destruction around them, proclaiming that hope is not dead. They were not all Christians. Some of them did not go to church. Most of the activists had no religious affiliation at all. But what I saw at Riverdale was a resurrection community. I saw the risen Christ, like the trickster he is, jumping out of the tomb yelling: Surprise! You can't keep hope down. You can't kill the love of God.

When I stood with those villagers in that decimated mobile home park, I knew what most people saw was just a bunch of low-class "trailer trash," as they were called on the blog sites in Williamsport. I knew many people either pitied the residents for being caught in circumstances they couldn't control, or thought of them as rabble-rousers, troublemakers, and trespassers. Some thought the villagers should just get out of the way and stop making such a scene.

Funny, those are just the kinds of things they used to say about Jesus and his disciples. That low-class carpenter's son and his low-life fishermen rabble-rousers, troublemakers, and trespassers. The religious authorities and the military police just wanted them out of the way. "Stop making such a scene!" So they crucified Jesus and figured the disciples would just scatter and fade away.

That's what eventually happened at Rivderdale. On the twelfth day, men in uniforms came and put up plastic orange fences. Police came and told the helpers that if they did not leave, they would be arrested. The villagers told the helpers they did not want them to go to jail. So the helpers, with tears in their eyes and lots of hugs for the villagers, packed up their tents.

Today, the water withdrawal plant is being built, and the village of Riverdale is nothing but a memory. But it is the memory that invokes the Trickster Jesus. The community of Riverdale that popped up on the site of the trashed park and planted themselves there for nearly two weeks was a sign to the world that God is alive and working for justice. What I saw was not a trailer park in Jersey Shore; I saw the upper room in Jerusalem with the Trickster Jesus moving among those gathered, breathing upon them— laughing them into new life that can come only from the resurrected Christ.

Commentary

In the next and last part of the sermon, the reader will note how the image of Bugs Bunny—a trickster figure recognized by millions of children and adults alike—bookends the sermon. Bugs Bunny is compared to Jesus in terms of irreverent humor, wit and cunning, and the ability to outsmart patriarchal powers bent on violent destruction. The sermon ends with an invitation to laugh, be creative, and join the carnival of God's "Sunday morning cartoons," even in the midst of the world's evil and destruction. Should the hearer join in the Easter laugh, it is hoped they will experience the confidence that comes with standing alongside the Trickster Christ, who will always "have the last laugh."

Sermon Text (continued)

A theologian named Sallie McFague puts it best: "We must believe… that life, not death, is the last word; that against all evidence to the contrary (and most evidence is to the contrary), all our efforts on behalf of the well-being of our planet and especially of its most vulnerable creatures, including human ones, will not be defeated. It is the belief that the source and power of the universe is on the side of life and its fulfillment. The 'risen Christ' is the Christian way of speaking of this faith and hope: Christ is the firstborn of the new creation, to be followed by the rest of creation, including the last and the least."[32]

Of course, nearly a year later, some will say, "You were fools. A table full of candles is nothing against the glaring lights of industrialization. Barriers erected from trailer home refuse are nothing against the bulldozers. Mobile home park residents chanting alongside protesters are nothing against the powers of the police. What difference did it make? You accomplished nothing. You were fools."

And don't they say that about us in the church? "You Christians are fools. Jesus' light is nothing against the darkness of evil. So what if he was resurrected?—What difference did it make? The world is still much like an abandoned mobile home park, with the waters of creation being sold to pad the pockets of the wealthy. Hunger, poverty, disease, injustice, violence, war, and death—those powers are still the law of the land."

And they would be right! But, you see, the church doesn't study those laws. Christians singing songs of joy, using water for baptism, eating little crusts of bread and sipping tiny cups of wine, being generous and offering compassion to our neighbors, laughing and juggling and telling jokes that erupt into the Easter laugh…these are what sustain us, surprise us with God's grace even as the Yosemite Sams are climbing up the ladder to saw us off and drop us down.

So go ahead and laugh and live. Dip your hands in paint and draw colorful murals. Giggle at the stuffy big shots who think they can have control over God's world and God's water. Smile when they come huffing and puffing with their big guns and bulldozers, yelling, "Say your prayers, Rabbit."

Chuckle and chortle, grin and guffaw! Because you know something that they don't know. We may be living in the long night of Good Friday, but God's Sunday morning cartoons are just around the corner. And the Trickster Jesus will always have the last laugh. Amen.

Reflection

After I preached this sermon I received pushback from a parishioner who had followed the saga of Riverdale in the local paper and was convinced that the owner of the trailer park was within his rights to sell the property as he saw fit. Rather than debate this with him on the spot, I asked if I could make an appointment to speak with him about it at a later time. He and his wife graciously invited me to their home to sit at their kitchen table and talk about our different perceptions of the situation.

As we talked, he conveyed to me how important it was for him that people's rights be respected, and shared his own experiences of times when he felt his rights as a property owner had been infringed upon by what he felt were unreasonable demands made by the government regarding environmental regulations. In turn, I shared with him my observations of how the rights of the residents to live peacefully in their homes had been violated. I was able to go into more detail about the injustices and hardships suffered by the residents (many of them elderly, disabled, and veterans) of Riverdale over the course of the ordeal. My parishioner expressed surprise that the details I shared had not come to light in the media portrayals of the situation and conceded that such information gave him a new level of understanding. The visit enabled both of us to gain new insights and share different perspectives.

This encounter confirmed for me the importance of maintaining strong pastoral relationships when engaging in Creation-crisis preaching. The fact that he trusted me enough to share his anger about the sermon attested to his willingness to express his feelings instead of quietly turning away and stewing without my knowledge. While it is difficult to receive criticism and feel the negative pushback, when we see those encounters as opportunities for building relationships and approach them with as much openness and judiciousness as we can muster, the results can be affirming to preacher and parishioner alike.

This is not to say that there won't be times when we have to "preach with our bags packed," as my mentor Karyn Wiseman has advised her students. In other words, we may need to be prepared to take leave of a congregation when we take a stand on an issue that is important but controversial (think white pastors preaching in favor of the abolitionist movement, or the civil rights movement; or pastors preaching on inclusivity and extending welcome to the LGBTQ community). But with Creation-crisis preaching, I have found that deep listening and finding common ground (along with common water or air), while building strong pastoral relationships of trust and good will, can go a long way toward engendering the process of repentance and healing necessary for our human and Earth community.

Notes

[1]Richard Lischer, *A Theology of Preaching: The Dynamics of the Gospel* (Durhmam, N.C.: Labyrinth Press, 1992), 16, 19.

[2]Michael E. Zimmerman, *Contesting Earth's Future: Radical Ecology and Postmodernity* (Berkeley: University of California Press, 1994), 364.

[3]Ibid., 364, quoting Donna Haraway, "The Promises of Monsters: A Regenerative Politics for Inappropriate/d Others," in *Cultural Studies*, ed. Lawrence Grossberg, Gary Nelson, Paul Treichler (New York: Routledge, 1992), 295–337.

[4]Zimmerman, *Contesting Earth's Future*, 364.

[5]Ibid., citing Haraway, "The Promises of Monsters," 297.

[6]Zimmerman, *Contesting Earth's Future*, 364.

[7]Ibid., 364–65.

[8]Catherine Keller, *Face of the Deep: A Theology of Becoming* (London; New York: Routledge, 2003), 192.

[9]Ibid., 193, citing Glen A. Mazis, *Earthbodies: Rediscovering our Planetary Senses* (Albany, N.Y.: SUNY Press, 2002), 196–98.

[10]Keller, *Face of the Deep*, 192, quoting Donna J. Haraway, *Simians, Cyborgs and Women: The Reinvention of Nature* (New York: Routledge, 1991), 201.

[11]Keller, *Face of the Deep*, 193.

[12]Ibid.

[13]Ibid.

[14]Charles L.Campbell and Johan H. Cilliers, *Preaching Fools: The Gospel as a Rhetoric of Folly* (Waco, Tex.: Baylor University Press, 2012), 68.

[15]Ibid., 70.

[16]Ibid., 39.

[17]Ibid., 103.

[18]Ibid., 104.

[19]Ibid.

[20]Ibid., 34, 35.

[21]Ibid., 36.

[22]Ibid., 71.

[23]Ibid.

[24]James H. Cone, *God of the Oppressed*, rev. ed. (Maryknoll, N.Y.: Orbis Books, 1997), 22.

[25]Ibid., 22., citing J. Mason Brewer, *American Negro Folklore* (Chicago: Quadrangle Books, 1968), 140.

[26]Cone, *God of the Oppressed*, 23.

[27]Ibid., 102.

[28]In the early church, the Sunday after Easter was observed by the faithful as a day of joy and laughter with parties to celebrate Jesus' resurrection. The customs of Bright Sunday, as it was called, came from the idea that God played a practical joke on the devil by raising Jesus from the dead. Easter was God's supreme joke played on death—"risus paschalis"—the Easter laugh! As Campbell and Cilliers describe it: "Christian carnivals and other carnivalesque celebrations embody the new age—the new, inverted order—that has broken into the world in Jesus Christ." (*Preaching Fools*, 77).

[29]The sermon was accompanied by key images projected onscreen through PowerPoint slides, including scenes from the cartoon described, as well as pictures from Riverdale.

[30]Some may object to the cartoon violence of the Bugs Bunny animated shorts. The cartoons are, of course, a product of their time (the 1940s) when concerns about children being exposed to cartoon violence simply did not exist. Coming on the heels of vaudeville and slapstick comedy such as the Three Stooges (also very violent), the cartoon

format is particularly entertaining because it can defy the laws of physics and real-world consequences. Bugs himself rarely uses blunt force, but rather relies on his wits and intellect.

[31]Campbell and Cilliers, *Preaching Fools,* 33.

[32]Sallie McFague, *The Body of God: An Ecological Theology* (Minneapolis: Fortress Press, 1993), 191.

7

Earth, Water, and Wind

A Trilogy of Creation-Crisis Sermons

"Instead of just telling us about Earth having a voice in preaching, show us. What would a sermon look like where the water itself was the speaker? What would the story of the woman at the well encountering the 'living water' of Jesus look like from the water's perspective?" These were the suggestions and questions posed to me by David Rhoads in a conversation about my project of creating an ecofeminist Christology for preaching. Rhoads, Professor Emeritus of New Testament Theology at The Lutheran School of Theology at Chicago, collector of ecological sermons for the book *Earth and Word*, and founder of the grassroots organization Lutherans Restoring Creation, suggested to me that using narrative criticism could help inform sermons that give voice to the other-than-human "characters" of the biblical story. So began a shift in my own preaching that opened a new way to think about how the *form* as well as the *content* of preaching could be shaped and influenced by ecofeminist theology.

As we have seen throughout this book, having concrete samples of the range of possibilities for ways that ecofeminist theology can either subtly or overtly influence our Creation-crisis preaching are helpful. This chapter, then, will pull together into one place both the criteria of an ecofeminist hermeneutic for Scripture and the guiding principles that shape an ecofeminist homiletic for preaching, and then provide examples of sermons informed by these criteria and principles. Preceding each sermon will be an explication of the ecofeminist hermeneutic for the biblical texts. Following each sermon will be an explanation of how the principles of ecofeminist theology were applied. The goal of this chapter is twofold: (1) to provide a model for preachers to see how homiletic theory and praxis can incorporate the values of ecofeminism, and (2) to help ecofeminist theologians see how their principles may be applied in the field of practical theology through the discipline of preaching.

A recap of the reasons that justify allowing ecofeminist theology to inform and expand homiletic theory is in order. John McClure reminds us that experiments in reading from differing social locations and experiences are nothing new to preachers:

> Commentaries by women, racial-ethnic minorities, and global partners are becoming standard reading prior to shouldering up to the task of sermon writing. Listening to interpretations by those on the margins of the community of faith or to strangers beyond the community is becoming more central to exegetical practice. Collaborative interpretation of the Bible with laity and the unchurched prior to sermon preparation is increasing.[1]

What this project argues is that the theology of ecofeminists, as well as marginalized voices of Earth and women, will make a robust contribution to a preacher's sermon preparation.

McClure is one of several homileticians (along with Christine Smith, Kathy Black, Charles Campbell, Stanley Saunders, Teresa Fry Brown, Cleophus LaRue, and others) who exemplify standing on the margins and listening to the "others" in order to open up "an integrative and critical conversation between and on behalf of *all* groups within the lifeworld."[2] It is in the margins, says McClure, "where participants become aware of other communities and of their common plight. The margins are also the places where people are most aware of the breadth and depth of the dangerous colonization of the lifeworld by the system of money and power, and of the need for strategies of resistance and hope."[3]

The term *lifeworld*, drawn from Jürgen Habermas, is synonymous with *public arena*. McClure describes it as the place of "everyday, ordinary communication, the world of discourse where we negotiate and share common meanings and values... According to Habermas, a strong and thriving lifeworld is necessary in order for there to be a social space in which critical thinking and decision making can occur."[4] Habermas is mainly concerned with the ways in which the colonization of capitalism and technology threaten the lifeworld: "In short, face-to-face communication on behalf of responsible, ethical, and life-enhancing cohabitation is being co-opted by impersonal patterns of exchange and control."[5] Nowhere is the colonization of the lifeworld more apparent, and the margins more clearly delineated, than at those places where God's Creation and women are jointly oppressed, abused, and made to suffer because of the androcentric system of money and power. We saw this with the situation of the Riverdale diaspora, for example, where both the community and the river's ecosystem were destroyed for the sake of financial gain. Thus the concerns of ecofeminism call for strategies of resistance and hope, especially where preachers stand in the pulpit speaking to a congregation made up not just of one's own parishioners but of the Earth-kin around us and those most vulnerable human-kin in our midst.[6]

An Ecofeminist Homiletic

Ecofeminism is a fusion of both ecology and feminism and draws together principles of both. In creating an ecofeminist hermeneutic for preaching, I join both an ecological and feminist hermeneutic that informs our exegesis and proclamation. In this process, Earth is seen as a *subject* in the text, with its own "horizon" (see explanation of Gadamer's "fusion of horizons" in chapter 1) that has a bearing on the preacher concerned with ecological ethics. Ultimately, one of the key tasks of ecological hermeneutics is "to retrieve the perspective or voice of Earth and Earth community of whom we humans are but one species."[7]

John McClure's "other-wise" ethic for preaching contributes to this reorientation to the other-than-human voice in Scripture. He calls for "listening to the textual margins" in order to access those voices that go unheard. "[O]ther-wise preachers," he suggests, "will have a keen eye for characters, ideas, and narrative actions that hover in the margins of the biblical texts. They will tend to ask questions such as: Who doesn't speak? Who's missing? Who goes nameless? Where is the voicing of the text ironic? What contradictions open the text toward other-wise interpretation?"[8]

Applied to an ecofeminist hermeneutic for preaching, those questions will intentionally listen for the nonhuman nature voices that do not speak in the text. We will seek to discover which of God's children of Earth are missing and nameless in the text, but who are nevertheless impacted by the ramifications of its interpretation. We will be curious as to the ways in which the voicing of the text is ironic regarding the three-way relationship between Creation, humankind, and the Divine. We will look for ways in which the text is opened up for an other-wise interpretation by looking for the contradictions and connections between the biblical text and contemporary issues raised by ecological theology.[9]

Values and Commitments for an Ecofeminist Homiletic

All of the principles and criteria listed below have been explored fully in previous chapters. Here they are only listed as a reference for analyzing the sermons included in this chapter. A Lutheran ecofeminist homiletic, drawing on an ecofeminist hermeneutic of Scripture, will include the following (not listed in any particular order):

1. The critique of patriarchy, hierarchy, instrumentalism, dualism, and othering, and a denunciation of misogyny.
2. An exiting of the influence of androcentrism on every homiletical authority through the decentering, deconstruction, and erasure of androcentric discourse.[10]
3. Critically examining one's use of language, metaphors, and symbols to allow for expansion of images for God beyond patriarchy and androcentrism to include the feminine and Creation in a positive way.
4. Critically engaging the presumed association between women and nature in a way that navigates between essentialism and constructivism. Ideally, the sermon will opt for a pragmatic "strategic essentialism"[11] that includes celebrating the association between women and nature as a means of reclaiming women's power on the one hand,[12] while avoiding an essential, biological connection between women and nature that reinscribes oppressive binaries on the other.
5. Altering "the cultural perceptions that both women and nature are either always available, passive, and subordinate or wild, evil, dangerous, and requiring control."[13] Instead, seek ways to invoke the shape-shifting/trickster aspect of both Creation and Jesus, emphasizing the creative, witty agency that upends pyramidic power structures and empowers the disenfranchised from below.
6. Reconnecting listeners with Creation, cultivating wonder, compassion, and respect for the nonhuman other. Ideally, a sense of relationship between the listener and the other-than-human aspect of Creation will be created.

7. Addressing contemporary issues of ecological justice (or lack thereof), and identifying patterns of environmental destruction, nonhuman animal exploitation and cruelty, and social injustice in order to erase the logic and illusion that such patterns are natural or divinely sanctioned.[14]

8. Attending to the cry of the oppressed as heard in the joint chorus of women and nature, and then prophetically calling for direct political action in order to proclaim God's liberation of both women and Creation.

9. Attending to different experiences of women and Creation across geographic areas, races, socio-economic strata, and cultures ("mapping").

10. Listening to voices on the margins—especially Earth and women—and "midwifing" their stories and perspectives into the preaching moment and the listeners' awareness.[15]

11. Confidently entering the public square with a public theology grounded in the teachings of the prophets and Jesus, as well as relevant church doctrines, but also informed by science, in solidarity with those who suffer and conversant with secular constituencies.

12. Applying the following aspects of Lutheran theology:

    a. Naming evil for what it is; helping listeners to discern anthropogenic evil against Creation.

    b. Reminding listeners of the hiddenness of God at those very places where we least expect to find God's presence, especially where women and Earth are jointly oppressed and suffering.

    c. Pointedly emphasizing not just human agency in addressing and correcting the oppression of Earth and women, but God's intention of love and surprising acts of grace to heal, restore, redeem, and bring resurrection out of eco-crucifixions.

With these twelve criteria in mind for creating a Lutheran ecofeminist homiletic for Creation-crisis preaching, we can analyze the sermons below to see how the theory actualizes in specific preaching contexts and events. For each sermon that follows there is a brief explanation of how the text(s) were interpreted from an ecofeminist perspective. After each sermon there is a discussion of how the principles of an ecofeminist homiletic were applied for that preaching instance. I will also mention some of the reactions from the congregation (where applicable) to give a glimpse of how the sermon was received.

A Trilogy of Ecofeminist Sermons

Sermon: "Earth Speaks: What's Next?"
Leah D. Schade
Texts: Genesis 2:18–24; Psalm 8; Mark 10:2–16

Applying the Ecofeminist Hermeneutic

This is a sermon I preached in October of 2012 at United in Christ Lutheran Church in rural Lewisburg, Pennsylvania, as part of a series entitled "Of Lambs and Limbs: A Preaching Series on Ecological Justice." The four-part series explored justice issues that affect "the least of these," including children and God's Creation. I include it here as an example of Creation-crisis preaching that incorporates ecofeminist theological principles and values, not just in terms of content, but in the form and performance of the sermon itself.[16] In this sermon you will begin to see how the ideas of Earth-as-body, Earth's co-creativity with God, the intrinsic value of Earth, and the relationship between Earth, its flora and fauna, human beings, and God are so intimately related. The sermon will also dramatically portray what it looks like when the relationships between these entities are violated by human beings. Also, from a homiletical perspective, the sermon illustrates what we might see in preaching when Earth is a central character in the biblical narrative. The sermon gives one example of what it might be like if Earth were to hear and interpret a biblical text. It also provides imaginative insight into the workings of God in response to suffering, from Earth's perspective.

Sermon Text

[Sung:] O, Lord, how majestic is your name in all of the Earth!

> I am Earth. I am Gaia. I am *ha-erets*.
> Birthed from your self-emptying
> I knew not who I was at first.
> Without shape, you molded me, atom by atom, molecule by molecule
> Until I saw that I was round and hot.

I could barely contain my excitement in having been created!

My surface burst and bubbled, molten lava shooting up from my depths.

You were patient with me

Until I cooled, my roundness hardening, forming great mountains of rock.

I hovered alone in space. But not lonely.

All around me, my siblings—

my sister moon and other planets joining me in our dance around Sun.

In the distance, my cousins—stars, supernova, comets, black holes.

All of us sing to you our cosmic song of praise:

[Sung:] How majestic is your name in all the cosmos, our Creator!

And then I felt something cool and blue enveloping me like a sheer curtain.

Air! Sky! You were breathing into me, your breath flowing all around me:

Ruah, your Spirit, surrounding me, inhaling, exhaling, wind blowing.

And what is this? I am wet.

Are these your tears of joy upon me?

I am wet all over, rain falling upon me, coursing down my mountains,

Pooling in my deep places, rising up from my depth in springs.

And then it was quiet. Just your breath, and the sound of water.

You were patient with me

Until I was ready. I wanted to know—what's next?

Ooh! What was that? Ooh! There it is again! Oh! That tickles!

What? What is all this? Things are moving within my waters.

Look at what you've done! I am alive! Life lives in me!

Oh, how you have blessed me!

Look—green algae! Yellow fish! Red earthworms! Blue birds! Orange insects! Purple frogs!

They dance and swim and fly and creep and make their home in me!

And it is not quiet! Buzzing and sloshing and splashing and cawing and whistling! Listen, they are all joining in the song of praise to you, their Creator!

[Sung:] O, Lord, how majestic is your name in all the Earth!

I am not patient now. I want to know—what's next?
Ooph! Ooph! Heavy!
Thump! Thump! Paws, claws, hooves, move
[Sound of galloping]
They race on me! They jump and climb and swing from branches.
Look—there goes the monkey! Zoom! There goes the zebra!
Fur and scales, brown and black, white and red.
Teeth, ears, eyes, noses, lambs and limbs—
Look at what you have done! Oh, how you have blessed me!
I am ready. What's next?

[Pretend to gently pull a rib from yourself. Pretend to hold a lump of clay in front of you. Look at it, rotating it. Slowly fashion it into a human being, like making a snowman, but a real person. Add the details—toes, fingers, face].

What is this? Who is this?
You drew him out of me. Out of my very soil. You fashioned him.
This at last is being from my being, and flesh from my body.
This one shall be called Adam, for he was drawn from my rib, from
　　my very body…

Gasp! You are breathing into him! You are giving him your Spirit,
　　your *Ruah!*
He must be very special.
I must be very special, that you would think to create him from me.

Oh, he is lonely. Yes—bring to him all that lives on me!
See what he will call them, see which one he will choose for a
　　companion. None?
Yes, let him sleep.

Oh, look—you are doing with him what you did with me.
From his rib—who is this? He likes her!
As I care for him, may he care for her.
May they care for me, as I care for them.

Look at what you have done!
What are human beings that you are mindful of them, mortals that
　　you care for them?
Yet you have made them a little lower than yourself
And crowned them with glory and honor.

You have given them dominion over the works of your hands…

[Double over in pain] Oh! Oww! Look what they have done!
[Cough] What has happened to my air?
What have they done to your *Ruah*?
Aahh! They are cutting into me!
My mountain—it's gone!
My forests—where did they go?
They are taking from me, drawing my essence out of me.
Why do they not use the Sun, as the plants do?

[Choking, gagging] What is that? That tastes horrible!
What are they putting into my water? What is this poison?
Look at my insects. They are dying. My bee hives—empty.
All of these dead fish!
My animals in cages. They live only to feed the one you have made.

And what is he doing to her? Stop!
You are doing to her what you are doing to me!
Why do you fight your brother? Why do you kill?
Why do you scream in rage!?
Why do you not sing with us the song of praise to your Creator?

[Sung, but voice dying out:] O, Lord, how majestic is your name…

Look at what they have done. They do not love me.
They are poisoning me, taking from me, drilling me, cutting me,
    choking me.
They are killing me.
I am afraid to ask:
What's next?
[Crouching with hand over head]

[Speaker 1 (male)]: *[stands and faces the congregation]*: And Jesus said: "Let the little children come to me; do not stop them; for it is to such as these that the kingdom of God belongs. Truly I tell you, whoever does not receive the kingdom of God as a little child will never enter it."

[Kneels down and puts arm around Earth. Lifts her up by the hand. Embraces her, placing hands on her head].

[Speaker 2 (female)]: And he took them up in his arms, laid his hands on them, and blessed them. Amen.

Analysis Using a Lutheran Ecofeminist Homiletic

This sermon is one example of what preaching might look like that takes seriously the idea that Earth is a character with agency in the biblical narrative. It is especially because Earth-as-subject has been de-voiced, disappeared, and unnamed throughout most of Christian history, particularly in sermonic form, that an ethical reorientation to Earth is necessary and urgent. The sermon dramatically illustrates what it might mean to preach an "eco-crucifixion." Earth is essentially gang-raped in this instance, left in a diminished, near-death state. But she is not left alone or without divine attention. A recapitulation of the gospel reading reminds the hearers that Jesus cares for all the children, including the Earth-child herself.

What kind of Jesus is this, who takes Earth into his arms and blesses her? In what ways does Jesus' incarnation bind him to the Earth that is both created by him (John 1) and bears him through the long evolutionary process that led to Mary's pregnancy and birth? Jesus' subsequent ministry and crucifixion place him in solidarity with women and Earth, who are also "crucified" —raped, tortured, humiliated, and relegated to the Golgotha garbage heaps of death and decay. Then, after this millennia-long Good Friday, the resurrection offers hope for the vast numbers of species, women, and habitats already sealed behind the tomb's rock. They are the "children" whom Jesus takes into his arms and blesses, offering new life and new hope.

Sermon: "I Am Water, I Am Waiting"

Leah D. Schade
Text: Genesis 1:1–23; Romans 8:18–25; John 4:1–42
  (The Woman at the Well)

Applying the Ecofeminist Hermeneutic

In the sermon "Earth Speaks," the creation story in Genesis is told from the perspective of Earth herself. In the sermon "I Am Water," we have Water's point of view. The interpretation is heavily influenced by Catherine Keller's *theology of becoming,* in which she parses just the first two verses of the beginning of Genesis in order to open a space to explore the depths of the chaotic *tehom.* She makes a distinction between "the depths" and water itself: "What of the waters (*mayim*) over or with which the spirit vibrates? These waters are distinguished from tehom: no longer tehom, not yet literal ocean (which must be separated out on day 'two.') So the *mayim* suggest (analogously to the earth *tohu vabohu*) the fluidity, the waves, the membranes of energy from which matter forms and stabilizes."[17] Keller also notes the way in which both chaos and the sea are inextricably tied to the feminine in a sexual way.[18] Unfortunately, patriarchy has subsequently demanded mastery of both the feminine and feminized Creation on behalf of the male/God. The sermon, however, plays with images of God breathing in Water and exhaling mist, joining Water with light in an almost orgasmic arc of color—the first rainbow. The Water then "gives birth" to Earth, contrasting its solidity against her fluidity. Thus the interpretation may be categorized as strategic essentialism that celebrates the creative interplay between God as masculine and Water as feminine.

But then the gender of Water takes on a shape-shifting quality (as water often does) and implies a masculine fluidity in its relationship with the female Earth, perhaps impregnating her as they comingle in her depths. Water again gender-shifts as it becomes a kind of amniotic fluid in which life germinates and springs forth. Water rejoices in seeing Earth draped in a rainbow of colors from plants and animals, just as Water was shot through with color from her joining with light at the beginning. Yet Water is not just agent of life, but also of death, as we are reminded in the Flood myth when Water mourns the dead within her depths. The ecofeminist hermeneutic of remembrance, then, is seen throughout the first part of the sermon, where a creative retelling of the Genesis story from Water's perspective invites us to read the Bible with fluidity and movement that washes away strict androcentric interpretations.

The aqua-hermeneutic is then carried into the story of the woman at the well, in which Water waits at the bottom of the cistern to quench her thirst. In the sermon, Water carries memories, so that when she encounters Jesus, she recalls their encounter at his baptism. Water is addressed by Jesus, named by him as *hudor zoe*, "living water," thus creating a relationship between them. We poetically follow Water across his lips on its journey through his body and its processes, affirming the humanity of Jesus. And just as Water secretly pooled within Earth millennia ago, so Water pools secretly within Jesus until the moment of his crucifixion. The spear of the soldier causes Jesus' water to "break," alluding to another kind of birth process, which Water cannot fathom at that point. Here the image of Sophia-Mer-Christ emerges, with Water flowing around him and from him.

Thus the first half of the sermon models a creative actualization by retelling the biblical narrative as Water's story. Human males are decentered, the woman at the well becomes the primary focal point, and a flattening of hierarchies occurs whereby Water is a partner alongside Jesus Christ.

Sermon Text

I am water. I am waiting.

In the beginning I waited in dark silence, my depths folding in on themselves, pushing me down into eternal *tehom*, the formless void.

I waited for God's breath to inhale me, free me from my liquid weight, to sweep me up into heights unknown, exhale me, floating in mists, my molecules dancing in darkness.

I waited…for light—and there was light! And it was good!

Light shining through me, creating something in me I had never known was possible—colors!

Red, orange, yellow, green, blue, indigo, violet—I was arched in ecstasy upon seeing my form transformed!

I waited…to push up and out and break and reveal…Earth! And there was Earth! Solid against my fluid. And it was good!

I waited…to join with myself again in droplet form and fall upon Earth as rain puddling in Earth's indentations, flowing down her peaks, coursing through her creases, washing her, gathering between her bosoms, soaking down into her depths, gathering silently beneath her skin, pooling gradually in her womb.

I am Water. I am waiting.

I waited for life! A crack of lightning surged through me, electrifying something within me that stirred slightly and grew. Atom by atom, molecule by molecule, cell by cell, tissue upon tissue, organ upon organ—look at all that is growing and moving within me! Swimming things, floating things, aggressive things, gentle things. Beings that take me into themselves as I take them into myself. I course through them, they course through me. I live in them, they live in me! I am alive—I make alive!

And look—there upon Earth—a rainbow has draped her! Green shoots, purple flowers, blue skies, yellow eyes, orange flesh, red blood.

I am Water. I am waiting…

I am waiting to recede. At God's command I broke forth in flood and rain, my depths rising, rising, rising, covering Earth, swallowing her colors. Only the ark remained, floating upon my surface. Look at all that is dead and floating upon my surface. I pull them into my depths, enfolding them into my eternal tehom. They are consumed by the swimming things.

I wait for Earth to reappear, for the dove to alight and cease his flight across my expanse, carried on God's breath. I wait for tentative toes to tickle into me, no longer afraid of me. I wait for light to shine through me …and now I am rainbow once again—this time joined with light as a sign of God's covenant.

I am Water. I am waiting…

I am waiting at the bottom of a deep well. I am waiting to quench her thirst.

I am waiting as Sun rises high in the sky, stealing my droplets with his heat, chasing me from sandy soil. I must gather myself quietly, in secret, beneath Earth's desert skin. Here in this well I wait.

She comes alone with her bucket that she drops down into me. I greet her with a splash from below. She draws me up and sets me beside a man.

She dips her clay cup into me and hands me to the man. I touch his lips with my coolness. He calls me *"hudor zoe,"*—"living water." I recognize that voice. I recognize these lips. I was poured over his body at the river. He played in me and rejoiced as God's breath once again spoke and light broke forth upon him.

Now I cascade down his throat and coat his belly. I course through him and take away the waste from his body. Later he will release me back into Earth. But part of me will remain in him, pooling beneath his skin, gathering in a secret place.

I am Water. I am waiting…

I am the sweat on his forehead cut by thorns. I am tears leaking from his eyes weeping in agony, falling to dusty soil far below his pierced feet.

I am breaking!! A spear pierces his side and I gush out, but what am I birthing this time? *Estauromenon*—crucified. I am crucified with the man.

I am Water. I am waiting…

I am waiting at the bottom of a shallow well, a bowl, a font.

I am waiting to be poured over the child's head. I am waiting as songs float over me and words are breathed around me, like God's breath moving over me at the beginning. I wait while a candle hovers over me, a token of Sun's flame, a reminder of what light can do to me, for this child, for these people.

I wait as hands cup me and draw me up and pour me over the child's head. I wash over flesh; I am once again *hudor zoe*, "living water"; I am alive, I make alive!

I am Water. I am waiting…

I am waiting to die and to make dead. I was sucked from the river and filled with chemicals meant to kill even the tiniest algae in me. I was forced into Earth with violent pressure such as I had never experienced, cracking her, fracturing her within her depths. Gas was released, and so was I, carrying the toxic substances that were meant only for Earth's deep places. Through fissures and seams I migrated from below. Onto concrete and streams I was spilled from above with my poisons.

I wait at the bottom of her well. She is afraid of me. I am dark and cloudy, brown and foul. I burn when a flame is held to me. Look at all that I have killed—microbes and fish, cattle and canine. Where is the dove? Where's is God's breath? Where are the toes I used to tickle?

I cannot quench her thirst. I am no longer *hudor zoe*. I am *hudor estauromenon:* "water crucified."

She carries me in clear glass jars, shows me to all who will see. "Will you drink this?" she asks. "Will you wash your children in this? Will you baptize in this? What will you do with this water?"

[Reader]: I consider that the sufferings of this present time are not worth comparing with the glory about to be revealed to us. For the creation waits with eager longing for the revealing of the children of God; for the creation was subjected to futility, not of its own will but by the will of the one who subjected it, in hope that the creation itself will be set free from its bondage to decay and will obtain the freedom of the glory of the children of God" [Rom. 8:18–21].

[Water]: I am Water. I am waiting. I am waiting for you. I am waiting, longing for you to be revealed as children of God, to set me free from my bondage to decay.

[Reader]: We know that the whole creation has been groaning in labor pains until now; and not only the creation, but we ourselves, who have the first fruits of the Spirit, groan inwardly while we wait for adoption, the redemption of our bodies. For in hope we were saved. Now hope that is seen is not hope. For who hopes for what is seen? But if we hope for what we do not see, we wait for it with patience" [Rom. 8:23–25].

Water: I am Water. I am filled with hope that God will make me *hudor anasteso*—"water resurrected." I am Water. I am waiting.

Analysis Using a Lutheran Ecofeminist Homiletic

This sermon is preached using four long pieces of flowing fabric: one dark blue (water), one iridescent (air), one multicolored (rainbow), and one a putrid green-and-brown tie-dye (fracked water). The flowing cloths help the listener to visualize the flowing and playful aspects of water. But the fabric is also used to convey water's destructive quality when the green and brown cloth becomes a whip and is used to evoke the fracturing of Earth. At the end of the sermon, the fracked water falls away to reveal both the iridescent and blue cloth layered together, a visual representation of *hudor anasteso,* water resurrected.

The sacrament of baptism figures prominently in this sermon. It is alluded to throughout the first half in the recounting of Creation and the Flood, two of the stories that figure prominently in most Lutheran baptismal liturgies. Again, Water has memory, and at the scene in the sermon where Water is waiting in the font, all of the memories of God's *Ruah*/breath/spirit, light, and Jesus' nomenclature of "living water" come together in the ritual of baptism. Thus, the ecofeminist principle of reconnecting listeners with Creation and the nonhuman other (in this case Water) is meant to cultivate a sense of the sacred as well as respect for this essential element in the sacrament of baptism.

But just as Water is rejoicing in being an agent of life, the scene abruptly shifts to Water being made a medium of death through the process of hydraulic fracturing for shale gas. Here the principles of addressing a contemporary ecological issue that is informed by science, as well as speaking in solidarity with those who suffer, are employed. The sermon, then, exemplifies the principle of listening to voices on the margins—women and water—and voicing their story and perspective. We follow Water's journey in the process of fracking, much as we did at the beginning when *he* washed over Earth, and again when *she* flowed through Jesus' body. (The gender-shifting here is meant to mirror the shape-shifting previously discussed.) However, this time the result is death upon death. The contemporary "woman at the well" now fears the water waiting there. Water declares itself *hudor estauromenon*: "water crucified." Thus it is joined in suffering to what Jesus suffered—both innocent, both killed. We cannot help but wonder if there can be any resurrection for this water, knowing that, as Rachel Carson taught us, these chemicals are not organic, cannot be removed, and poison all life with which they come in contact.

It is at this point when the Word is proclaimed from Romans 8:18–21. Water hears the Word reminding her that she is to be set free from her bondage to decay. She then addresses the listeners directly, calling for them to set her free. In this way, the sermon is *leafing,* prophetically calling for action from the listeners in order to liberate both the women who suffer with poisoned well water from fracking, as well as Water itself. Thus human agency and a response to the preached Word are invited. But this is not where the sermon ends, for the reading of Romans 8 continues with verses 22–25, which remind the listener—including Water—of the hope that comes through faith. The final words of the passage, "we wait for it with patience," are meant to be the "a-ha" moment for the listener who has heard the refrain, "I am Water, I am waiting," repeatedly throughout the sermon. It is finally a waiting filled with hope in the God who can redeem Water and transform her into *hudor estauromenon*—"water resurrected." While it is not as overt, the theme of God's hiddenness is implied here. For just as water was hidden within Earth, within wells, and within Jesus, waiting to be reborn, so we hope against all evidence to the contrary that God is somehow hidden within the brown, toxic water of fracking, working a miracle invisible to our eyes.

Sermon: "I Am Ruah: A Sermon on Climate Disruption Preached from the Perspective of the Holy Spirit"

Leah D. Schade
Texts: Genesis 1:1–8; 2:4a–8; Matthew 12:30–32; John 20:19–23

Applying the Ecofeminist Hermeneutic

In order to lend perspective to this final sermon, it is helpful to remember Mark Wallace's notion of Earth suffering a crucifixion by invoking the image of the "cruciform Spirit." He offers a novel image of Earth as the continually crucified Spirit of God. The Holy Spirit, according to Wallace, is embodied in and through Earth and suffers just as Jesus did on the cross—this time, under the continual siege of ecological sin. By seeing the Holy Spirit as the feminine aspect of God, which then becomes embodied in the natural world, he builds on Sallie McFague's notion of Earth as God's body, but shifts the focus to the third person of the Trinity, as well as incorporating the Divine Feminine. He then makes the connection to Christ's crucifixion:

> If God's body—this small planet that is now under siege by continued global warming, deforestation, the spread of toxins, the chronic loss of habitat—continues to suffer and bleed, then does not God, in some sense real but still unknowable and mysterious to us, also suffer and bleed?... If it is the case that when the earth, God's body, suffers, then God's Spirit suffers as well, then we can say that the Spirit of God is "Christ-like"

or "cruciform" because the Spirit suffers the same violent fate as did Jesus—but now a suffering not confined to a onetime event of the cross, as in the case of Jesus, but a suffering that the Spirit experiences daily through the continual debasement of the earth and its inhabitants… [T]he Spirit bears the cross of a planet under siege as she lives under the burden of humankind's ecological sin.[19]

The sermon below is an illustration of the notion of the Spirit crucified by the burning of fossil fuels and climate change. Building on one of the meanings of the Hebrew word *ruah* as a mother bird, the sermon is a creative actualization of Ruah's perspective of this planet. The sermon takes a long view of Earth's story and creates a narrative amplification of the Spirit's interaction with Earth and its flora and fauna, especially human beings, and particularly Jesus.

Sermon Text

I am all the air there ever was. I am Ruah, *pneuma*, the breath of God. I am the wind of memory.

You cannot see me, but you know I exist because you can feel me, see what I do, listen for me. You know me as the Holy Spirit. I issued forth from God from before the beginning.

I moved over the waters of Creation, as gases and hot steam from volcanoes bursting on this young planet. In the oceans God formed the tiniest bacteria—the beginning of organic life! They took in my carbon dioxide and released my oxygen, which flew across the waters and lands, so that I hovered over this planet as a mother bird flutters over her nest egg. And what a beautiful orb God had created—swirling blues, soft white snows, and solid greens and browns.

It is I who gives life to all that breathes. I move between plants and animals, all of whom thrive in the exchange, the sharing of balance. Plants take in carbon dioxide and give off oxygen. Animals take in oxygen and give off carbon dioxide.

You, too, Human, are part of that sacred exchange. God blew me, the exhalation of the plants, into your lungs as you emerged from the warm, wet womb. Earthling—you are *adamah*, the one whom God formed from Earth and blew into your nostrils the breath of life. I know every cell of your body, and I carry the memories of all other cells through which I have passed.

This oxygen–carbon-dioxide interchange takes place at the very basic level of your body. Your lungs are like trees through which these sacred gases are exchanged. Your blood is like Earth's water where the mystery of life courses in an endless cycle of give-and-take. The air you inhale was once exhaled by the brontosaurus. The air you exhale will one day be inhaled by your sons and daughters living far across the globe. I am all the air there ever was and will be. I am Ruah. I am the wind of memory.

Before your kind emerged on the orb, that brontosaurus roamed a planet thick with vegetation and teeming with other massive thundering lizards of all kinds—flying and scampering, red-toothed and thick-muscled, scaled and spiny. For 165 million years they flourished—until the days when the great fire rained from the sky, and I burned and smoked, extinguishing the lives of so many, their bodies falling into the mud of all the dying vegetation. I grieved at the loss of so much life, all the cells I had nurtured, all the greenery I had caused to flourish, now sinking into the depths of time and the stony grip of mountains and riverbeds, beneath ice sheets and vast stretches of flat lands. But God assured me that life would arise again, with even greater variety and texture.

I am Ruah, and I carry the memory of the Great Turning. Together over many millions of years we coaxed the sacred exchange to renew itself again. Little by little, life returned to the planet in colors of all shapes and forms—growing, swimming, flying, galloping. This time I learned to sing! In the whistle of the warbler. In the sonorous bellows of the deep-diving whale. And in your own voice! I, Ruah, God's breath, sing through you! [sung:] "Sing to the Lord a new song." Take me into your lungs and sing with me: [sung:] "Sing to the Lord a new song. Earth contains marvelous things! I too will praise God with a new song!"

Beautiful! The same singing I heard from Miriam after I blew across the Sea of Reeds and allowed the captive Israelites to walk to freedom on dry ground. The same song I heard from Mary when she opened herself to me and God formed the tiniest zygote in her womb—the one who would become Jesus. In Mary another great Turning had begun, and her song inspired her Son. He would sing her song with the women and fishermen and tax collectors when they would gather to break bread on the Sabbath. Oh yes, Jesus loved to sing! He would take me into his lungs and burst into song for any reason at all, or for no reason at all.

I hovered over him as he emerged from the baptismal waters. I filled his lungs and issued forth from him in his words, his vocal cords vibrating with the teachings, his whispers of healing, his exhaled exhortations. But just as he was breathing into the world new life and new hope, others were using me to conspire against him. They breathed threats against him, hissing their plans for his demise.

But Jesus did not cower in fear before them. He warned them: "Therefore I tell you, people will be forgiven for every sin and blasphemy, but blasphemy against the Spirit will not be forgiven. Whoever speaks a word against the Son of Man will be forgiven, but whoever speaks against the Holy Spirit will not be forgiven, either in this age or in the age to come"[Mt. 12:31–32].

I am Ruah. I am all the air there ever was. I carry the memory of his final hours. With each gasp as he hung from the crude scaffold of crossed planks, my power grew weaker. The weight of his body crushed his lungs, forcing me out of him. The carbon dioxide overwhelmed the balance, causing a cascading effect in his blood, his brain, his heart. He used his last bit of air for prayer, and then exhaled for the final time.

I grieved at the loss of this life, all the cells I had nurtured, all the hope I had caused to flourish, now sinking into the depths of time and the stony grip of the tomb. But God assured me that life would arise again, with even greater power and energy.

I am Ruah. I carry the memory of that Great Turning. Three days later, God blew me into his nostrils—this *adamah*, this Divine Earthling—filling his lungs, coursing through his newly pulsing veins and arteries. In his lungs the sacred exchange of oxygen and carbon dioxide lifted him up, raised him from death. He arose from the heart of the Earth with power—my power, the power of the Holy Spirit. And in that upper room he breathed me onto those women and fishermen and tax collectors: "Receive the Holy Spirit."

And then he sent me to them as his own power. On the day of Pentecost I blew into that upper room, lit the holy fires above each of them. They could not see me, but they knew I existed. They could feel me, see what I did, listen for me speaking through them. I am Ruah. I carry the memory of their power, which God has exhaled into you: Earthlings who are baptized with water and the Holy Spirit. I filled your lungs and issued forth from you in your words that echoed his teachings, his healing, his exhaled exhortations. You were breathing new life, new hope into the world. In you the sacred exchange was happening—you were the lungs of the body of Christ!

But others were using me to conspire against you, against him, against all life on this precious orb. You remember those dinosaurs and plants from those many millions of years before? The carbon from those fossilized forms had been locked away, safely buried beneath millennia of gravity and pressurized stone. The sacred exchange in the land and air above continued undisturbed as life unfolded, diversified, flourished across the face of the orb. But then your kind learned to unlock the heat within the stone, to dig deep for the black oily remains, to fracture the rock and release the gases held safely miles beneath the surface.

As your kind swarmed the globe, the sacred balance began to tilt. You tore the trees—the planet's lungs—from forests and jungles. Grey toxic fumes rose from your factories, your cars, your power plants, hovering over your cities, choking and smothering. Pipes spread across the land, jutting into the sky, leaking the gases, shooting flames into me. This was an unholy fire. In just 200 years, 165 milllion years of Creation was being undone by the very ones who were the shining light of that Creation.

The carbon dioxide and methane overwhelmed the oxygen, trapping heat and causing Earth's fever to rise. This was blasphemy against the Spirit—the unforgiveable sin. For if the very essence of life, God's breath, Ruah, is destroyed, there can be no breath, no life for anyone or anything. It is unforgiveable because there is no return. Once the balance tips too far, the cascading effect on the oceans, the ice sheets, the mountains, and the climate cycles falls too fast to stop.

I am Ruah. I am all the air there ever was. With each final gasp of the last of each species, my power grew weaker. The weight of the concrete and steel crushed Earth's lungs, forced me from so many bodies. I grieved the loss of so much life, all the cells I had nurtured, all the hope I had caused to flourish, choked by the fumes from the stony grip of those fossilized remains. I was suffocating with fear. But God assured me that life would arise again, with even greater power.

I am Ruah. I am carrying back to you the memory of those fateful years. Receive this memory of the Great Turning: God filled the lungs of the remaining singers and they sang the song of Miriam, of Mary, of Jesus. They were filled with the Holy Spirit and used their air for prayer, lifting their voices in songs of protest and peace. They called for the burning to stop, for the sacred remains of the brontosaurus and her kin to remain in their burial grounds safely in the heart of the Earth. They called for the balance to be restored. They breathed in together as they marched, as they testified, as they taught and healed and spoke words of exhortation: Do not blaspheme the Holy Spirit. Use this power for life, for hope, for peace. They learned to draw upon Sun and Ocean, Earth and me—the Wind—to generate their power and restore the sacred balance.

I am Ruah. I am all the air there ever was. I am *pneuma*, the breath of God. I am the wind of memory. You cannot see me, but you know I exist because you can feel me, see what I do, listen for me. I am the Holy Spirit, and you are part of the sacred exchange, the Great Turning. I know every cell of your body, and I carry the memories of all other cells through which I have passed. I am carrying your memories to your daughters and sons who will breathe the air your exhale.

[sung]: Sing to the Lord a new song. Earth contains marvelous things! I too will praise God with a new song!

Analysis Using a Lutheran Ecofeminist Homiletic

In this sermon the human is decentered from its assumed pinnacle in the biotic order by being placed within the context of the larger and longer story of Earth's life, including the Cretaceous Era (age of the dinosaurs) and the Paleocene Era (age of the mammals). At the same time, the sermon is designed to create a sense of relationship between the listeners and Ruah by the reminder that the air of God's breath is essential to their lives and is intimately familiar with every cell of their bodies. In this way, the listeners are meant to feel an affinity for the Holy Spirit from the beginning of the sermon and become personally invested with the story.

The sermon also employs a time-shift, in that Ruah is actually speaking to them from a point in the future. The listeners hear the story of Earth's past and the three great "turnings" (the recovery from the mass extinctions at the end of the age of dinosaurs, Jesus' incarnation through Mary's encounter with the Holy Spirit, and the resurrection of Jesus Christ), followed by a retelling of the current state of Earth's and Ruah's demise. But this last is told in the past tense because Ruah as "the wind of memory" is speaking from a time after a fourth "Great Turning." Thus the listeners realize that they are hearing this Word from a period earlier than the one from which Ruah is speaking.

This decision to preach proleptically was driven by the need to help the listener see beyond the Good Friday of the climate crisis and envision at least the Vigil of Easter, and even the resurrection itself. Ruah shares a vision of a resurrected future of herself and our planet as if this future already existed. This prochronism engenders an eschatological proclamation whose intention is to spark the desire in the listeners to act in such ways as to realize the beginning of this Great Turning in our present time. Thus the sermon includes references to direct political action such as unified prayer, marches, and protests, as well as practical actions of turning away from fossil fuels and embracing alternative forms of cleaner energy (an example of *leafing*).

As in the sermon "I Am Water, I Am Waiting," this sermon employs a visual representation of the other-than-human character.

A sheer fabric laced with feathers is draped across the preacher's shoulders to imply the "mother bird" aspect of the Holy Spirit. Not only does this engender the Divine Feminine in a concrete way, it also provides the listener with a means by which to connect visually with the enigmatic Third Person of the Trinity. In this sense, the sermon engenders *flowering* (consciousness-raising) in a tangible way [a video of this sermon can be viewed at www.creationcrisispreaching.com].

One of the marginalized voices that is midwifed—brought to the listener's consciousness—in this sermon is that of the brontosaurus and its kin. If we imagine the geological layers beneath our feet as the sacred burial grounds of God's creatures from 165 million years ago, we might begin to see those creatures and plants as having been created by God and thus worthy of our moral consideration. Thus the mining, drilling, and fracking for the carbon fuels from those remains is not only an offense of the Holy Spirit, but also a desecration of those creatures of the Cretaceous Era carefully and respectfully buried within the heart of the Earth—the best carbon-sequestering system that could have ever been designed. The invoking of this memory by Ruah serves a dual function in the sermon. First, it implicitly brings the realm of science (both paleontology and climatology) into conversation with the spiritual and religious realm. Second, it exposes the pattern of environmental destruction and exploitation as unjust.

Perhaps the most provocative aspect of the sermon is the eco-hermeneutic applied to Jesus' injunction against blaspheming the Holy Spirit. In this sermon the unforgiveable sin is interpreted as anthropogenic climate change. The voices that conspire for the use of fossil fuels and the deforestation of the planet are, in a sense, speaking against the Holy Spirit. And those voices include all of the human race, for we are each connected with and culpable within the global economic system fueled by this environmental devastation—though, certainly, it is the poorest citizens of the Two-Thirds World who are the least culpable while being most significantly and immediately vulnerable to the suffering of Ruah.

And yet, as with the mass extinctions following the Cretaceous Period and Jesus' crucifixion, Ruah is assured by God that life will arise again. God's agency of restoration through the Holy Spirit brings forth the song of freedom, healing, and "turning," leading to the sung ending of the sermon. In this way, Ruah's and Earth's resurrection is glimpsed by the congregation, an example of *fruiting*—transforming the listeners at a fundamental level of faith.

The sermon is intended to be preceded by an opening hymn in the service entitled "Earth and All Stars"[20] (or "Earth and All Kin"—see www.creationcrisispreaching.com for a free download of the lyrics I rewrote for the hymn). This enables the congregation to quickly call to mind the verse Ruah sings in the middle and end of the sermon and to join in the singing. The hymn after the sermon is "Canticle of the Turning,"[21] which not only invokes the "turning" alluded to in the sermon, but also allows the congregation to echo Mary's song after she is filled with the Holy Spirit. Thus the sermon is framed liturgically by a communal inhaling and exhaling of the breath of God.

Conclusion

We close by remembering that preaching can bring a word of hope, empowerment, and courage for us to resist the demonic powers that seek to dominate us and this planet we call home. Through Creation-crisis preaching that incorporates the concerns of ecofeminist theology, clergy and congregations can begin to see how their ministry can, in a very contextual way, bring Jesus to meet the modern-day "women at the well," speaking for and with both Earth and those most vulnerable in a ministry of reconciliation and resistance to injustice. This preaching has a Word to say to the "powers and principalities" and the society that exists beyond the church walls. It is a Word that puts the systems of domination (and those they hold in thrall) on notice that the crucifixions they perpetrate will not be the final word, nor will their oppressive reign endure without resistance.

And yet, even as we do all we can to resist andropogenic[22] evil, teach our children to cherish and protect Earth, speak out against eco-injustice, and change hearts, minds, practices, and laws through our preaching, sometimes it seems all we see is Earth's crucified body crumpled and dying all around us. However, as we stand with the women at the tomb of the crucified Earth looking at the enormous stone blocking our way, the biblical story reminds us that the Resurrected One will call our names and open our eyes to Creation transformed to new life. An ecofeminist homiletic urges us to return again and again to the biblical accounts of the resurrection to recover sacred memory and hope.

What can we learn about resurrection from the biblical texts? I believe the key is in how Jesus appeared: the same, yet different; transformed, yet with scars remaining. So, too, will be the resurrected Earth. This has enormous implications for preachers standing at the intersection of the oppression of Earth, women, children, and their communities. Earth, too, will bear the scars, as do those most vulnerable who bear the brunt of suffering when Creation is violated. Nevertheless, we proclaim that new life will emerge in ways that are sure to surprise us with God's grace.

Like the women going to the tomb on Easter morning who wonder, "Who will roll the stone away?"—who know nothing at that point other than defeat and death, but who make that journey to the tomb out of their love and faithfulness—we, too, must walk to the tombs of our crucified Earth today. The women did not go thinking they could save Jesus. They went because that is what they were called to do. Likewise, we do not do this work thinking we can "save" the planet. We do this because it is what we are called to do. We are not called to be successful. We are called to be faithful. And we can with confidence proclaim that when we arrive at the tomb we are met by the resurrected Christ and Easter joy!

Notes

[1] John S. McClure, *Other-Wise Preaching: A Postmodern Ethic for Homiletic* (St. Louis: Chalice Press, 2001), 15.

[2] Ibid., 109.

[3] Ibid.

[4] Ibid., 103.

[5] Ibid., 104.

[6] For example, in a sermon I preached on Matthew 13:31–33, 44–50, I focused on the vulnerability of the "nature" characters in the parables and in Jesus' teachings in the Sermon on the Mount. Drawing on images from Isaiah, I compare the Earth to a sanctuary and the Earth-kin as fellow pew-mates of the listeners. Further, in their role as Jesus' didactic assistants, I speak of the seeds, birds, fields, pearls, and fish as "Sunday school teachers." And I ask listeners if they would want their teachers' dwelling places destroyed, polluted, or turned into industrial zones.

[7] McClure, *Other-Wise Preaching*, 8.

[8] Ibid., 139.

[9] Norman Habel's book, *An Inconvenient Text: Is a Green Reading of the Bible Possible?*, is an example of how ecotheology engages in critical reading with Scripture. Habel notes that there are some passages in the Bible that are not "green" (having a positive theology of nature) but "grey," in which God and humans are depicted as destroying and devaluing parts of creation. He asks serious questions as to how and whether it is possible to recover and redeem these texts from an ecological perspective, or whether they must be set aside, much the same way passages that advocate slavery have been reduced in importance in the last two hundred years. (Norman C. Habel, *An Inconvenient Text: Is a Green Reading of the Bible Possible?* [Hindmarsh, South Australia: ATF Press, 2009].)

[10] The concept of "exiting," as previously explained, comes from John McClure, *Other-Wise Preaching*.

[11] A reminder that this idea is drawn from Serene Jones, *Feminist Theory and Christian Theology: Cartographies of Grace* (Minneapolis: Fortress Press, 2000), 44.

[12] Celia Deane-Drummond, "Creation," in *The Cambridge Companion to Feminist Theology*, ed. Susan Frank Parsons (Cambridge, UK: Cambridge University Press, 2002), 191.

[13]Bernice Marie-Daly, *Ecofeminism: Sacred Matter/Sacred Mother* (Chambersburg, Pa.: Published for the American Teihard Association for the Future of Man Inc. by Anima Books, 1991), 5.

[14]Wendy Lynne Lee, *Contemporary Feminist Theory and Activism: Six Global Issues* (Ontario, Can.: Broadview Books, 2010), 196.

[15]I choose the term "midwifing" recognizing that the preacher is not the one giving birth to these stories and voices, but simply assists them, albeit in a very active and agential way, into the sermon. The preacher cannot presume to speak for others, but must be in mutual partnership with those with whom she or he is working. For example, as was seen in the sermon about the community of Riverdale, the residents already "birthed" their experience into the world. As the preacher, I simply provided the means by which their story could be heard in one congregational context.

[16]The performance of this sermon can be found at the following site: http://www.youtube.com/watch?v=r9UT8nKADdg

[17]Catherine Keller, *Face of the Deep: A Theology of Becoming* (London; New York: Routledge, 2003), 232.

[18]"Tehomic iconography — as oceanic, as turbulent, as natural, as below, as dark, as womb or as abortion – outfitted an entire western legion of shadowy femininities" (ibid., 31).

[19]Mark I. Wallace, *Finding God in the Singing River: Christianity, Spirit, Nature* (Philadelphia: Fortress, 2005), 23–24.

[20]"Earth and All Stars," text: Herbert F. Brokering; music: David N. Johnson; copyright Augsburg Publishing House, 1968.

[21]"Canticle of the Turning," text: Rory Cooney, based on the Magnificat; music: Irish traditional; text copyright GIA Publications, Inc., 1990.

[22]This is my ecofeminist variation on Celia Deane-Drummond's term "anthropogenic evil," shifting the concept to focus more on the oppressive patriarchal aspect of human evil committed against Creation.

Bibliography

Adams, Carol J. *Ecofeminism and the Sacred.* New York: Continuum, 1993.

(ATSDR), Center for Disease Control Agency for Toxic Substance and Disease Registry. *Health Consultation;* Chesapeake Atgas 2h Well Site – Leroy Hill Road, Leroy – Leroy Township, Bradford County, Pa. November 4, 2011.

Boff, Leonardo. *Cry of the Earth, Cry of the Poor.* Maryknoll, N.Y.: Orbis Books, 1997.

Bond, L. Susan. *Trouble with Jesus.* St. Louis: Chalice Press, 1999.

Brueggemann, Walter. *Genesis: A Bible Commentary for Teaching and Preaching.* Atlanta: John Knox Press, 1982.

Campbell, Charles L., and Johan H. Cilliers. *Preaching Fools: The Gospel as a Rhetoric of Folly.* Waco, Tex.: Baylor University Press, 2012.

Charleston, Steven. "The Isaiah Factor: Prophetic Words That People Can Hear." In *Earth and Word: Classic Sermons on Saving the Planet,* edited by David M. Rhoads. New York: Continuum, 2007.

Chopp, Rebecca S. *The Power to Speak: Feminism, Language, God.* New York: Crossroad, 1989.

Clements, John M., Aaron M. McCright, Chenyang Xiao. "An Examination of the 'Greening of Christianity' Thesis among Americans, 1993–2010." *Journal for the Scientific Study of Religion.* Vol. 53, no. 2. 2014.

Cone, James H. *God of the Oppressed.* New York: Seabury Press, 1975.

Deane-Drummond, Celia. *Christ and Evolution: Wonder and Wisdom, Theology and the Sciences.* Minneapolis: Fortress Press, 2009.

_____."Creation." In *The Cambridge Companion to Feminist Theology,* edited by Susan Frank Parsons. Cambridge, UK: Cambridge University Press, 2002.

_____.*Eco-Theology.* London: Darton Longman and Todd, 2008.

d'Eaubonne, Françoise. *Le féminisme ou la mort.* Paris: P. Horay, 1974.

Eaton, Heather. *Introducing Ecofeminist Theologies.* London; New York: T&T Clark International, 2005.

Eckert, Penelope, and Sally McConnel-Ginet, "Communities of Practice: Where Language, Gender and Power All Live." In

Language and Gender: A Reader, edited by Jennifer Coates. Malden, Mass: Blackwell, 1998.

Florence, Anna Carter. *Preaching as Testimony*. Louisville, Ky.: Westminster John Knox Press, 2007.

Gadamer, Hans-Georg. *Truth and Method*, 2nd revised edition. New York: Crossroad, 1991.

Gamson, William A., and David S. Meyer. "Framing Political Opportunity." In *Social Movements and Culture*, edited by Hank Johnston and Bert Klandermans. Minneapolis: University of Minnesota Press, 2001.

Gebara, Ivone. "Ecofeminism." In *Dictionary of Feminist Theologies*, edited by Letty M. Russell and J. Shannon Clarkson. Louisville, Ky.: Westminster John Knox Press, 1996.

_____.*Longing for Running Water: Ecofeminism and Liberation*. Minneapolis: Fortress Press, 1999.

Habel, Norman C. *An Inconvenient Text: Is a Green Reading of the Bible Possible?* Hindmarsh, South Australia: ATF Press, 2009.

_____."Guiding Ecojustice Principles." In *Readings from the Perspective of Earth*, edited by Norman C. Habel, The Earth Bible series. Cleveland: Pilgrim Press, 2000.

_____.David M. Rhoads, H. Paul Santmire, editors. *The Season of Creation: A Preaching Commentary*. Minneapolis: Fortress Press, 2011.

_____,and Peter L. Trudinger. *Exploring Ecological Hermeneutics*, Society of Biblical Literature Symposium Series. Atlanta: Society of Biblical Literature, 2008.

Hall, W. David. "Does Creation Equal Nature? Confronting the Christian Confusion about Ecology and Cosmology." *Journal of the American Academy of Religion*. Vol. 73, no. 3. September 2005.

Hauerwas, Stanley. "The Church's One Foundation Is J.C. Her Lord; or, in a World without Foundations: All We Have Is the Church." In *Theology without Foundations: Religious Practice and the Future of Theological Truth*, edited by S. Hauerwas, N. Murphy, M. Nation. Nashville: Abingdon Press, 1994.

Jerving, Sara. "The Fracking Frenzy's Impact on Women." The Center for Media and Democracy. http://prwatch.org/news/2012/04/11204/fracking-frenzys-impact-women. http://PRWatch.org: November 29, 2011. Accessed April 4, 2012.

Johnson, Elizabeth A. *Women, Earth, and Creator Spirit*. New York: Paulist Press, 1993.

Johnston, Hank. "A Methodology for Frame Analysis: From Discourse to Cognitive Schema." In *Social Movements and Culture*, edited by Hank Johnston and Bert Klandermans. Minneapolis: University of Minnesota Press, 2001.

_____,and Bert Klandermans, "Cultural Analysis of Social Movements," in *Social Movements and Culture*, edited by Hank Johnston and Bert Klandermans. Minneapolis: University of Minnesota Press, 2001.

Jones, Robert P., Daniel Cox, Juhem Navarro-Rivera. *Believers, Sympathizers, and Skeptics: Why Americans Are Conflicted about Climate Change, Environmental Policy, and Science: Findings from the PRRI/AAR Religion, Values, and Climate Change Survey*. Washington, D.C.: Public Religion Research Institute and American Academy of Religion, 2014.

Jones, Serene. *Feminist Theory and Christian Theology: Cartographies of Grace*. Minneapolis: Fortress Press, 2000.

Kearns, Laurel, and Catherine Keller, editors. *Ecospirit: Religions and Philosophies for the Earth*. New York: Fordham University Press, 2007.

Keller, Catherine. *Apocalypse Now and Then: A Feminist Guide to the End of the World*. Boston: Beacon Press, 1996.

_____.*Face of the Deep: A Theology of Becoming*. London; New York: Routledge, 2003.

Kelly, Mark. "Lifeway Research Studies Global Warming Beliefs among Protestant Pastors." http://www.lifeway.com/Article/LifeWay-Research-studies-global-warming-beliefs-among-Protestant-pastors. April 16, 2009. Accessed July 13, 2014.

King, Ynestra. "The Ecology of Feminism and the Feminism of Ecology." *In Healing the Wounds: The Promise of Ecofeminism*, edited by Judith Plant. Philadelphia: New Society Publishers, 1989.

Lee, Wendy Lynne. "Restoring Human-Centeredness to Environmental Conscience: The Ecocentrist's Dilemma, the Role of Heterosexualized Anthropomorphizing, and the Significance of Language to Ecological Feminism." *Ethics and the Environment*. Vol. 14, no. 1. 2009.

_____,*Contemporary Feminist Theory and Activism: Six Global Issues*. Ontario, Canada: Broadview Books, 2010.

_____."Fracking Is a Variety of Environmental Rape Abetted by the Law: Governor Corbett's Pennsylvania, Inc." Raging Chicken Press, http://www.ragingchickenpress.org/2011/12/15/fracking-is-a-variety-of-environmental-rape-abetted-by-the-law-governor-corbetts-pennsylvania-inc/. December 15, 2011. Accessed October 19, 2012.

Lischer, Richard. *A Theology of Preaching: The Dynamics of the Gospel*, revised edition. Eugene, Oreg.: Wipf and Stock, 2001.

Lustgarten, Abraham. "E.P.A. Finds Compound Used in Fracking in Wyoming Aquifier." November 13, 2011. http://www.propublica.org/article/epa-finds-fracking-compound-in-wyoming-aquifer. Accessed March 21, 2012.

Marie-Daly, Bernice. *Ecofeminism: Sacred Matter/Sacred Mother.* Chambersburg, Pa.: Published for the American Teihard Association for the Future of Man Inc. by Anima Books, 1991.

McAdam, Doug. *Political Process and the Development of Black Insurgency, 1930–1970* Chicago: University of Chicago Press, 1982.

McClure, John S. *Other-Wise Preaching: A Postmodern Ethic for Homiletics*. St. Louis: Chalice Press, 2001.

_____.*The Roundtable Pulpit: Where Leadership and Preaching Meet.* Nashville: Abingdon Press, 1995.

McFague, Sallie. *A New Climate for Theology: God, the World, and Global Warming*. Minneapolis: Fortress Press, 2008.

_____."An Earthly Theological Agenda." In *Ecofeminism and the Sacred*, edited by Carol Adams. New York: The Continuum Publishing Company, 1993.

_____.*Metaphorical Theology: Models of God in Religious Language*, 2nd print ed. Philadelphia: Fortress Press, 1984.

_____.*Models of God: Theology for an Ecological, Nuclear Age.* Philadelphia: Fortress Press, 1987.

Merchant, Carolyn. *The Death of Nature: Women, Ecology, and the Scientific Revolution.* San Francisco: Harper & Row, 1980.

Midgley, Mary, "Is a Dolphin a Person?" In *The Essential Mary Midgley*, edited by David Midgley. Oxford and New York: Routledge, 2005.

Moe-Lobeda, Cynthia D. *Resisting Structural Evil: Love as Ecological-Economic Vocation*. Minneapolis: Augsburg Fortress, 2013.

Moltmann, Jürgen. *Crucified God*. Minneapolis: Fortress Press, 1993.

Newsome, Carol A. "Common Ground: An Ecological Reading of Genesis 2—3." In *The Earth Story in Genesis,* Earth Bible. Sheffield, England: Sheffield Academic Press, 2000.

Ngien, Dennis. "Theology of Preaching in Martin Luther." *Themelios* 28.2, Spring 2003. Accessed March 6, 2013. http://www.biblicalstudies.org.uk/pdf/themelios/luther_ngien.pdf.

Osborn, Stephen, A. Vengosh, N. Warner, R. Jackson. *Methane Contamination of Drinking Water Accompanying Gas-Well Drilling and Hydraulic Fracturing.* Durham, N.C.: Center on Global Change, and Division of Earth and Ocean Sciences, Nicholas School of the Environment, Duke University. April 14, 2011.

Osmer, Richard R. "Teaching as Practical Theology." In *Theological Approaches to Christian Education,* edited by Jack L. Seymour and Donald E. Miller. Nashville: Abingdon Press, 1990.

Patrick Center for Environmental Research, The. "A Preliminary Study on the Impact of Marcellus Shale Drilling on Headwater Streams." Philadelphia: The Academy of Natural Sciences of Drexel University, 2012. Accessed March 21, 2012. http://www.ansp.org/research/environmental-research/projects/marcellus-shale-preliminary-study/.

Rae, Eleanor. *Women, the Earth, the Divine.* Maryknoll, N.Y.: Orbis Books, 1994.

Ramberg, Bjorn. "Hermeneutics." In *Stanford Encyclopedia of Philosophy.* First published Nov. 9, 2005. Accessed December 26, 2010. http//plato.standford.edu/entries/hermeneutics.

Ramshaw, Gail. *God Beyond Gender: Feminist Christian God-Language.* Minneapolis: Augsburg Fortress, 1995.

Ravetz, Tom. "Reenlivening the Dying Earth," *Journal for the Renewal of Religion and Theology,* December 2006.

Riley, Shamara Shantu. "Ecology Is a Sistah's Issue, Too." In *Ecofeminism and the Sacred,* edited by Carol Adams. New York: Continuum, 1993.

Rootes, Christopher. "Environmental Movements." In *The Blackwell Companion to Social Movements,* edited by David A. Snow, Sarah A. Soule, and Hanspeter Kriesi. Malden, Mass.: Blackwell Publishing. 2007.

Rose, Lucy Atkinson. *Sharing the Word: Preaching in the Roundtable Church.* Louisville, Ky.: Westminster John Knox Press, 1997.

Ruether, Rosemary Radford. *Gaia & God: An Ecofeminist Theology of Earth Healing*. San Francisco: HarperSanFrancisco, 1994.

_____.*New Women, New Earth: Sexist Ideologies and Human Liberation*. New York: The Seabury Press, 1975.

Santmire, Paul. "American Lutherans Engage Ecological Theology: The First Chapter, 1962–2012, and Its Legacy." Presented at the Convocation of Teaching Theologians, Trinity Lutheran Seminary, Columbus, Ohio, 2012.

_____.*Nature Reborn: The Ecological and Cosmic Promise of Christian Theology*. Minneapolis: Fortress Press, 2000.

_____.*The Travail of Nature: The Ambiguous Ecological Promise of Christian Theology*. Philadelphia: Fortress Press, 1985.

Sawtell, Peter. "Three Layers of Environmental Preaching." Eco-justice Ministries, www.ecojustice.org. Accessed May 9, 2011. http://www.eco-justice.org/3layers.asp .

Schüssler Fiorenza, Elisabeth. *Bread Not Stone: The Challenge of Feminist Biblical Interpretation*. Boston: Beacon Press, 1984.

Shiva, Vandana. *Staying Alive: Women, Ecology, and Development*. Atlantic Highlands, N.J.: Zed Books Ltd., 1989.

Sittler, Joseph. "Called to Unity: Redemption within Creation." In *World Council of Churches Meeting*. New Delhi, India, 1961, reprinted 1985.

Smith, Christine M. *Preaching as Weeping, Confession, and Resistance: Radical Responses to Radical Evil*. Louisville, Ky.: Westminster/John Knox Press, 1992.

_____.*Weaving the Sermon: Preaching in a Feminist Perspective*. Louisville, Ky.: Westminster/J. Knox Press, 1989.

Snow, David A. "Framing Processes, Ideology, and Discursive Fields." In *The Blackwell Companion to Social Movements*, edited by Sarah A. Soule, David A. Snow, and Hanspeter Kriesi. Malden, Mass.: Blackwell Publishing, 2007.

Solberg, Mary M. *Compelling Knowledge: A Feminist Proposal for an Epistemology of the Cross*. Albany, N.Y.: State University of New York Press, 1997.

Swedish, Margaret. *Living Beyond the "End of the World": A Spirituality of Hope*. Maryknoll, N.Y.: Orbis Books, 2008.

Von Rad, Gerhard. *Genesis: A Commentary*. Translated by John H. Marks. Philadelphia: The Westminster Press, 1961.

Wallace, Mark I. *Finding God in the Singing River: Christianity, Spirit, Nature.* Philadelphia: Fortress, 2005.

_____.*Green Christianity: Five Ways to a Sustainable Future.* Minneapolis: Fortress Press, 2010.

Warren, Karen J. "Feminism and the Environment: An Overview of the Issues." In *Philosophy of Woman: An Anthology of Classic to Current Concepts,* edited by Mary Briody Mahowald. Indianapolis/Cambridge: Hackett Publishing Company, Inc., 1994.

White, Lynn Townsend Jr. "The Historical Roots of Our Ecologic Crisis." *Science.* Vol. 155, no. 3767. March 10, 1967.

Williamson, Clark M., and Ronald J. Allen. *A Credible and Timely Word: Process Theology and Preaching.* St. Louis: Chalice Press, 1991.

Wink, Walter. *Engaging the Powers: Discernment and Resistance in a World of Domination.* Minneapolis: Fortress Press, 1992.

Zimmerman, Michael E. *Contesting Earth's Future: Radical Ecology and Postmodernity.* Berkeley: University of California Press, 1994.

Index

A

Air, as character in scripture (*see also* Ruah; Holy Spirit), 179–85
androcentrism, 9, 106, 109–10, 125, 139, 166
andropogenic, 185, 187
anthropocentrism, 6, 9, 22, 65, 84, 109, 125
anthropogenic evil, sin, 77, 132, 136, 137, 167, 187
Assisi, Francis of, 26, 83, 85, 121

B

baptism, 118, 159, 173, 177, 180
Barth, Karl, 1, 14, 28, 130
biocentric, 62, 67
birth, 9, 37, 85–87, 93, 98, 117, 122, 126, 142, 143, 148, 168, 172, 173, 175, 187
Bond, L. Susan, 10, 15, 120, 136, 137, 188
breath, breathing (*see also* Ruah; Holy Spirit), 61, 73, 86–87, 158, 169–83
Buber, Martin, 66
Bugs Bunny, Br'er Rabbit, 153–54, 158, 161
Bulgakov, Sergii, 130, 135

C

Campbell, Charles (and Johan Cilliers), 13, 140, 150–52, 161, 164, 188
capitalism, critique of, 20, 22, 93, 137, 164
carnival, 140, 151, 158, 161
Carson, Rachel, 19, 177
chaos, chaos theory 118, 140–42, 173

Charleston, Steven, 53–54, 61, 188
child, children (and nature), 55–59, 68, 78–82, 86–90, 93, 98, 113–14, 124–25, 132, 135, 165, 168, 171–72, 175–76, 185, 186
Chopp, Rebecca, 12, 72, 90, 188
Christ. *See* Jesus Christ, or Christ
Christian, Christianity, 1–4, 6–7, 11, 14, 17, 21, 23–28, 37, 43, 50, 57, 59, 68, 73, 86, 89, 103, 104, 106, 112, 114, 115, 119, 121, 125, 137, 140, 159, 161, 172, 186, 189, 190, 192, 193
Christology, 3, 7, 9, 10, 13, 28, 84, 111, 117, 119–22, 125, 130, 131, 134, 136, 139, 140, 152, 163
church, also ecclesia, 1, 7, 8, 10, 14, 28, 47, 48, 53, 56, 58, 63, 68, 70, 73, 103, 104, 117, 120, 121, 125, 126, 129, 144, 147, 149, 154, 157, 159, 161, 167, 185
Clements, John M., 2, 6, 14, 188
climate, climate change (*see also* global warming, 1, 2, 3, 7, 15, 19, 47, 50, 61, 87, 88, 90, 94, 123, 134, 178–79, 182–84
Cobb, John, 36, 67, 103, 114
community of faith, 59, 63, 69, 110, 164
Cone, James, 106, 115, 153, 161, 188
consciousness-raising, 12, 44, 45, 47, 49–51, 184
constructivism, 99, 102, 166
Cosmic Christ, 84, 89, 102, 111, 122
Council of All Beings ritual, 75
Creation (*see also* Earth), 1–3, 5–7, 9–11, 24–29, 32, 46–51, 54, 56–59, 65, 68, 69, 71, 72, 76–78, 82–89,

104–13, 119–25, 130, 132, 134–43,
146, 147, 149, 156, 159, 165–68,
173, 176–79, 182, 185, 186
agency of, 89, 137, 140, 141, 147,
166, 172
as subject rather than object, 3,
6, 33, 34, 140, 165, 172
as teacher, 147, 148, 186
suffering of, 10, 50, 66, 81, 86,
102, 111, 132–39, 167, 168,
176–79, 184, 186
voice of, 7, 12, 18, 27, 33, 34, 64,
69, 70, 75, 77, 82, 85, 107, 108,
111, 163–67, 172, 177, 184
Creation or Nature, terminology,
5–6
Creation-care, 2, 3, 30, 45, 51, 52, 74
Creation-crisis, 39, 63, 120, 122, 151
Creation-crisis preaching, 11, 12,
17, 26, 27, 33, 34, 39, 45, 47,
52–55, 64, 67, 70, 71, 101, 111,
119, 129–39, 152, 160, 163, 167,
168, 185
Creation-crisis preaching
strategies, 12, 39, 41, 42, 45, 127,
164, 165
flowering, 12, 49, 50, 55–58, 78,
149, 184
fruiting, 12, 52, 55, 57, 58, 78,
83, 88, 184
leafing, 12, 38, 50, 51, 55, 56, 58,
78, 83, 177, 183
creative, creativity, 3, 7, 12, 13, 34,
75, 76, 84, 87, 101, 104–11, 119,
120, 135, 139, 140, 147, 152, 158,
166, 168, 173, 174, 179
cross, crucifixion (see also eco-
crucifixion), 3, 4, 5, 11, 13, 14,
49, 81–89, 103, 119, 122, 127–40,
150–55, 157, 172, 173, 178, 179,
184, 185

D

d'Eaubonne, Francoise, 94, 112,
188

Deane-Drummond, Celia, 13,
23, 98, 100, 102, 112, 113, 122,
130–38, 186–88
decentering, 73, 125, 146, 166
deforestation, 2, 35, 87, 88, 178, 184
DiLorenzo, Anthony, 13, 118, 131,
134, 135, 138
dinosaurs, 180–84
Divine Feminine. See God,
Feminine aspects
domination, 2, 4, 10, 21, 22, 25, 38,
94, 95–100, 103, 104, 107, 111,
114, 115, 119, 134, 185
dualism, 13, 94, 97, 100, 124, 166

E

Earth
as character in scripture, 168,
172
Earth's story, 77, 108, 131, 179
Earth (see also Creation), 2–9, 21–
29, 32–36, 48, 54–58, 65, 69–72,
76, 79–92, 96–15, 119, 121–23,
125, 129–31, 134–43, 146, 151,
152, 161–67, 168–72, 173–94
Earth and women. See Women and
nature/Earth/Creation
Earth community, 29, 33–35, 65,
70, 77, 103, 110, 121, 139, 151,
161, 165
Earth Day, 19, 20, 77
Earth, agency of. See Creation,
agency of
Earth, as body and/or as God's
body, 85, 87, 88, 104, 107, 115,
124, 125, 137, 152, 162, 168–72,
173, 172–78, 185
Earth, as teacher. See Creation, as
teacher
Earth, suffering of. See Creation,
suffering of
Earth-kin, 12, 64, 77, 78, 83, 85, 87,
88, 165, 186
Easter, 13, 82, 85, 89, 122, 137,

140, 143, 144, 147–49, 153–55,
    158–61, 183, 186
Eaton, Heather, 97, 103, 104, 112,
    188
ecclesia. *See* church
eco-crucifixion (*see also* eco-
    resurrection), 4, 5, 83, 87, 167,
    172
ecofeminism, 5, 8, 13, 14, 17, 22, 23,
    84, 94–103, 106, 110, 113, 119,
    120, 124, 129, 139, 140, 164, 165
ecofeminist Christology, 3, 9, 10,
    13, 111, 117, 118–22, 125, 130,
    131, 134, 136, 140, 163
ecofeminist hermeneutic, 109, 110,
    163, 165, 166, 168, 172, 173, 178
ecofeminist homiletic, 7, 13, 65,
    111, 126, 128, 145, 163, 166, 167,
    172, 176, 183, 185
ecofeminist theology, 3, 7–15,
    92–94, 103–6, 108, 110, 119, 135,
    136, 137, 139, 163, 164, 185
eco-hermeneutics, 13, 18, 30,
    32–34, 37, 58, 63, 84, 143, 165,
    184, 189
Eco-Justice Ministries, 47, 193
eco-location (*see also* mapping), 12,
    39, 62, 64
ecological hermeneutics. *See* eco-
    hermeneutics
ecological justice, 45, 167, 168
ecological sin, 4, 5, 178, 179
ecological theology. *See*
    ecotheology
ecology, 8, 14, 15, 17, 18–23, 28,
    33–36, 38, 60, 67, 70, 75, 82, 94,
    95, 99, 104, 112, 115, 122, 127,
    161, 165, 189–94
    deep ecology, 17, 20, 22, 23, 67,
        75
    radical ecology, 21, 22, 36, 161,
        194
    reform environmentalism, 19,
        36
economy, economic systems, 3, 21,

35, 44, 46, 59, 63, 76, 94, 96, 149,
    152, 167, 184, 191
eco-resurrection (*see also* eco-
    crucifixion), 4, 5, 10, 71, 82, 87
ecotheology (also ecological
    theology), 9, 10, 12–15, 17, 21,
    23, 28–30, 32, 40, 45, 72, 105,
    124, 166, 186
ecowomanism, 112, 113
emancipation. *See* liberation
embodiment, 4, 28, 71, 123–27, 134,
    136, 150, 151, 161, 178
environmental crisis, 4, 32, 33, 38,
    80
environmental justice (*see also*
    ecojustice), 20, 49, 53, 63, 70, 94,
    112
environmental movement, 12,
    17–20, 23, 35, 38, 39, 41–43, 46,
    192
environmental preaching, 7, 38, 42,
    45, 47, 49, 52, 61, 193
epistemology, 95, 96, 127, 128, 129,
    137, 193
erasure, 64, 65, 109, 166
essentialism, 94, 99, 102, 111, 124,
    129, 140, 148, 166, 173
    strategic, 102, 111, 148, 166, 173
ethics and morality, 4, 5–7, 11, 14,
    23, 29, 32, 37, 39, 41–43, 46, 48,
    49, 52, 59, 62–68, 72, 95, 96, 109,
    120, 121, 128, 129, 132, 134, 135,
    140, 152, 164, 165, 172, 184
Evangelical Lutheran Church in
    America (ELCA), 29, 92
evil, 50, 59, 80, 81, 98, 102, 108, 128,
    131, 132, 134–36, 151, 155, 158,
    159, 166, 167, 185, 187, 193
evil, anthropogenic. *See*
    anthropogenic evil, sin
evolution, 13, 19, 20, 104, 123, 131,
    132, 135, 136, 138, 172, 188
exit, exiting, 13, 108, 109, 166, 186
exploitation, 10, 21, 24, 26, 32, 57,
    65, 97, 98, 103, 142, 167, 184

F

face, of nature (also visage), 64–65

faith, 2, 43, 57, 69, 77, 87, 88, 106, 109, 125, 128, 145, 147, 149, 159

feminism, feminist, 9, 10, 13–15, 23, 33, 34, 39, 72, 89–91, 94, 95, 101, 110, 112–15, 120, 122, 123, 127, 128, 137, 138, 142, 165, 186–94

Florence, Anna Carter, 12, 64, 70–72, 90, 189

fossil fuels, 2, 80, 90, 179, 183, 184

Fox, Josh, 93

fracking, 13, 35, 40, 66, 71, 90, 92, 93, 111, 112, 153, 177, 178, 184, 189, 191

fracking, effects on women, 92–94, 112, 153, 174–78

fracking, water issues, 40, 46, 47, 71, 92–94, 111–12, 152, 155–60, 172–78

frame, framing, frameworks, 7, 12, 13, 27, 29, 30, 34, 41, 42–45, 47, 49, 51, 53, 59, 60, 77, 84, 120, 128, 185, 190

Francis, Saint, *See* Assisi, Francis of

fusion of horizons, 30–32, 37, 165

G

Gadamer, Hans-Georg, 18, 30–32

Gaia, 98, 119, 168, 193

garden, gardener, gardening, 13, 25, 57, 74, 78–82, 87, 91, 143–50

Gebara, Ivone, 94, 96, 104, 112, 114, 189, 190

gender, 8, 15, 23, 44, 62, 95, 99, 102, 103, 105, 106, 115, 118, 120, 126, 127, 139, 140, 146, 173, 177, 188, 189, 192

global warming (*see also* climate change), 14, 19, 47, 61, 94, 178, 190, 191

God, 3–5, 8–10, 11, 14, 24–29, 32, 35, 37, 43, 47, 48, 52, 55–59, 60, 63, 65, 67–69, 72, 77, 79–83, 84–89, 91, 104, 105–14, 118, 120–27, 130–32, 135–40, 144, 147, 148, 150, 151, 154–62, 165, 167, 168, 171, 173–75, 178–82, 184–86, 188, 191

as Creator, 5, 24–27, 52, 57, 79–83, 168–171, 174–76, 179–83

as Father, 105, 114, 115

as masculine, 173

as Mother, 100

breath of (*see also* Ruah; Holy Spirit), 174–83

feminine aspects of, 100, 124, 146, 178

God's activity of healing Creation, 3, 35, 39, 51, 77, 87, 176, 184

God's presence in Creation, 57, 58, 67, 71, 167

hiddenness of, 4, 13, 89, 128, 129, 151, 152, 167, 178

household of, 70

images of, 115, 123–27, 166, 192

suffering of, 4, 85, 168, 178

surprise of, 13, 87, 140, 143, 151, 154, 159, 186

transcendence/immanence of, 27, 28, 125

God's body. *See* Earth, as God's body

Goddess, 100, 102, 105, 140

Good Friday, 4, 84–89, 122, 140, 159, 172, 183

gospel (also Good News), 2, 3, 11, 14, 39, 71, 72, 83, 102, 111, 114, 128, 129, 140, 143, 150, 151, 154

grace, 5, 8, 27, 48, 59, 89, 128, 139, 140, 150, 151, 154, 159, 167, 186

grandmother, figure, 144–50

green Christianity, 6, 7, 36, 90, 91, 194

green preaching (*see also* Creation-crisis preaching), 12, 17, 27, 76

H

Habel, Norman, 9–10, 15, 18, 32, 33, 36, 37, 186, 189
Habermas, Jürgen, 164
Hall, W. David, 5, 6, 14, 189
Haraway, Donna, 140–142, 161
healing, 3, 8, 51, 72, 75, 77, 81, 100, 119, 123, 126, 129, 161, 180, 181, 184
    environmental, 53–54, 61
hegemony, 109, 111, 119, 137, 139
hermeneutic of suspicion, 34, 120
hermeneutic, ecofeminist, 109, 163, 165
hermeneutics (see also eco-hermeneutics), 23, 31, 32, 34, 37, 104, 110, 137, 173, 192
Hessel, Dieter, 18, 36
hierarchy, 10, 13, 22, 25, 29, 63, 65, 67, 68, 72, 73, 94–96, 100, 103, 105, 107, 111, 114, 119, 123, 124, 128, 145, 151, 166, 174
Holy Humor Sunday, 140, 153, 154
Holy Spirit, 27, 32, 100, 135, 150, 172, 178, 183, 184, 178–85
    as cruciform Spirit, 4, 89, 178, 179
    blasphemy against, 181, 182, 184
    suffering of, 4, 89, 178, 179
home, 71, 78, 79, 82, 84, 121, 124, 149, 152, 156, 157, 159, 160, 169, 185
homiletics (see also preaching; proclamation), 7–8, 11, 64, 70, 109, 191
    and ecofeminism, 7, 9, 11, 13, 106, 110, 139
    homiletics, and ecotheology, 27, 32
Homiletics, Academy of, 15
hope, 3, 8, 10, 13, 26, 29, 35, 42, 45, 49, 59, 64, 65, 71, 72, 82, 83, 86, 87, 89, 113, 122, 125, 129, 131, 134, 137, 148, 152, 155, 156, 157, 159, 164, 165, 172, 176, 178, 180–82, 185, 193
humor, 140–42, 151, 153, 154, 158
hydraulic fracturing (see also fracking), 1, 35, 40, 46, 92, 93, 176, 177

I

I Thou, I-Ens, 66, 90, 115
incarnation, 13, 105, 113, 119, 122, 123, 130, 131, 132, 134, 135, 172, 183
injustice (see also justice), 3, 10, 33, 39, 42, 47, 65, 68, 88, 150, 159, 160, 167, 185
instrumentalism, 13, 21, 93, 94, 96, 97, 166
Interfaith Power and Light, 15, 74
Interfaith Sacred Earth Coalition, 40, 41, 45, 46, 59

J

Jesus Christ, or Christ, 3, 4, 7, 10, 13, 27, 39, 53–55, 58, 59, 62, 63, 68, 76, 77, 81, 84, 85, 87, 106, 114, 115, 117–55, 158, 159,161, 163, 166, 167, 171–74, 177–88
    and connection with Creation, 87, 102, 111, 135, 143–47, 172, 177
    and gender, male/female, 103, 115, 119, 120, 123, 126, 132
    as shape-shifter and/or trickster, 126, 139, 140, 142–44, 151, 153–55, 158, 159, 161, 166
    as Sophia-Mer-Christ. See Sophia-Mer-Christ
    challenging patriarchy, 114, 115
    Cosmic Christ. See Cosmic Christ
    crucifixion and/or resurrection of. See crucifixion and/or resurrection

images of, 117, 119, 127, 132, 139, 144, 145, 185
incarnation of. *See* incarnation
suffering of, 85, 86, 128, 177–79
Johnson, Elizabeth, 103, 114, 190
Jones, Serene, 102, 114, 186, 190
justice (*see also* ecological justice; injustice), 2, 4, 7, 11, 13, 14, 23, 29, 33, 35, 44, 45, 56, 64, 65, 71, 72, 82, 101, 113, 118, 125, 156, 158, 167, 168
environmental (*see also* ecological justice), 20, 49, 53, 70, 94, 112

K

Keller, Catherine, 3, 14, 23, 36, 85, 91, 104, 114, 141, 142, 161, 172, 173, 187, 190
kenotic, self-emptying, 68, 73, 120, 130
Kingdom of God (also Peaceable Community), 11, 15, 37, 55, 147, 171
kinship with Creation (*see also* Earth-kin), 29, 124, 131
language, 15, 34, 43, 51, 54, 81–91, 95, 98, 105–7, 114, 115, 123, 126, 127, 137, 166, 189–92
metaphor, 9, 17, 27, 28, 49, 52, 69, 73, 95, 98, 103, 105, 107, 115, 123, 124, 126, 127, 142, 143, 154, 166
models, 123–27
symbol(s), 4, 5, 11, 42, 46, 95, 98, 103, 1057, 121, 130, 132, 134, 142, 150, 153, 166
laugh, laughter, 87, 151–54, 158–61
law
God's law in nature, 77, 80
law and gospel, 72, 83, 128, 155
least of these, the, 7, 11, 50, 63, 67, 68, 74, 75, 82, 127, 168
Lee, Wendy Lynne, 9, 10, 15, 65, 89, 90, 111, 187, 190

Levinas, Emanuel, 64–66, 89
liberation, 33, 65, 71, 94, 96, 100–102, 106, 114, 123, 126, 130, 140, 146, 167, 177
lifeworld (*see also* Habermas), 164–65
Lischer, Richard, 8, 10, 11, 15, 140, 161, 191
listening, 34, 63, 64, 70, 79, 87, 155, 160, 164, 165, 167, 177
liturgy, liturgical, 11, 23, 29, 30, 70, 76, 84, 104, 108, 127, 177, 185
lived experience, 106, 128
love, 71, 72, 87, 88, 91, 124, 150, 186, 191
of Creation, 4, 27, 56, 58, 65, 77, 87, 88, 130, 171
Divine (God's, Christ's, Spirit's), 27, 55, 85, 86, 87, 89, 123, 126, 135, 136, 148, 150, 151, 154, 156, 157, 167
Luther, Martin, 28, 130
Lutheran, 3, 4, 5, 12, 18, 28, 36, 37, 92, 127, 163, 177, 193
Lutheran ecofeminist Christology, 3, 137, 140, 152
Lutheran ecofeminist homiletic, 128, 166, 167, 172, 176, 183
Lutheran perspective on ecotheology, 28–30
Lutheran theology, 4, 5, 10, 28, 83, 89, 127–130, 136, 140, 151, 167
Lutheran theology of preaching, 4, 11
Lutherans Restoring Creation, 15, 30

M

Madonna and child, 132, 135, 136, 138
mapping (*see also* eco-location), 12, 39, 55, 59, 62, 64, 72, 73, 75, 167
Marcellus Shale (*see also* fracking), 92, 111, 192

margin, margins, marginalize, 63,
    69, 70, 72, 73, 84, 103, 108, 109,
    152, 164, 165, 167, 177, 184
Marie-Daly, Bernice, 97, 99, 100,
    102, 112, 113, 187, 191
Mary Magdalene, 143, 144, 148
Mary, mother of Jesus, 132, 135,
    136, 172, 180, 182, 183, 185
McAdam, Doug, 41, 60, 191
McClure, John, 12, 13, 64, 65, 89,
    90, 109, 111, 115, 164, 165, 186,
    191
McFague, Sallie, 25, 36, 115, 122,
    123–127, 137, 158, 162, 178, 191
memory, 158, 185
    sacred, 177, 179, 180, 181, 182,
        183, 184, 185
Midgley, Mary, 64, 66, 89, 90, 138,
    191
misogyny, 100, 103, 113, 145, 166
moral or morality. *See* ethics and
    morality
Mount Saint Alphonsus Retreat
    Center, 117, 119, 131–32, 136,
    138

N

narrative (*see also* story), 6, 13, 24,
    49, 76, 108, 110, 127, 137, 149,
    153, 163, 165, 168, 172, 174, 179
natural gas (*see also* shale gas), 1,
    56, 92, 93
nature (Creation), 5, 6, 9, 13, 14,
    19–24, 48, 56–58, 66–68, 76–78,
    84, 89–98, 103, 107, 108, 112,
    113, 121, 125, 132, 136, 137,
    140–43, 145, 147–52, 165–67, 186
    and children. *See* children, and
        nature
    and women (*see also* women
        and nature/Earth/Creation),
        94–102
    rights of, 90
Nature or Creation, terminology.
    See Creation or Nature,
    terminology
neighbor (*see also* Earth-kin), 12,
    39, 59, 62–66, 72–75, 155, 156,
    159
nonhuman beings (*see also* other-
    than-human beings), 6, 10, 25,
    27, 65, 68, 69, 71, 76, 78, 84,
    90, 95, 107, 109, 115, 125, 132,
    134–36, 141, 165, 166, 167, 177

O

oikos (household), 69–71
ontology, 22, 64, 70, 84, 95, 97, 109
oppression, 3, 7, 9, 20, 24, 29, 32,
    33, 42, 63, 65, 72, 87, 88, 93, 94,
    96, 99–102, 106, 109, 110, 114,
    119, 123, 125–30, 137, 140, 146,
    165–67, 186, 187
othering, 13, 94, 96, 97, 103, 166
other-than-human beings (*see also*
    nonhuman beings), 6, 9, 12, 13,
    19, 29, 34, 59, 64–66, 68, 70–72,
    76, 77, 84–85, 90, 108, 110, 111,
    115, 121, 129, 134, 165, 166, 183
other-wise homiletic, 64, 109, 165,
    166,
Other-wise Preaching 64, 109

P

panentheism, 26, 27
parable(s), 39, 44, 49, 53, 54, 62, 63,
    76, 77, 101, 123, 145, 151, 186
pastor(s), pastoral issues, 11, 14,
    52, 76, 78, 92, 190
and preaching, 1, 3, 43, 44, 48, 50,
    51, 60, 107
and relationships with
    parishioners, 59, 72, 127, 159–61
patriarchy, 9, 10, 13, 22, 23, 91, 93,
    94, 95–106, 111, 113–15, 119, 120,
    123, 124, 126–28, 130, 137, 140,
    143, 145, 152, 158, 166, 173, 187
Peaceable Community. *See*
    Kingdom of God
Pennsylvania, 1, 40, 46, 51, 56, 60,

61, 78, 83, 88, 92, 111, 144, 149, 168
and fracking, 41, 92–94, 191
Hildacy Farms Natural Lands Trust, 78–83
Loyalsock State Forest, 56–59
Media, 78
R. B. Winter State Park (Halfway Dam), 83
Riverdale Mobile Home Park, 46, 47, 152–61
Susquehanna River, 18, 40, 46–47, 60
Susquehanna River Basin Commission, 46
tire incinerator in Central PA, 43
Pentecost, Day of, 181
play, playfulness, 117, 118, 139–43, 152, 157, 161, 173, 175, 176
power
corporate, 44, 47, 48, 59
of Creation, 137, 142, 144, 159
and domination, 4, 23, 46, 68, 101, 104, 115, 128, 137
empowering, 38, 100, 102, 110, 166, 181, 182, 185
and evil, 151, 155, 158, 159
of God, 5, 13, 24, 115, 119, 125, 135, 140, 181
of Jesus Christ, 122, 125, 135, 181
patriarchal, 100, 113, 119, 143
political, 40, 46, 137
power structures, 58, 101, 104, 113, 115, 139, 164, 166
powers that oppress, 42, 63, 114, 119, 128, 140, 185
and preaching, 11, 39, 70, 110, 140, 185
and privilege, 54, 97, 111, 121
of Ruah/Holy Spirit, 181, 182
shared, 70, 90, 124, 135
The Powers (Walter Wink), 14, 106, 114, 185, 194

those in power, 97, 128, 137, 151, 159
those lacking power, 69, 97
and trickster, 150–59
and wealth/money, 21, 46, 82, 128, 159, 164, 165
of women, 102, 113, 129, 166
pray, prayer, 30, 46, 59, 86, 88, 89, 108, 147, 156, 181, 182, 183
preaching (see also homiletics; proclamation), 1, 3, 4, 60, 70, 71, 101, 139, 160, 183
and context, 7, 32, 63, 71–73, 77, 83, 88, 106, 110, 130, 149, 167, 183, 185, 187
conversational, 68–70
and dialogue with other disciplines, 8, 11, 33
environmental, 3, 53, 76, 77, 122, 139, 172
form and content of, 70, 84, 96, 163, 168
as memory, 10, 70, 85, 158, 177, 179, 183, 184, 185
as "midwifing", 140, 167, 184, 187
preaching fools, 13, 150–52, 154, 155, 159, 161, 188
prophetic, 3, 13, 53, 58, 71, 89, 120, 160, 167, 177
preaching, Creation-crisis. See Creation-crisis preaching
process theology, 103, 104, 114, 115, 194
proclamation (see also preaching), 5, 10, 11, 13, 14, 35, 37, 39, 59, 63, 68, 69–71, 73, 77, 84, 89, 96, 102, 110, 111, 119, 122, 131, 134, 140, 150–52, 155, 157, 165, 167, 177, 183, 186
prophet, prophetic, 3, 8, 13, 46, 53, 58, 61, 71, 89, 120, 167, 177, 188
Public Religion Research Institute (PRRI), 2, 14, 190

public theology, 41, 59, 88, 130, 139, 167

R

racism, environmental, 20, 48, 112, 113, 120
Rae, Eleanor, 96, 98, 106, 108, 112, 113, 192
rape, rape of Earth, 98, 107, 111, 126, 191
redemption (*see also* salvation), 37, 51, 84, 91, 108, 120, 140, 176, 193
    of Creation, 51, 84, 91, 108, 120, 140
Reformation Lutheran Church Media, PA, 78, 149
relationship, 66, 72, 80, 94, 114, 124, 135, 160, 173
    between children and nature, 56
    between God and Creation, 26, 27, 84, 107
    between God, humans and Creation, 25, 27, 48, 123, 166, 168
    between humans and nature, 19, 24, 25, 29, 35, 48, 56, 66, 67, 69, 70, 77, 78, 80, 90, 121, 166, 168, 183
    between pastor and parishioners. *See* pastor(s), pastoral issues
    between preacher and listeners, 71, 72, 160
    between women and men, 120
    between women and nature. *See* women and nature/Earth/Creation
    with the "other," 64
rhetoric, 12, 42–45, 49, 50, 58, 83, 88, 150, 151, 155, 188
    of action versus inaction, 44–45
Rhoads, David M., 30, 61, 163, 188, 189
Rootes, Christopher, 19–21, 35, 192
Rose, Lucy Atkinson, 68–72, 90

roundtable pulpit, 68, 69, 90, 191
Ruah (*see also* Holy Spirit; breath), 169, 170, 171, 177, 185
Ruether, Rosemary Radford, 94, 97, 112, 120, 193

S

salvation (*see also* redemption), 3, 5, 10, 37, 51, 81, 84, 117, 119, 121, 122, 131
Samaritan, The Good, 59, 62–63
Santmire, H. Paul, 15, 18, 23, 28–30, 36, 37, 66, 89, 115, 121, 137, 189, 193
Sawtell, Peter, 47–49, 52, 61, 193
Schüssler Fiorenza, Elisabeth, 110, 115, 193
science, 11, 14, 34, 35, 95, 107, 111, 138, 167, 177, 184, 188, 190, 192
    environmental, 19
    of interpretation (hermeneutics), 31
    and religion, 8
    and technology, 24, 26
Season of Creation, 9, 15, 189
shale gas (*see also* natural gas; fracking), 39, 94, 111, 177, 192
shape-shifting, 13, 119, 126, 139, 140, 143, 166, 173, 177
Sittler, Joseph, 28–29, 84, 91, 193
Smith, Christine, 39, 59, 110, 115, 116, 164
social movement theory, 12, 39, 40–60
    framing (*see also* frames, framing, frameworks), 42, 47, 49, 51, 52, 60, 61, 189, 190, 193
    meaning construction, 12, 44, 50
Solberg, Mary M., 13, 122, 127–30, 13638, 193
Sophia-Mer-Christ, 13, 117, 119, 132, 136, 139, 173
Spirit. *See* Holy Spirit

Spirit and Truth Worship Center, Yeadon, PA, 149
story (*see also* narrative), 54, 77, 86, 108, 145, 155, 163, 187
  biblical, 76, 185
  Christ's Passion/Resurrection, 84
  and climate disruption, 178–85
  Earth/Creation's story, 25, 36, 84, 86, 87, 115, 192
  Easter, 137, 143–50
  Jesus' parables about nature, 144–145
  loaves and fishes, 38
  of Riverdale Mobile Home Park, 153–61
  "The Fall" in Genesis, 77, 80
  Water's story, 172–78
strategies for Creation-crisis preaching. *See* Creation-crisis preaching strategies
suffering (*see also* Creation, suffering of; God, suffering of; Jesus Christ, suffering of; Holy Spirit, suffering of), 4, 63, 85, 109, 117, 121, 126, 128, 129, 130, 134
surprise. *See* God, surprise of
Swedish, Margaret, 38, 39, 59, 121, 137, 193

T

tehom, tehomic theology, 86, 141, 142, 172, 174, 175, 187
testimony, 64, 65, 70, 71, 75, 88, 109, 149, 189
theodrama, 131–36
theology, 8, 25, 27, 28, 34, 1035, 121, 123, 125, 127, 128, 131, 136, 137, 140–42, 164, 172, 187, 188
  and Creation-crisis preaching, 26
  ecofeminist. *See* ecofeminist theology
  ecological. *See* ecotheology

Lutheran. *See* Lutheran theology
  of nature, 23, 28, 36, 103, 120, 122, 186
  of preaching, 10–11, 15, 140, 161, 191, 192
theology of the cross (*see also* cross, crucifixion), 11, 128, 129
  and nature, 122, 151
  ecofeminist, 4, 14, 127–30, 136, 152
  feminist, 13, 127–30
transformation (*see also* Creation-crisis preaching strategies, fruiting), 10, 39, 43, 44, 45, 49, 52–55, 58, 64, 72, 88, 125, 134, 135, 137, 150, 178, 184, 185
trickster, 13, 119, 137, 139–61
  Jesus as. *See* Jesus Christ, as shape-shifter and/or trickster
Trinity, 113, 114, 178, 184
truth, truth-telling, 54, 58, 71, 103, 104, 111, 129, 147, 148, 151
Turning, the Great, 180–84

U

United in Christ Lutheran Church Lewisburg, PA, 149, 168

V

voice, 163, 175, 180, 184, 187
  of ecofeminism, 8, 11, 111, 164, 177
  preaching giving voice, 10, 57, 107, 163, 187
voice, of Creation. *See* Creation, voice of
voices
  joined, 46, 59, 63, 69, 182
  unheard, 69, 70, 75, 77, 82, 107, 108, 164, 165, 167, 172, 177, 184
vulnerable (also those most vulnerable)
  (*see also* least of these), 26, 55, 56,

59, 68, 75, 119, 125, 126, 129, 135, 137, 143, 153, 159, 165, 184–86

W

Wallace, Mark I., 4–5, 14, 27, 36, 67, 75, 89–91, 178, 187, 194
Warren, Karen, 95, 96, 107, 112, 194
water, 1, 17, 18, 39–41, 46, 51, 57, 58, 63, 65, 69, 73, 75–82, 87, 88, 91, 104, 118, 119, 141, 142, 144, 152, 154, 155, 156, 158–60, 163, 169, 171, 172–81
    "living water", 17, 163
    as character in scripture, 172–78
    and fracking. *See* fracking, water issues
wealth. *See* power: and wealthy/ money
White, Lynn Townsend, 2, 14, 17, 23, 24–26, 36, 194
Wink, Walter, 4, 14, 114, 115, 194
wisdom, 13, 119, 130, 134, 135, 138, 146, 148, 188
wisdom and wonder, 13, 134, 136, 138, 188
Wisdom, the Divine Feminine, 135, 146
witty agency of Creation, 140, 141, 166
woman at the well, 163, 172–78, 185
women and fracking. *See* fracking, effects on women
women and nature/Earth/ Creation, 3–10, 13, 21, 22, 65, 93–114, 119, 124, 129, 130, 136, 142, 143, 146, 148, 165–67, 172, 186
wonder, 13, 67, 78, 116, 134–38, 166, 188
Word of God or God's Word, 10, 140
works righteousness, ecological or environmental, 5, 89

Z

Zimmerman, Michael, 17, 21, 22, 23, 36, 140, 141, 161, 194